COMPLETE BOOK OF
FRESH WATER FISHING

OUTDOOR LIFE

COMPLETE BOOK OF FRESH WATER FISHING

◉

By P. Allen Parsons

Drawings by Ray Pioch

◉

OUTDOOR LIFE · HARPER & ROW
NEW YORK

DEDICATION

To my daughter Nan,
and my son Lowell

Contents

Foreword

When I was asked to write a foreword for this book I was inclined to refuse. I thought, "It probably will be just another average book on fishing, so what can I say except a few words showing appreciation in a formal way."

But because I have known the author for many years, have respected his knowledge of fishing, and loved his enthusiasm for the sport I decided to do it.

After I had read the galley proofs I was glad that I did. It is a splendid work. The information is sound and interestingly written. All the fresh water fish are discussed, with word sketches of the different species covering their habits and nature. It describes the tackle to use and how to use it in a way to catch fish.

The personal incidents pertaining to the author's experiences with the different fishes are particularly interesting. They show an understanding of fish, which is transferred to the reader.

P. A., as he is affectionately known to many, has given us a worth-while book, one that I shall be proud to add to my angling library. I am sure that many others will also.

Ray Bergman
Nyack, New York

COMPLETE BOOK OF
FRESH WATER FISHING

The Fisherman's Clothing

MOST OF US dress for our first fishing trips by putting on an old jacket and pair of pants. If going after trout, we don hip boots, stick a can of worms in one pocket and a package of hooks in another, pick up a rod and the simplest elements of tackle, and are serenely confident that we are properly equipped. At one time I did not have hip boots so I would put on a pair of sneakers and wade the icy streams of early season, priding myself on my hardiness. But a season or two of this back-to-nature folly, with its warning rheumatic pains, cured me. I became convinced that to get the utmost pleasure out of fishing it was important to be properly clothed and equipped.

JACKETS AND VESTS

High in importance is the trout fisherman's jacket or vest. It is preferable to get one short enough so when you are in waist-deep water, as you often will be, gear in the side pockets won't get wet. When I last fished the Madison River and some of its tributaries, I packed my fishing jacket in my duffel bag without emptying its pockets. On returning, I emptied them and put away the contents. Here is a list of the various items that I took from that one jacket: three fly boxes, one with dry flies, another with wet flies and nymphs, and the third with bucktails and streamers; gut clipper; a bottle of dry-fly oil; leader box, fisherman's pliers; pocket scales and linear measure; hook file; insect repellent; tobacco pouch and pipe; can of line dressing with its pad for greasing my dry-fly line; polaroid glasses; and an extra reel filled with a sinking Dacron line, to be used if I found conditions favoring wet flies or nymphs.

That is a rather lengthy list. A tyro might think that toting around all those articles was unnecessary, but each had its use and was needed at one time or another. The problem is how to carry them.

The trout fisherman who contents himself by wearing an old jacket normally will find two fairly shallow side pockets with or without flaps, an outer breast pocket without a flap, and an inside breast pocket. He does not have the room in that jacket to carry his accessories. Moreover, if he puts a normal-sized fly box in either of the side pockets there is nothing to hold it in, and he may lose it. The answer is a jacket or vest specially designed for the trout fisherman, with many pockets tailored to hold objects safely. To illustrate: One famous specialist in sporting goods lists a fishing jacket with eight pockets, some of which are even on the long sleeves. The pockets are expandable and have button closures for safety. There also is a large back pocket and a wool pad for drying flies. The price is $22.50. The same company also lists a fishing vest with eight pockets for tackle and an expansion rear pocket for gear. It has a front zipper closure and zipper and button closures on pockets. There also is a detachable waterproof creel of nylon mesh. This too is priced at $22.50. Both garments are sand color.

Another well-known sporting goods outfit lists a very practical vest with four large zipper pockets which will safely hold large fly boxes, eight small pockets of bellows construction with adjustable snaps, and a large rear pocket which will hold lunch package, rain jacket, and extra gear. It also has a landing-net ring, loops for rod butt and tip, zip-on mesh creel, and lamb's-wool pads for wet and dry flies. It too is sand color. The price is $18.75.

Another dealer offers a medium-weight jacket of windproof, water-repellent poplin with corduroy-lined collar and cuffs. This jacket has seven pockets—four in front, one large in the rear, and two zipper pockets inside for fly books. The breast pockets are buttoned. It is priced at $13.85. Its forest-green color is, in my opinion, superior to those mentioned earlier, for green or dark brown is less visible to the fish than sand or tan, and the good fisherman strives to keep from being seen by the fish. In pockets and design I like the others better.

The beginner, reading of the clothing best suited to the fisherman's needs, and the prices asked by first-class dealers, may feel that fishing is an expensive sport, for to this type of equipment must be added the basic tools of the sport such as rod, reel, line, leaders, and lures. If he is budgeting, he

Angler at left wears multi-pocketed fishing vest, waist-high waders, and long-billed cap. His partner favors a jacket with ample pockets on front and sleeves, and a pair of "hippers," lightweight version of the hip boot. *Hodgman Rubber Co.*

can get the various items piece by piece and thus gradually accumulate a
first-rate outfit. My own represents the purchases of years. Good equipment, properly used and cared for, will last almost a lifetime. I am still
using a fishing vest that I bought nearly twenty years ago.

If the angler looks around he often can pick up bargains—not cheap
equipment, which rarely is a bargain, but gear that is well made. For instance, shortly after World War II I saw in the window of a sporting goods
store on lower Broadway, New York City, an army field jacket and an
airman's vest. Their utility as fisherman's clothing impressed me. I went
into the store and examined the garments. The field jacket had two large,
deep side pockets with flaps, and two smaller outside breast pockets. It
was olive colored, well made, and shower resistant. As I recall, I bought it
for about $7.50.

The vest has a label in the inside, "Vest, Emergency Sustenance Type."
It has two deep inside pockets with snap fasteners, and on the outside five
smaller pockets, also with snap fasteners. It cost me about $4.

TROUSERS

The trout fisherman's trousers are of less importance than the jacket or
vest. But there is one thing to insist on—deep pockets with buttoned flap
or zippered closures. You will want to have your wallet, with money and
fishing license, handy and safe. Also, it is well to get the trousers either with
ski-trouser bottoms or with straps equipped with button holes which attach
to buttons on the trouser legs, to tighten them around the ankles. Trousers
with ordinary leg bottoms have a disconcerting way of riding up your legs
when you don boots or waders. A reliable dealer, from whom I bought
mine, catalogs such trousers made of water-repellent brown poplin, with
reinforced seat and legs, for $10.60.

HATS

The fisherman's hat is of minor importance but it should shield the eyes,
and an old felt hat or cloth cap will do. It should be large enough to set
well down on the head. It is annoying, in a wind, to have to keep clutching
at your hat to prevent it from blowing off. Many anglers like the long-
billed caps favored by commercial fishermen for they keep the sun out of
your eyes. But do not purchase one with a cardboard-stiffened visor. In
rain such a visor becomes little more than pulp.

SOCKS

The trout fisherman will need heavy wool socks for his waders. The favorite type of waders today is the "stocking foot." These require wool socks inside and outside the waders' feet. The wading shoes are worn over the outside pair. The socks not only make the fisherman more comfortable but they also prolong the life of the waders by guarding them from abrasion. On your return from fishing, wring out the outside socks and place them where they can get sun and air. When they are dry, slap them against a post or tree to free them from the sand which inevitably accumulates in them. The inner pair will probably be damp from perspiration and should likewise be dried and aired. You will need several pairs of such socks. They are stocked in long and short lengths. My preference is for the short lengths as they are less bulky. You can get good quality socks for $1.50 to $2.

WADERS

The advantage of waders over hip boots is apparent. Even on the smaller eastern trout streams the fisherman often comes upon a stretch of water too deep for hip boots but which offers good prospects for a trout or two. Full-length waders reaching to the chest used to be heavy. At the end of a day's fishing the angler might well be exhausted from dragging all the weight around. But now you can get them in light weights, and with proper care they are quite durable. The prices asked by various dealers differ considerably. I have before me the catalog of a reliable sporting goods mail-order house with whom I have done business for a number of years. They offer a stocking-foot extra-light wader of rubber-coated nylon with reinforced feet and ankles for $16.85. The wading shoes to go with them are of duck, solid counter, and have felt soles. An extra-full bellows tongue and brass-screened eyelets let the water out but stop sand and fine gravel from coming in. The wading shoes cost $14.45. That company offers a package deal of waders, wading shoes, and suspenders for $30.

Another one of the long-established companies offers nylon zephyrweight stocking-foot waders. The fabric is coated on each side with natural rubber. These are priced at $19.95. The company also lists lightweight stocking-foot waders at $14.25. The wading shoes to go with these waders sell for $8.50 with rubber soles and $18.50 with felt soles. Leather-and-canvas wading shoes with leather hobnail soles are priced at $27.

Here we come to the best type of sole for wading shoes. So far as I'm concerned, rubber soles for wading are an anathema. No matter whether they are heavily corrugated or plain, to me they mean *slip*. It takes all the pleasure from wading and fishing if you have to devote more attention to your footing than to your casting. Several of my fishing friends use rubber-soled wading shoes and like them, but I don't. The best all-round soles for all types of water are leather with hobnails of soft iron. But in my experience it does not take long before the hobnails are worn flat and smooth, and then the leather soles become slippery and dangerous. Also, such wading shoes are heavier than the all-canvas and felt-soled ones. I find the felt soles functional and very satisfactory.

WADING SANDALS

If you have waders or hip boots with rubber soles you will do well to equip yourself with wading sandals. These have hard felt soles, are made of heavy-duty leather, and are offered in only one size to fit any boot. They strap on over the heel and also over the toe. Many sporting goods stores stock an arrangement of chains to go over the sole. I have used them and they are satisfactory until the chain links begin to come apart. These wading sandals cost $6.

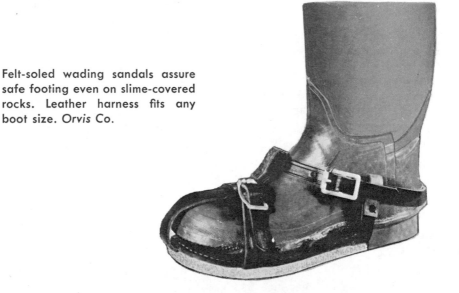

Felt-soled wading sandals assure safe footing even on slime-covered rocks. Leather harness fits any boot size. *Orvis Co.*

PLASTIC WADERS

Plastic waders are offered by many dealers. Plastic is a wonderful substance but my experience with it as wader material is not to its credit. Those I had were too frail and their seat was split within the first week of use. Some day the manufacturers will come out with a plastic wader that will combine strength with lightness and that can be marketed at a lower price than rubber or rubberized material.

Waders will last much longer if used with care. Avoid walking where sharp stubs are liable to puncture the fabric. Avoid as much as possible sharp-edged rocks. When you have finished your day of wading, turn your waders inside out and let them dry in a cool, shady, airy place. Then turn them outside in. Store them away from any heat and in a cool, dry, dark place.

HIP BOOTS

Strangely enough, hip boots often cost about as much as waders. Felt-soled hip boots at one of the three representative houses I have mentioned cost $32.50 a pair; with cleated soles (presumably of rubber) a pair costs $21.50. The second of the dealers charges $22.95 for hip boots, type of sole not mentioned so presumably of rubber. The third offers rubber hip boots at $15.90 a pair.

Until recently, when your felt soles wore thin there were only two alternatives—junk the boots or find a dealer who stocked wading sandals. Now separate felt soles are available which have a special adhesive to cement them over worn-thin soles. I bought a pair for my hip boots and they work fine. Price $5.

Rubber boots cannot be turned inside out as can the waders. Roll down the tops as far as possible to let the insides of the tops dry out, for they are likely to be damp from perspiration. Stuff dry newspapers down the legs and inside the toes. When you store them, do not let them flop down on the floor and acquire folds. Folds in rubber, if left for a while, tend to get stiff and then to crack. Stuff the whole length of each boot with dry newspapers and hang them up by the straps, away from any heat. Use newspapers because this type of paper absorbs dampness from the air and the boots should dry thoroughly.

FOOTWEAR FOR BOAT FISHERMEN

The boat fisherman will be happier if he has footwear suited to the occasion. Many boats leak and it is most unpleasant to have your feet in water for most of the day. My favorite shoe for boat fishing is a pair of featherweight shoe pacs with rubber bottoms and lightweight leather tops. I paid $10.50 for them. When I am on a fishing vacation I like to have a pair of moccasins to slip my feet into after taking off my waders. Mine are oil-tanned leather and cost $7.50. They are tough enough for hard duty.

SHIRTS

The fishing shirt is a minor detail. Whether it is wool or cotton depends on season and location. If you are going away in spring or fall, when you can expect both cool and warm weather, go prepared for both. Do not use a shirt that is white, yellow, or other light color. Such shirts make you too conspicuous to the fish.

RAINWEAR

The fisherman can expect all types of weather, cold or hot, clear or rainy. It is wise to carry with you in the big rear pocket of your fishing jacket a lightweight rain shirt. This can be of waist length—which together with your waders will give you complete protection—or it can come below the knees. The latter serves well for the boat fisherman. These cost from $18 to $20. A three-quarter length parka made of sheeting coated with rubber is priced at $12.95. A featherweight rain suit of shirt and trousers is made of balloon cloth base with rubber coating. The shirt is hooded, thus giving the wearer complete protection. The shirt is priced at $10.90 and the trousers at $5.95. Let the rain pelt down and the wind blow, if the boat fisherman's feet are protected with rubber shoes he can fish dry and warm in such a rain suit.

CHAPTER 2

Lines and Leaders

THE FISHERMAN'S LINE is important. If he uses care in selecting the right one, he will fish with more comfort and greater pleasure. Also, he will cast better and catch more fish. My first fly line was selected with no knowledge of the best type or size for my rod. It was a cheap enameled line, tapered HFH, while my rod was 9½ feet long and weighed 6 ounces. The enamel soon cracked and slivered. Where it cracked, the line momentarily "hung" in the guides on the cast, slowing up and holding back, thus shortening the length of the cast. Also, the line was too light for the rod, and it took a lot of strength to get it out for just a fair distance. After several fishing excursions I was thoroughly fed up with it, took it off the reel, and used it for tying parcels. That was all it was good for. Then I saw the folly of trying to save a little money and bought a tapered HCH silk line. As I added other fly rods of varying lengths and weights, I bought lines specially adapted to each rod. That brings us to the demonstrated fact that one line will not do for all rods.

If you are well enough advanced in your fly fishing to own several fly rods, and if they vary in weight and length, you should have a reel for each line suited to a particular rod. We are likely to acquire three different types of fly rods: a rather short, light one of about 3 ounces, 7½ feet long, for use on small streams where the trout run small and overhanging trees make long and heavy rods impractical; one of medium length, 8 feet, weighing about 4 ounces, for the average stream and average trout; the third longer and more powerful, say, 9½ to 10 feet long and weighing 5½ to 6 ounces, for larger rivers where big fish abound, and to use when fly fishing for salmon and black bass. Note the different lines to which each of these three types is adapted. The little rod requires an HEH nylon line, the middle size can be used with an HDH, but if it is of rather stiff action an HCH works a little better, while the longer and heavier rod requires a GAG. Using the big rod with the HEH that does so well with the little rod would involve work, not pleasure, and the GAG line on the little rod would just about ruin the rod.

You won't want to take the time while on a stream to switch lines on the reel you have on your rod. If you have a floating or greased line on your reel, are fishing dry flies and find the trout are not rising to the surface, you will want to change to a sinking wet-fly line to get your flies down to the depth where the fish are lying. If you have in a pocket of your fishing jacket another reel loaded with a Dacron or sinking line, the change from one reel to another is simple.

FLY LINES

Fly lines are made of silk or nylon and each type has been treated with a non-enamel dressing, which gives it slickness and also added weight. A fly line must be silky smooth so as to flow through the guides and have enough weight to shoot forward easily. Unlike bait and spin casting, where the weight of the lure plus the propelling power of the rod carries the line out, in fly fishing it is the line weight added to rod propulsion that carries out the fly. That gives importance to the finish of the fly line. A good fly line will not be kinky or sticky.

Silk or Nylon.   Which is better, silk or nylon line? Each has some advantages. The nylon line is a little cheaper and is more durable. The silk line, even though well cared for, properly dried after use, and dressed often with line dressing, will lose some of its slickness and strength with age. Also, some silk fly lines may become sticky and not cast well, even though made by a first-class manufacturer.

My experience has been that if you are lucky enough to get a *good* tapered silk fly line, of weight suited to the length and weight of the fly rod on which it is to be used, flexible yet reasonably stiff, of vacuum finish, it is slightly superior. Such a line in a 30-yard length costs about $11, and in 35-yard length $12. Tapers available are HEH, HDH, HCH, GBG, GBF, and GAF. The first and last letters of each group of three refer to the diameter of the tapers at each end. The middle letter gives the diameter of the belly of the line where the weight is that carries out the line on the cast. The heavier the rod, the more weight is needed in the line's belly.

Nylon tapered lines come in HEH, HDH, HCH, GBG, GAG, and GAF, in both 30- and 40-yard lengths. Prices range from about $10 for the HEH to $13 in 40-yard length GAF. Nylon lines from a reputable maker are *good* lines, make no mistake about that, and the fact that they cast just about as well as the best silk line, and are more durable and dependable, makes them the better buy, all things considered.

The following chart shows how to fit your line to your rod.

Rod length and weight	Double taper	Torpedo head	Level
7½ to 8 ft.	Nylon HDH	Nylon HDG	Nylon E
3½ to 4¼ oz.	Silk HEH	Silk HEH	Silk F
8½ to 9 ft.	Nylon HCH	Nylon HCF	Nylon D
4¾ to 5½ oz.	Silk HDH	Silk HDG	Silk E
9 ft.	Nylon GBG	Nylon GBF	Nylon C
5½ to 6½ oz.	Silk HCH	Silk HCF	Silk D
9 to 9¼ ft.	Nylon GAG	Nylon GAF	Nylon B
6½ to 7 oz.	Silk GBG	Silk GBF	Silk C

The beginner who wishes to keep expenses down until he has profited by experience can get along quite nicely with one tapered line if he has but one fly rod. He can use it for wet-fly fishing in shallow water where no split shot is needed to take the leader and fly down. The advantage of a tapered line is that the leader end of the line, being of finer diameter than the belly, lands on the water with little if any disturbance, and consequently is less likely to alarm the fish.

Types of Fly Line

6'	30'	6'
to Reel	DOUBLE TAPER LINE	*to Leader*

16'	20'	6'
to Reel	WEIGHT FORWARD LINE	*to Leader*

LEVEL LINE

New Fly-Line Classification.   During the last year or so another system for marking fly lines has been developed by line manufacturers. Although many sporting goods stores still stock fly lines graded in the old system discussed above, anglers would be wise to be familiar with the new system as well.

The new system marks fly lines by weight rather than by diameter. Each line is assigned a number, 1 through 12, which corresponds to a particular weight. Every fly line bearing a certain number, regardless of material or taper, will have the same weight.

The weight of the fly line is determined by weighing the first 30 feet of line. That is the length most fly casters have overhead during their forward and back casts, the length that directly affects the play of the rod. The weight is measured in grains. The following table gives the new fly-line sizes with their corresponding weights.

Size	Weight in Grains
1	60
2	80
3	100
4	120
5	140
6	160
7	185
8	210
9	240
10	280
11	330
12	380

The average angler will generally use sizes 6 through 10, the others being too light or too heavy for routine fly fishing for trout, bass, steelhead, or salmon.

Fly lines are also graded according to type—level, double taper, forward taper (torpedo head), or single taper; and according to whether they are floating, sinking, or intermediate lines. Intermediate lines float when dressed and sink when not dressed. Thus a floating double-taper line, size 7, would be marked DT-7-F. A sinking level line, size 8, would be marked L-8-S, etc.

Lines for Dry-Fly Fishing.　　The dry-fly line should float and the leader sink. If the line sinks, it will cause the fly to sink also. Some lines now on the market have built-in floatability attained by tiny air chambers in the line, by a hollow core, or by a special finish. But all types of fly line except the sinking lines should be greased at intervals with one of the preparations on the market. Likewise, the leader should be treated with leader-soak or rubbed with something that will have the same effect. My friend the late Fred Hollender, a skilled fly fisherman, would rub his leader with toothpaste, and since he put me on to it, I like to carry a tube of it in my pocket.

Lines for Wet-Fly Fishing. A sinking line is fine for wet-fly fishing in lakes, ponds, and streams where there are deep pools or depths greater than average. It takes the leader down to where the lunkers are lying. Those of Dacron have a higher specific gravity than those of silk or nylon, thus carrying the fly or nymph down to where the deep-lying fish are. They too come in tapers ranging from HEG, HDG, HCF, and GBF to GAF, the price advancing a dollar with each taper from $9 to $13.

Torpedo-Head Lines. For bass fishing with bugs and poppers, the torpedo-head line has its advantages. This line has a long belly, a short, heavy section, followed by a long tapered end. These lines make distance casting easier and the tapered end lands on the water with more delicacy, thus increasing your chances of taking wary fish. Tapers vary on such lines. Some come with a long final taper, others with short. For bass-bug fishing, choose the short taper; for long casts with flies on lakes, ponds, and the larger streams, either for trout or bass, take the long taper.

Here I must add that most trout taken on flies are caught within 30 to 40 feet of the fisherman who moves with caution and is careful to be neither seen nor heard by the fish. Distance with casts is not often an advantage except on the large rivers of the Rockies and the Pacific Coast. The cautious fly fisherman who realizes that trout are sensitive to sound and motion, knows where a fish is likely to be lying, and is able to make delicate casts averaging about 35 feet, will outfish the man who strains for distance with full-arm casting.

Level Lines. Level lines have the advantage of being considerably cheaper than tapered lines. For instance, a large sporting goods house handling only high-quality fishing supplies offers a nonsinking level line claimed not to waterlog, crack, or peel, length 25 yards, at the following prices: Size E, $2.50; D, $2.75; C, $3; and B, $3.25. It is claimed that this line will float all day without dressing. This same line in 30-yard lengths and tapered with the same bellies as the level line costs about $7 more. The beginner and the man who must budget his expenditures can get a lot of pleasure out of such a level line. It does not permit such delicate casting as a tapered line, but it will take plenty of fish.

In the summer of 1959 I was fishing the streams, lakes, and beaver ponds of northeastern Washington. My son and son-in-law, at the first lake we fished, outfished me consistently. Each was using a sinking line, and on that day I had forgotten to bring along a reel loaded with such a line. The trout, mostly brookies, were on the bottom feeding on snails. I tried to get my leader down to them by weighting it with split shot. I ended that day with only two trout as against a total of fourteen for my companions. The next day, having provided myself with the reel loaded with Dacron line, I did much better. Such lines are particularly useful early in the season when the water is still so cold that the trout are sluggish and feed on the bottom.

Care of Fly Lines.   When you invest in a fine tapered line, don't think it is going to wear long and satisfactorily without care. Tapers gradually shorten with use. If at the end of a day's fishing you find the knot connecting the line with the leader has become too tight to unfasten readily, cut the line at the knot. Your line will last longer if you change the tapered end often so that the taper on the reel becomes the end to which the leader is tied. By having an extra reel this may be done without much bother. Obviously when you transfer the line from one reel to the other, the leader end of the line becomes the end which is fastened to the spool of the extra reel. Then, after some use, it may be wound back again on the spool of the first reel.

A fly line will pick up coarse sand and dirt during a day's fishing. If not removed, this will act as an abrasive as the line passes through the rod guides. At the end of several hours of fishing, take a soft cloth and gently rub down the line to remove the dirt or sand. I find that storing my fly lines over the winter on drying reels prevents them from developing kinks.

If you find it necessary to splice two lines together, first scrape the ends of both lines with a razor blade. Then fray both ends of the lines to be joined, each for about an inch, using a needle. Then spread apart the frayed ends and push them together so they enmesh. Wrap them tightly with waxed thread or silk for about ½ inch, stopping your wrapping to clip off the unwrapped ends of the lines. Then continue the wrapping over the entire splice and about ⅛ inch of the unscraped line on each side. Roll down the splice with a bottle to make it smooth and even, then give it three coats of varnish.

Backing.   Backing is a good thing if you are going to fish waters where large fish may be expected. As the average fly line is only 30 yards long, it follows that a lunky, active, and powerful fish like a steelhead trout can run it out in short order, Monofilament makes a very good backing and is of such a fine diameter, being strong for its weight, that it takes much less space on a fly reel than a fly line. A 20-pound-test monofilament backing is adequate for outsized trout and steelheads. Fasten it to the spool end of your casting line. A 10-pound-test monofilament is quite strong enough for most waters and the average trout.

Line Dressing. When dry-fly fishing you should dress your line a number of times during the day with a good line dressing, designed to keep your line on the surface of the water and prevent it from sinking. A sinking line inevitably pulls the dry fly under water, causing drag, and rarely will a trout take a dragging fly. Most good tackle stores carry dressing pads which are impregnated with a dry-fly line dressing. I have used Mucilin, an English preparation, for years with good results. It has the merit also of serving as a fly dressing to make a dry-fly float. The price of these preparations usually is under a dollar.

LINES FOR BAIT CASTING

In fly fishing, the weight of the line activated by the rod gets out the fly, which is practically weightless. But in bait casting, the weight of the lure sent forward by the rod carries out the line. Thus there is much difference between the two methods of fishing. When first I began to cast for bass and pickerel, my line was 6-pound test, of fine diameter, and undressed silk. At the start of my casting it worked fine, but soon with repeated casts and retrieving it became waterlogged. The length of the casts became progressively shorter and casting became work. As each cast went out, a fine spray from the line wet hand, wrist, and arm. I did not realize what was the trouble until later I saw in a tackle shop a waterproofed, hard-braided casting line. I bought it and no longer was annoyed by being sprayed, and my casts were made with less effort.

The bait caster is faced with the fact that a heavy lure can be cast with ease on a light line such as a 6-pound test on his reel, but that when he switches to a light lure, he must also use a light line. Furthermore, in recent years, there has been a pronounced trend toward lighter lures. As in the case of fly casting, where a line of one weight will not do well with rods of varying weights but does its best with the rod to which it is fitted, so here for best results the angler should carry with him an extra reel or two loaded with casting lines of varying strengths. Then, should he switch from a lure of one weight to another, he can get the most out of his fishing. A waterproof line of 8- to 12-pound test will handle well plugs weighing up to about ⅜ ounce; for lures weighing up to ⅝ ounce use a waterproofed 15-pound-test line; and for the really big lures a 20-pound-test line works better.

A first-class dealer catalogs 50-yard spools of good line, two spools connected, at the following prices: 9-pound test, price per spool, $1.45; 12-pound test, $1.50; 15-pound test, $1.60; 18-pound test, $1.70; 25-pound test, $1.90. As compared with tapered fly lines, these prices are very low, and it pays the fisherman to carry with him an extra reel or two loaded with lines suited to the varying weights of lures in his tackle box.

LINES FOR SPINNING

It now is common knowledge that spinning enables the fisherman to get longer casts than is possible in either fly or bait casting, and with lures lighter than those used when bait casting. These range in weight from a low of $\frac{1}{16}$ ounce up to $\frac{1}{2}$ ounce, and the spinning fisherman has the advantage of using a line that is practically all light leader and so less visible to the fish. In spinning you have the choice between a monofilament line and one that is braided. Braided monofilament lines used with the heavier spinning lures are likely to get twisted, and then they kink. Ordinary single-strand monofilament lines are likely to be like fine wire and come off the spinning reel in corkscrewlike curls. Recently the Du Pont Company, developers of nylon, came out with Stren, which has more strength and less give than monofilament. It is stronger than nylon monofilament, of equal diameter, limper, and more flexible. It overcomes the handicap of wiriness in the ordinary monofilament, and in my experience is preferable. Most of the line makers now offer lines of this material.

I have before me the catalog of a first-class dealer. It offers 100 yards of a 2-pound-test Stren, diameter .0047 inch, at $1.25; 4-pound test, diameter .0070 inch, at $1.55; 6-pound test, diameter .0087 inch, $1.85; 8-pound test, diameter .0101 inch, $2.25; 10-pound test, diameter .0114 inch, $2.50; 12-pound test, diameter .0125 inch, $2.75; 14-pound test, diameter .0136 inch, $3. To give you an idea, a 4-pound-test line will handle lures up to $\frac{1}{2}$ ounce in weight. Unless you are fishing waters where game fish get really big and rambunctious, a 4-pound- or 6-pound-test line is quite sufficient for ordinary fishing. Just set the drag on your reel to a little less than the breaking point of the line.

LEADERS

Just as no one line will do for all types of fishing, there is no one size or length of leader suited to all kinds of conditions. The leader is important for it is the connecting link between line and lure, and the less visibility it has, the more likely it is to get a wary fish to accept the lure. Therefore length, calibration or diameter, and color are all to be considered.

Before synthetics such as nylon were developed and placed upon the market, there was only one leader material available, and that was silkworm gut. Gut is good but open to criticism for several faults. It must be dampened in a leader box before it is used so that it casts upon the water flat and straight, without curling. Furthermore it may deteriorate with age. I recall the time when I carried over from one season to another a package of fine gut leader points to tie to the ends of leaders which I had shortened by cutting off flies when changing patterns. The points looked as good as new. But after losing several good fish because the point broke when I tried to hook the fish, I got wise and tested them by pulling on them. There was not a sound point in the lot.

Then Japanese synthetics came on the market. When new they looked like the answer to a fisherman's prayer, but they got stringy and disintegrated after little use. They were no good at all. Then came nylon and other synthetics. The leader problem was solved. The material is strong for its calibration, it does not require dampening before use, and in my experience does not deteriorate from one season to another. Some fishermen say there is some stretch to the material. I have not been conscious of it. When using gut leaders I always tied the leader end to the fly with the conventional turle knot, which is made by threading the leader tip through the eye of the fly, tying a slip-knot loop in the end, then passing the loop over the fly and drawing the knot tightly over the eye of the fly. It worked fine with gut and was secure, but I found nylon more slippery than the gut and the nylon would pull free from the fly. I changed to the barrel wrap and have had no trouble since.

Primarily the selection of a leader depends upon the condition of the water. When trout fishing, if the water is high and colored, making the leader less visible to the fish, it may be as short as 7½ feet and tapered to 2X or even 1X. But such a leader is likely to be ineffective if the water is low and clear and the trout wary. Then you need greater length and a much finer terminal point, and a 9-foot or even a 12-foot leader is desirable, tapered to 4X or even 5X. With such fine leader points, a hand that is heavy on the strike will lose many fish. Such an angler must school himself to be gentle and do little more than raise his rod when a fish rises to the fly.

Tapered leader tips vary widely in strength according to the type of leader materials used. For instance, one fine representative tackle company carries three different types of leaders. In the case of one type of leader, the strength of the terminal tip, 4X, is given as 1.75-pound breaking point; in the second it is given a breaking point of 2½ pounds; in the third 4 pounds. In the heavier leaders 1X strength is rated at 3½ pounds; in the second type of leader this same 1X is rated at 6-pound test; in the third at 7-pound. So it is well, where possible, to select tapered leaders on the basis of point test. The usual X rating is too variable to be of much help.

The advantage of a tapered leader is that, if it is well made, the butt sections have sufficient weight to carry the leader well out on the cast, and make the finer sections land straight and delicately on the water.

Where the water's surface is disturbed, as in a strong current, and you are fishing a large fly, say from size 6 up to size 10, a 7½-foot leader tapered to about a 3-pound test will do very well. But under ordinary conditions I am a strong believer in 9-foot leaders tapered to 3 or 4X, or roughly 2- to 3-pound test.

On hard-fished streams, particularly in the East where brown trout prevail, leader length and fineness is important in dry-fly fishing after the spring run-off. I know men who on such waters use leaders anywhere from 12 to 20 feet long, tapered to 5X or even 6X. Any length beyond 12 or perhaps 14 feet is beyond my capabilities. Not only is there the question of ability to handle such a length when casting, but also that of netting a fish after it has been whipped and brought in close enough to be netted. When I am waist-deep in a strong current, trying to net a trout and at the same time keep my footing, I have to extend my left arm holding the rod as high as I can stretch so as to get the fish close enough to net. Otherwise the knot connecting the line with the leader is quite likely to stick in the tip-top of the rod and then there is trouble. Of course, it is possible to splice the leader to the line but the splicing adds an element of risk. Once when I had made such a splice, just as I was about to net a two-pounder the splice came apart. So now I don't bother with it.

In wet-fly fishing the length of the leader is not as important as in dry-fly fishing. A 7½-foot leader is often long enough. This applies not only to streams but to trout ponds and lakes where much of the fishing is wet fly. A leader tapered to about 2X, roughly 3-pound test, makes a good all-round leader for such fishing. If the water of the pond is calm and the fish pretty choosy, switch to a 9-foot leader treated with a sinking preparation. For some unknown reason, wary trout in calm water are likely to ignore a fly tied to a floating leader but take it if the leader is sunken.

Bass are not nearly as leader-shy as are trout. In bugging for bass, a

6- or 7-foot length of level leader of about 7-pound test will do all right. Bluegills and other sunfish rise well to the fly and give good sport on a fly rod. A 7½-foot leader tapered to about a 2-pound test does very well on these fish.

Atlantic salmon are powerful fish. A good all-round leader for them is a 9-footer tapered to about 10-pound test. If the salmon in the river run extra large, a leader tapered to about a 17-pound test is better.

For leader tippets to replace shortened leader tips, you can get at any sporting goods store coils of nylon of any pound test you want. Be guided in this by the pound test of the leader ends you are using. Cut off as much of the nylon as you need, and attach to your leader end by using the barrel wrap.

Leaders of synthetic material such as nylon are much more reasonable in cost than silkworm gut. I prefer the knotless leaders to those of strands of varying diameters. I believe the knots in a knotted leader are visible to the fish, for I have seen trout nip at a knot in my dry-fly leader. A leading supplier offers these knotless leaders as follows:

7½ ft. 1X 3.5	lb. test	....	$.40
7½ ft. 2X 2.9	lb. test	....	.40
7½ ft. 3X 2.25	lb. test	....	.40
7½ ft. 4X 1.75	lb. test	....	.40
9 ft. 1X 3.5	lb. test	....	.50
9 ft. 2X 2.9	lb. test	....	.50
9 ft. 3X 2.25	lb. test	....	.50
9 ft. 4X 1.75	lb. test	....	.50

CHAPTER 3

The Fisherman's Accessories

THERE ARE MANY accessories that will add to the fisherman's pleasure. He does not have to get them all at once but as he finds the need for them. There is a lot of fun in assembling an outfit. Some items are used constantly; others may be required only occasionally.

FLY FISHING ACCESSORIES

Fly Boxes. The fly fisherman must have a box in which to carry his flies. Before modern plastics were available, I bought several metal fly boxes. These boxes had a number of cozy little compartments, each with a transparent lid activated by a spring. The lid worked well at first, but inevitably the wire springs got rusted and stubborn; in order to take a fly from a compartment I had to pry the lid open. That is pretty exasperating when the trout are rising and time is valuable.

I turned to plastic boxes, but they were brittle and easily broken. When I stored them over winter in a chest with moth balls or similar insect repellent, the fumes affected the plastic so that the boxes became cloudy and were no longer transparent.

The best fly boxes that I have come across are of Tenite, which is transparent and astonishingly tough. It is claimed that you can stand on a box made of this material without breaking it. They measure 7 x 4 x 1½ inches and cost about $1.25 each.

Line Drier. To dry or store lines a line drier is a necessity. I use a wooden line drier with a 5-inch cylinder. The drier is 13 inches long, 6 inches high, and 7 inches wide. Price: around $3.25.

A well-equipped fly fisherman begins the day. He carries a wicker creel, landing net, fly boxes, and wears special fly-holding hat. He is selecting a fly from a tough, transparent Tenite box. *Ontario Dept. of Lands & Forests.*

Container for Leaders.   Some sort of container is needed in which to carry leaders. When I used leaders of silkworm gut, I carried a metal leader box containing pads to dampen the leaders and keep them from curling in casting. Such a box isn't needed with the modern nylon or other plastic leaders. I have found that an old leather wallet with just two compartments is satisfactory. It is wide enough to hold the leaders without jamming.

Magnetic fly box (left) keeps flies anchored in strong wind. Box below has a magnifying glass on the cover to aid in changing flies and matching natural insects. *Orvis Co.*

Fisherman's Knife.   Did you ever leave the water to sit on the bank and dress your fish and find you had no knife with you? Or have you found the knife you carry has somehow got badly rusted? My fisherman's knife is 5 inches long, rust-proof all over, has an extra-sharp blade, and these added features: hook disgorger, ruler, scaler, bottle-cap remover, magnetic tip, hook sharpener and straightener. It costs $5.

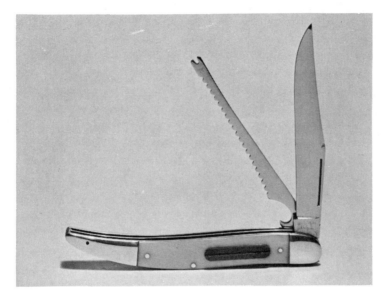

Rustproof fisherman's knife is equipped with cutting blade, combo hook disgorger and scaler blade, bottle opener, and hook sharpener-straightener. Knife is 5 inches long. *Orvis* Co.

Gut Cutter.   An essential is a gut cutter to take off a fly in changing to another pattern, and to clip off surplus gut after tying on a fly. A handy gadget is a clipper, patterned after the well-known nail clipper, with a little stiletto to pierce the eye of the hook when it is clogged with the varnishlike stuff fly tyers use, and a little disgorger. It sells for about 75 cents.

Wading Staff.   When you are fishing a big rushing river, you may feel the need for the support of a wading staff. My friend, the late Lou Noe, always carried a stout bamboo long-handled landing net and used it as a wading staff. I tried it and it gave me a feeling of security, as I could probe ahead with it and feel out the stream bottom. I used to do some skiing and reasoned that one of my ski sticks with a steel spike at the bottom would make a good staff. I removed the little hoop of leather and wood above the spike, and had an ideal wading staff. I lashed it to a strong cord to loop over my shoulder when not using it, and now probe my way along rocky and slippery river bottoms with ease.

Water Thermometer.   The value of a water thermometer will be pointed out in the chapter on water temperatures. One firm catalogs a fish-finder thermometer for $2.50, and also offers a fisherman's barometer for $8.95. A special dial designed for fishermen indicates whether fishing conditions are good or bad.

Polaroid Glasses.   Polaroid glasses are very useful to the angler. They not only serve as sun glasses but also cut out the glare on the water that makes it impossible to see the fish under the surface. The glasses weigh only 1 ounce, cost about $3.

Knot-Tying Vise.   Most of us feel, when tying knots, that we need an extra hand. That need is especially felt when tying barrel knots for putting on a tippet to the end of a leader, or in tying a tapered leader where sections of nylon or gut in varying sizes are knotted together. A practical knot-tying vise that solves this problem is available. The two sections of gut are gripped firmly in two uprights, leaving the hands free to knot them together. Price: around $2.50.

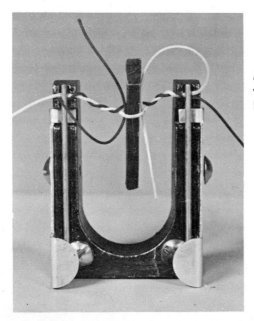

Many anglers use a knot-tying vise for splicing lines, tying barrel knots. *Orvis Co.*

Pliers. I bought Sargent "Sportmate" pliers some years ago, and always carry them with me on a fishing trip. They have parallel jaws, a wire and hook cutter, and act as wrench, pocket vise, hook disgorger, hook, wire, and nail straightener and shot crimper. Every now and then some fisherman gets a hook imbedded in his flesh. The orthodox way to get the hook out of the flesh is to run the barb on through and bring it out of the flesh. Then it is possible to cut off the barb with a wire cutter and work the barbless hook back again the same way it came in. The wire cutter on these pliers lets you do just that. They are priced at about $2.95.

Rod Case. A good fishing rod needs protection when it is traveling. The cloth cases in which many of them come cannot shield them from hard knocks. Each rod deserves a metal container with screw-cap top. Such cases range in price from $6.50 to $8.25, depending on the rod's length and whether it is in two or three pieces.

When you are going to distant fishing waters—either by train, plane, or car—you are likely to take with you more than one rod, and to carry them loose in their cases can be exasperating. Several years ago I got a rod-carrying case of heavy canvas with leather handle and fittings which holds three to four rods in their metal cases. It costs from $6.70 to $7.15, depending upon size.

Insect Repellent. Mosquitoes, black flies, and "no-seeums" can make the angler miserable in the North Woods in May and June. The fisherman should protect himself with a good repellent or a head net. There are several good repellents on the market, among them "2-C," which will not damage or stain equipment and materials and has no offensive odor and "OFF!," which can be applied to skin and clothing without harm.

Landing Net. There are a number of different types of landing nets on the market. I have made long fishing trips by rail and have found that the conventional landing net offers the biggest transportation problem. It is difficult to pack in a duffel bag and is stiff and unyielding. What is needed is a net that can be carried in a small container and assembled at the stream. Such a net can be obtained for about $4.95. It is full size when assembled, with a folding steel frame that fits snugly into a pocket-sized leather pouch only 5½ inches square.

Creel. The conventional willow creels are fine when you can go by car to the place you intend to fish. But when you have to go by rail or plane they become a nuisance, always sticking out and getting in the way. A collapsible creel of canvas which folds flat and is easily packed sells for around $5.95.

Hone.   You will need a small hone to sharpen hooks. Touch up your hook every now and then, and you'll lose fewer fish. All tackle stores carry them, and the price is usually less than a dollar.

Fly-Line Dressing.   For dressing your dry-fly line so that it will float, there are a number of preparations. I have used Mucilin paste for years, and like it. There also are dressing pads impregnated with Newton's Streamline Dressing. Mucilin sells for 60 cents for the paste in cans and 65 cents in liquid form. The pads cost 50 cents. Dry-fly dressing in small bottles is available for $1 at all tackle stores.

A fly and leader soak is needed in wet-fly or nymph fishing to get your fly down where it will do the most good. Also, in dry-fly fishing it is needed to sink the leader. Fly and leader sink, in a nonleak bottle with a brush applicator, sells for around 50 cents in most stores.

ACCESSORIES FOR THE BAIT FISHERMAN

Minnow Trap and Pail.   A minnow trap is an essential for a bait fisherman. Usually any lake or pond that has game fish will also have its minnows. Be careful not to keep any small game fish that might enter the trap. A glass trap which sells for around $8 does a good job of luring minnows if it is placed in the right spot and properly baited with cracker crumbs. After setting it, be sure to visit it soon for the minnows that enter it will soon leave when the bait is exhausted. You will find further details on placing and operating it in the chapter on baits.

To keep minnows alive and healthy the fisherman must have a minnow pail. Made of polyethylene, with outer and inner buckets, floating and self-aerating, it sells for about $5.95.

Landing Net.   The boat fisherman needs a long-handled landing net. One 42¼ inches long with a cork grip can be purchased for about $13.50.

Tackle Boxes.   The handiest type of tackle box has two or three compartmented trays that work on the cantilever principle. Usually of metal or plastic, they range in price from about $2.50 up to $18 or more, depending upon finish and quality.

Chair Back.   If you have ever sat on a backless seat in a boat all day, leaning forward, backward, and sidewise trying to relieve your aching back, you realize that a chair back is not a luxury but a necessity. I take one with me whenever I go boat fishing. It enables one to fish in comfort. A nice one with an aluminum frame and foam-rubber cushion weighs only 45 ounces and folds compactly. It is priced at $5.40.

Glass minnow trap is a handy item for the bait fisherman who wants to be sure he won't be caught short. *Orvis* Co.

Life Preserver. When you go fishing on a lake where the water may get disturbingly rough, it gives you ease of mind to have with you either a boat cushion filled with kapok, which will keep you afloat in case of boat swamping, or a life-saver vest, also filled with kapok. The first lists at about $3.90 and the second at about $4.40.

Cooler. It is disheartening to carry home a fine catch of fish and find they have spoiled. A portable cooler is the remedy. A leakproof cooler with fiber-glass insulation and separate ice compartment, which can be used either with ice or a cooling material, sells for $13.50 and up. The same company carries "Perma-Ice," a material that will keep fish and foods cold for hours, comes in units, and lasts for years. These units, measuring 12 x 3½ x 1¾ inches, are priced at $1.69 per unit.

Fish Finder.   This is the newest in fishermen's accessories. It utilizes an electronic device which can locate and track moving fish. The sound of a moving fish comes back to the device and is heard in the earphones of the operator. It operates on a single 9-volt dry battery. It weighs 4 pounds and the battery 1 pound. It sells for $48.95, and the battery for $1.35.

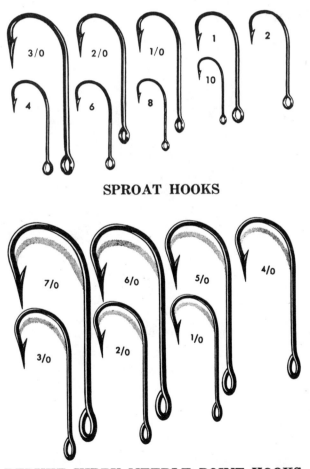

SPROAT HOOKS

DELUXE KIRBY NEEDLE POINT HOOKS

Actual sizes of two of the most popular types of fish hooks used in fresh-water fishing. *Pfleuger Co.*

CHAPTER 4

The Fisherman's Baits

AT ONE TIME or another practically all of our fresh-water game fishes will take almost any type of flesh that is properly presented to them on a hook. It may be the flesh of fish, animal, insect, frog, fowl, crustacean, worm. All are acceptable if the fish is in a feeding mood.

WORMS

The earthworm heads the list of baits because of its attractiveness to practically all of our fishes. This creature is important not only to the fisherman but to the soil, and so to the farmer and gardener. Charles Darwin considered the earthworm so useful that he wrote a book on the subject, *The Formation of Vegetable Mould Through the Action of Worms*. In it he describes how the earthworm adds humus to the soil through the disintegration of rocks and vegetable matter by means of humus acids which it generates. He does not mention its great value to the bait angler, to whom it is a standby.

Look for earthworms where the soil is fertile, black loam being specially good. If the soil is dry, the worms will be found deep where ground moisture still exists. When such is the case, you will bring the worms closer to the surface if several hours before you go fishing you soak the selected spot with a few pails of water. The worms may be kept alive and happy by placing them in a wooden pail or box filled with good garden loam and storing them in a cool, dark place. When you store the worms for some time, they should be fed by scattering a little cereal, corn meal, chopped suet, coffee grounds, or bits of hard-boiled egg on the surface of the earth in the storage box or pail.

41

In use, hook the worm under the collar, then again through the head or body, leaving the ends to wiggle to attract the fish. Discard dead or mangled worms. Worms should be lively on the hook to be most effective. Before you take them on your fishing excursion, it is well to let them scour and toughen by placing them in sphagnum moss, first soaking the moss in water, squeezing out the surplus and leaving it merely damp. Nurserymen and florists make much use of this type of moss in preparing rooted plants for shipment, and the moss may be obtained from them.

Nightwalkers, the large and lively members of the worm family, are nocturnal in habit. Look for them on lawns. To take them, equip yourself with a flashlight or lantern with a thin, transparent red cloth or red tissue tied over the lens or glass. Red light is less alarming to this wary worm than white or yellow. As they are sensitive to soil vibrations, don sneakers, walk softly, and sneak up on them. When you see one it is likely to have its rear extremity anchored in its hole. Seize it quickly. If you pull on it at once you will probably pull it apart. Keep a firm grasp on it. The muscular effort of the worm is spasmodic. When its hold in the soil appears to be lessened, pull it a little farther out of the soil, and then wait for another muscular relaxation. Store nightwalkers the same way as ordinary earthworms.

Manure worms, called redworms by many, are found in manure piles. In my opinion they are inferior to the other two kinds just mentioned, as they are softer and do not hold to the hook as well. Hooked as described, all of these worms will live for some time and be lively on the hook.

I have found nothing better for a "worm bank" than a compost heap. I have a garden with both flowers and vegetables. To bring up the fertility of the soil I have made a practice of raking up grass cuttings and dead leaves and putting them, with vegetable waste from the garden, into a flat-topped heap in a shady corner of the garden. It takes from one to two years for the heap to disintegrate into rich mould like the leaf mould you find in forests of deciduous trees. Worms find their way to the heap from the garden, aid the decomposition of the vegetable matter, and before long the pile is alive with them. The process is helped by wetting down the pile with a hose several times during the summer.

MINNOWS

Minnows are an important bait for bass, the pike family, crappies, and trout. Consult the fish laws of your state to learn what, if any, are the restrictions on their capture and use. Some states ban their capture in specified waters. Other states forbid their use in various waters because many good fishing lakes have been practically ruined by the introduction into them of trash fish that were used as bait. Do not use carp or goldfish as bait for that reason.

Where legal, minnows may easily be taken with a minnow trap baited with fragments of food such as cracker crumbs. These traps are made of galvanized wire or glass, the design of each type being similar. The typical wire trap is rectangular. The funnels may number from one to four. The glass trap is usually round.

Glass traps are most effective in streams, and commercial bait dealers often use them. "Raising Bait Fishes," Circular 35, Fish and Wildlife Service, U.S. Department of the Interior, gives useful advice on the various kinds of minnows and their capture. Walk along the bank of a stream and study the water closely to locate a minnow school. Having sighted one, go upstream from the minnows and seek a spot where there is little current, with water depth less than a foot. It is likely that you will find such a spot near the bank. Scoop out a shallow depression into which the trap may be set, bait the trap with cracker crumbs, and place it in the depression with the funnel opening facing downstream. Some of the cracker crumbs will float downstream, thus making a chum. The minnows will follow this chum into the trap. The trap must be visited within a few minutes to remove those minnows that have been captured. If this is not done, the minnows will escape as soon as all the crumbs have been eaten.

Using one of the wire traps, my method has been to prowl along the shorelines of a pond or lake, either afoot or in a boat. Usually the minnows stick close to weed beds in the shallows where they are safer from predatory fish. Having located them, I sink my baited trap, taking care to attach to it a rope with a stick of wood for a float. This is to make it easy to find the trap again. While a brightly painted piece of wood as a buoy makes it easier for you to relocate your trap, it also is so conspicuous that a conscienceless person may see it, lift your trap, and rob it of its minnows. I have had it happen. In one instance the trap itself was gone.

Another way to collect minnows is with a baited lift net. This net is square, with ropes attached to the corners meeting above it at a single rope which in turn is attached to the tip of a pole. Cracker crumbs are wetted and tossed into the water over the sunken net to draw the minnows. Most states specify the maximum size of these nets. Here too consult the laws of your state.

After capture the minnows are placed in a minnow pail which has an inner container of wire netting or of galvanized metal with a bail for lifting it out of the pail with its contained minnows. The inner container is perforated to let the water escape when lifted, making one of the minnows easy to capture and hook. The angler, having selected a minnow, lowers the container into the pail again. It is necessary to aerate the water in the pail at intervals to keep the little fish alive. To do this, empty out some of the water, and refill it with fresh water from the lake or stream you are fishing. If you are in a boat, keep the minnow pail out of the sunshine by placing it under a seat. Water-aerating minnow pails have now been placed on the market. They are an improvement.

There are several different ways of hooking a minnow. The simplest is to hook it through both lips. If care is used to keep from grasping the little fish too tightly, thus hooked it will keep lively for some time. Another way is to hook it lightly through the back just behind the dorsal fin, just deep enough to hold the minnow without injuring the spine, taking in with the hook little more than the skin and a bit of flesh. For trolling you can kill the minnow and run the hook through the mouth, down through the body, and then out. It is well to do this so that the minnow's body is curved and will spin through the water. With this hook-up, use a swivel or two to avoid twisting the line.

As minnows are so popular and effective as a bait, here is a brief summary of the range and characteristics of some of the tougher species that best withstand handling and hooking, and are durable on the hook. The information given is based upon Circular 35.

Suckers are widely distributed, ranging from northern Canada down into Georgia, Arkansas, and Oklahoma. This fish is durable in the minnow pail and a good bait for walleyes and muskies.

Fathead minnows, which reach a maximum length of 3½ inches, are found throughout southern Canada and from Lake Champlain west to North and South Dakota, and south to Kentucky and the Rio Grande. Their preferred habitat is ponds, streams, and shallow lakes. The lateral line appears on only half of their bodies. The male in spawning season has a black head and tubercles on the snout and under the chin. They are good bait for panfish and are also used for pike.

Creek chubs may be identified by a black spot at the base of the dorsal fin, the large mouth, which comes back to a location below the eye, and a small barbel just above the mouth corners and concealed in a groove. In this species the male is considerably larger than the female. The latter

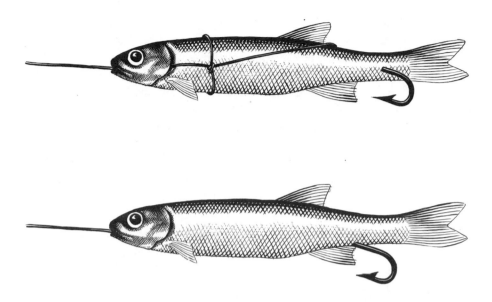

Two ways to hook a minnow: Run the line through the mouth, out the gills, tie it around the body, then back to the hook, which is embedded in tail (top). Or run the hook into the mouth, through the body, and out below (bottom).

has a maximum length of 5 inches. These fish are very tough and tenacious of life. They are often called horned dace, and are found in creeks and rivers from Montana and New Mexico to the Atlantic Coast and south to Florida.

Golden shiners are found from Canada to Florida and throughout the eastern United States. They are the most popular of baits, their color making them conspicuous and attractive to the pikes, bass, and panfish.

Hornyhead chubs, excellent bait for members of the pike family, are durable on the hook. They are found from the Hudson River to the Rockies and south to Oklahoma. Their preferred habitat is large creeks and the smaller rivers with swift water and gravel bottom.

LARVAE

Hellgrammites, the unlovely larvae of the Dobson fly, are tough, tenacious of life, and active on the hook. They are one of the best baits for both large-

and smallmouth bass. Walleyes and catfish will fall for them and they are an excellent lure for lunker yellow perch. They are found in trout streams and are good trout bait. They live in their pre-adult state for several years, hiding under rocks in rivers, creeks, and brooks, preying avidly upon the larvae of other insects. They can be captured by holding a fine-mesh net below a rock in the stream bed, then raising the rock and letting the current sweep the hellgrammites into it. Make certain that this is legal in your state. They can be stored in a wooden box containing damp sod and rotting leaves.

To hook a hellgrammite, grip it just below the head to escape the painful nip of its pincers and run a sharp No. 8 or 10 hook under the collar. If it is a big one, a No. 6 hook will be better. A thick, large hook will not only be so heavy as to kill a small hellgrammite but also spoil its natural action as it drifts along in the current. Use a hook of thin wire. Unless the current is heavy, you will not need split shot on your leader. Cast about 45 degrees across the stream into a current that takes the bait into promising water and let it drift down on a fairly slack line. You will have to follow the technique of the fisherman using artificial nymphs. Watch that line closely. If it twitches at the point where it enters the water, chances are that a trout has taken it. Your reaction to that signal depends upon whether your hellgrammite is small or large. If the former, pause for a moment, then strike. If the bug is large, allow several seconds to give the trout time to gorge it. You will have to do some experimenting here to time your strikes properly. Timing that works well one day in a particular stream may not always work on another day or on another water. Keep the bug off the bottom for if it gets a chance it will grip rock with its tail pincers. Should it do so a hard pull or strong jerk will loose the hook from the collar, and you have lost your bait.

The larva of the fishfly is another underwater bug upon which trout feed heartily. It resembles the hellgrammite but is different. It isn't a fast-water bug but frequents the more placid trout-stream water where the bottom is of mud, gravel, and stones mixed together. These fishfly larvae are tough enough to stand considerable use and are quite active on the hook. Fish them as you do hellgrammites. You can store them in a cool cellar in damp moss, sod, or rotting leaves.

Gall worms are found in the galls of giant ragweed, goldenrod, and other weeds with woody stems. They can be located by looking for the noticeable swelling on weeds of that type. When cut into with a sharp knife, the swellings will be found to contain a small worm or grub. Gall worms are effective bait when ice fishing for panfish. A similar bait is the meal worm, which may be found in stale corn meal. This too is attractive to panfish and is used in ice fishing.

Catalpa worms are the larvae of the catalpa sphinx moth which is decidedly partial to the leaves of the catalpa tree. This moth lays its eggs upon the leaves, and when the caterpillars hatch from the egg they feed avidly upon the leaves all summer long. They are weird-looking creatures, noticeably black and white. Each bears upon its tail a prominent black horn, which looks like a no-touch affair but is quite harmless. When the caterpillars become fully adult, they descend from the tree and burrow in the ground. There they hibernate for the winter.

Catalpa worms are hard to surpass as bait. Other types of caterpillars are soft and mushy, too much so for effective bait, but these worms have surprisingly tough skins and cling admirably to the hook. Run a fine wire hook through the skin from one side of the worm to the other, then back again in another spot. These worms last a long time on the hook and withstand freezing.

Caddis worms are well known to most fishermen. They are found in those little bundles of twigs, sand, and tiny pebbles glued together with a secretion from the mug itself. To collect them, use a fine-mesh net and scoop

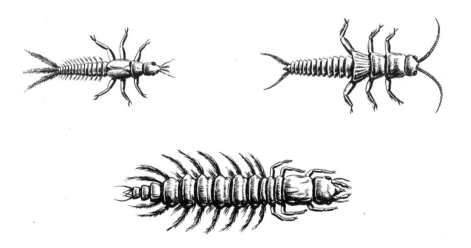

Some favorite natural baits: the May fly nymph (top left), stone fly nymph (top right), and hellgrammite.

them up along the bottom. You have the choice of two ways to fish this worm, either taking it from its case or fishing it by hooking it through the rind of its case without killing the worm. As the worm is only about 1 inch long, you will need a small, thin wire hook, about a No. 14. Fish it on the bottom.

Stone fly nymphs are another fine trout bait. Wade along a trout stream in May or June and you will see the abandoned cases of the stone fly on the rocks. Like the hellgrammites, they are found under rocks on the stream bed or in masses of woody debris. Those under rocks may be gathered by overturning the rocks and letting the current wash the bugs into a fine-net screen. Those in the debris or on sunken logs are gathered by hand. Use a thin No. 12 hook, running the hook under the bonelike structure at the head so it does not injure the frail flesh. They do not store well; at best they will live for only a day or two. Carry them in a bait can and cover them with watersoaked leaves.

CRAWFISH

Also called crayfish, crawdads, and crabs, crawfish are widely distributed over the continent, and in the softshell phase are an excellent bass bait. Looking like miniature lobsters, they usually are brownish or olive in coloration. They are found in brooks, creeks, and rivers as well as in ponds and lakes. Some varieties dig burrows in coarse sand, and may be located by spotting the small mounds of freshly dug sand next to the holes. There are different varieties, some being tiny, while others may reach a foot in length. They are bottom dwellers, hiding under waterlogged logs, rocks, and masses of weeds. In the South they are plentiful in swamp waters. They are not easy to capture. Their ability to scurry backward or forward is frustrating. They feed upon small animal life such as tadpoles, water snails, insect nymphs, tiny fishes, and carrion, largely at night. They shed their shells several times yearly, and at that time, in their soft-shell stage, they are helpless and become the prey of various forms of animal life. Then they stay close to their burrows. They are found most easily in the hot months of July and August.

About as good a way as any to capture crawfish is with minnow traps baited with meat fragments or bits of fish. If you can locate their burrows by the telltale mounds of sand, dig them out, making quick grabs as they try to escape. Seek them under rocks and masses of debris where they often dig their burrows. Then it is possible to catch them with a landing net or a quick hand. In captivity the shell shedding may be speeded up by stuffing them, like pigs for market, on fish or meat fragments. They may be kept in a wooden pail in a cool place with a lot of dampened grass or water weeds. Hook them through the tail and fish them just off bottom. Otherwise, if allowed to touch bottom, they are likely to crawl under a rock or into a mass of tangled weeds and get hung up.

FROGS

Frogs are a good bait for bass and for members of the pike family. Here, as in the case of minnows, some states place restrictions upon their capture. Some have open and closed seasons as well as bag limits. Consult your state laws before going on a frog hunt. Most weedy and shallow ponds and lakes, as well as creeks and brooks, have them in quantity, especially if the water is warm. A long, stiff cane pole with a stout line of about the pole length, with a No. 8 gaudy wet fly such as the Scarlet Ibis or Parmachene Belle, or even a bit of red flannel, is an effective rig. Get someone to paddle you slowly along the weedy edge of suitable water. When you spot a frog, either among the lily pads or on the bank, hold your pole so that the fly dangles just before its mouth. Chances are that it will snap at the fly, even jump for it. Then the frog may be swung into the boat, freed from the hook, and placed in a wire cage or a box with a sliding lid. If the latter, be sure the box is perforated with small holes to allow air to enter.

Or, if the law permits, cruise at night along the banks of weedy waters, equipped with a flashlight or a lantern with a reflector. Directing the light along the shore and among the weeds, you will be able to spot the frogs by the reflection of their eyes. With pole, line, and fly you will then be able to take them. For bait purposes the small frogs should be sought. A long-handled scoop net can be used instead of rod and line. When I was a youngster I would creep up on a frog sitting on the shore and catch it with a butterfly net or a quick pounce with the hand. One of my favorite lures for pickerel was a skinned frog's leg, impaled on a hook and skittered along the surface among the lily pads.

Frogs may be kept in a wooden box perforated with many small holes, placed partly under water, and filled with rocks high enough so that the frogs may sit on them above water. In going to your fishing water, carry the frogs in a perforated box partially filled with damp grass or weeds.

The frog is hooked through both lips. It will stand little casting and soon dies under this punishment. Years ago when I used frogs much more than today, I found the best way to fish them was with a long cane pole and a line about the length of the pole. Then I would skitter the frog over patches of open water among the lily pads where bass or pickerel might be hiding, imitating the action of a frog trying to escape from an enemy. This method of fishing was very effective, and, being less hard upon the frog than casting, enabled it to live longer. Even if it died it was still an effective bait.

GRASSHOPPERS AND CRICKETS

These insects are good bait for trout, smallmouth bass, and most panfish. Look for grasshoppers in a grassy field. Two men, one at each end of an 8-foot length of mosquito netting, usually can gather a number of these insects if they move rapidly through a meadow. Or one man alone, equipped with a long-handled butterfly net of the same material, can capture them fairly easily by tracking one down as it jumps ahead of him in the grass, and then bringing down the net swiftly over the hopper. Another good way is to go out at night equipped with a flashlight. Spotting a hopper, you can easily pick it up as they are sluggish at night and dazzled by the light. There are two good ways to store them. Cut a piece from an old inner tube large enough to tie over the mouth of a mason jar. Cut a cross in the rubber large enough to admit your hand. The rubber enables you to insert your hand, pick up a grasshopper, and withdraw it without the others in the jar escaping. The other way is to use a bottle with a perforated metal cap and a small neck. When you want to take out a hopper, only one at a time can pass through the mouth.

Crickets can be found under stones and boards, and in the open on lawns and fields. Carry them in a jar or bottle. A cricket should be hooked carefully under the collar so it will stay alive. A grasshopper may be hooked the same way, or by running a thin wire hook through the body from mouth to tail.

SALMON EGGS

Salmon eggs are much used for steelhead trout in those states and provinces where such bait is legal. Sporting goods stores in such areas sell preserved eggs of this type. Or you can make such "goop," as it is called, by mixing old eggs with fresh, using a little salt as a preservative. Aging this mixture adds to its effectiveness.

CHEESE

Cheese as a trout bait is being used widely with success, particularly in California. Smelly cheese is the best. Break off a piece about the size of a horsechestnut, putting it in the open right hand and with the other hand work it until it is pliable. Then press it flat and mold it around the hook. Work it so that the portion at the bend of the hook bulges out somewhat, then taper it along the shank toward the hook's eye.

THE EPHEMERAE

Insects of the *Ephemerae* genus are so important as trout food both in nymph and adult forms that it is worthwhile to sketch briefly their remarkable lives. Those of us who have seen swarms of these insects rising from the water, dancing in the air, dapping on the surface of the water, and dropping finally to die there, have been impressed with this mystery of life. These insects are among our most beautiful, not in their coloring but in their delicacy of form.

For several years the insect lives in the bottom ooze, in sand or gravel, an unlovely thing, always hungry, and gaining strength by preying upon small organisms. Feeding greedily, it fattens, becomes too large for its skin, sheds it, and assumes another form. It is a voracious predator and itself is preyed upon by the trout. It has to fight and feed to live and to learn the wiles of escape. Enough of them must escape for the race to carry on.

Finally the day arrives for which this underwater life has been preparing them. With the last shedding of the skin, they bid farewell to their larval stage. An entirely new creature emerges, a creature of the air with wings to fly, and sex organs fully formed to insure the perpetuation of the race. But now, in one of Nature's great mysteries, we have a creature perfect in appearance yet imperfect in a significant way. Life must renew itself by feeding. The *ephemerae* have no mouths to feed, no stomachs to digest. So their life is short, ephemeral as their name implies. They must mate and die. Unsocial in their underwater existence, now they have become social. They pair in a nuptial flight. The climax of their strange existence has come, and with it death. They fall to the water and put the trout into a frenzy of feeding. Windrows of their frail bodies may be washed to the shore.

Nymphs and Larvae.   Immature insects are known as nymphs or larvae. A larva is a form more primitive than the nymph. It does not have any external evidence of rudimentary wings. A nymph hatches from the egg in a more advanced form; it may have visible rudimentary wings and its mouth resembles that of an adult.

The famous May fly is a splendid example of the various metamorphoses through which aquatic insects pass. It is easy to identify this beautiful insect: its antennae are short and stiff, its mouth is nonfunctional, and its transparent wings are netted and veined. It usually has three long hairlike tail threads. Like others of the family, its early life is spent in fresh water. The nymph may shed its outer skin as many as twenty times. Thus almost the entire life of the creature is spent in the nymph form. The nymphs may hide under stones or seek shelter in the sand or cling to underwater vegetation.

In due time the nymph seeks the surface by crawling or swimming. Its skin cracks and the fly emerges, takes wing, and flies away. Then it is known as in the subimago stage. It seeks rest and in a varying period of time, which may be within an hour or up to a day, the final skin is shed and the full adult May fly emerges. While some of this family may live for several days, they cannot eat and soon die.

These interesting insects of the *Ephemerae* genus are important to the fisherman. Their nymphs are imitated by artificial nymphs; their adult form by various types of artificial dry flies such as the duns and spinners. Their larvae make good bait where legal.

CHAPTER 5

Fly Casting

MOST MEN AND women who have taken up fly casting and practiced it to any extent usually rate it as the most pleasurable of fishing methods, the most sporting, and the most fascinating. The light weight and beauty of the equipment, the delicacy and grace of the casting, together with the charm of the artificial fly patterns, put fly fishing out in front of all other methods.

The fly fisherman does not have to capture, store, and carry messy baits alive or dead. If the fish he captures isn't needed as food or is undersize, it can be restored to the water unhurt, to live, gain weight, and be more desirable another day.

Fly fishing is good conservation, especially on trout water. I remember the objections that were raised when my friend and fishing companion Frank Valgenti, Jr., for fifteen years the chairman of the New Jersey Fish and Game Council, succeeded in having passed regulations restricting stretches of several trout streams to fly fishing only. Letters to the council and to newspapers claimed that this was class legislation aimed at favoring a select few, and that the rank and file were being barred from what was their right. These objectors thus showed their ignorance. The legal limit of trout on the portions of streams reserved to fly fishing had been reduced to four, one half of that on the unreserved stretches. If there was prejudice, it was against the fly fisherman. The fly fisherman could restore to the stream a small trout without harm; while the small trout having gorged a hook baited with a worm is so badly injured that few of them live after being restored to the water. Thus fly fishing is a sound conservation measure. Also, fly fishing is not an art hard to acquire. It can be easily and quickly learned by anyone.

FLY RODS

The early fly rods were long and heavy, tiring to use and awkward to cast. Before the middle of the last century they were being offered by tackle dealers as "light" when they weighed a total of 3 pounds! They were made of wood, usually of bethabara or greenheart, often with a lancewood top joint. Such rods obviously were not made for single-handed casting, but required the use of both hands. Our makers doubtless were influenced by the English, who felt that anything under 16 feet was too short, and anything under 32 ounces too frail to land a trout of several pounds. Today English rodmakers recognize the value of light rods.

Some years ago an elderly New Jersey sportsman died, and his executor invited me to look over his collection of fly rods and make bids on any that took my fancy. The sportsman had been a wealthy man, able to indulge in the best rods available. I looked them over in keen anticipation. There was not a rod that did not belong in a museum. There was only one

Fiberglass fly rods are light, strong, and inexpensive. This two-piece rod comes in lengths of 7'9", 8'6", and 9'. *Shakespeare Co.*

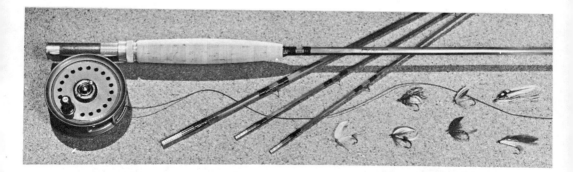

For those who can afford one, a fine split-bamboo rod, hand-crafted by an expert, is still the best, possessing a life and spring unequaled by any other type of fly rod. *Orvis Co.*

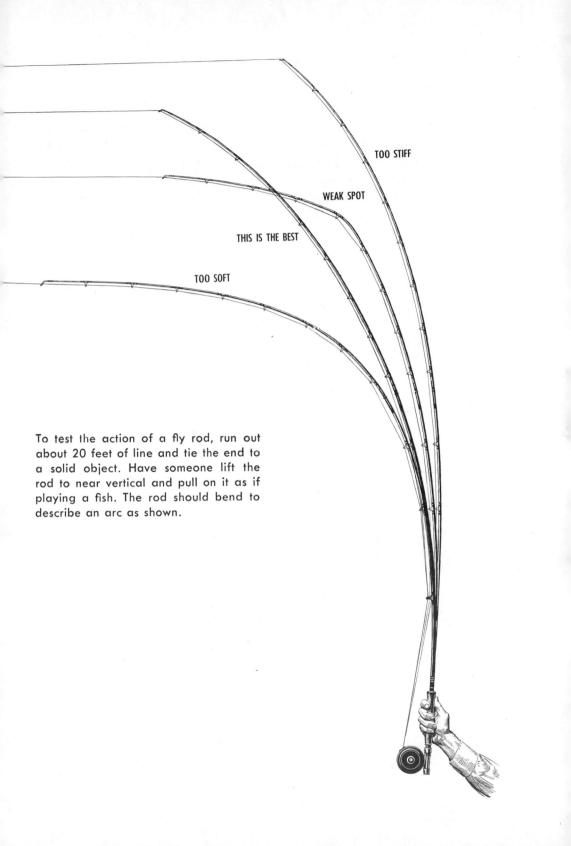

TOO STIFF

WEAK SPOT

THIS IS THE BEST

TOO SOFT

To test the action of a fly rod, run out about 20 feet of line and tie the end to a solid object. Have someone lift the rod to near vertical and pull on it as if playing a fish. The rod should bend to describe an arc as shown.

split bamboo. It was about 15 feet long, had five joints, and weighed 12 ounces. The others were of wood, long and stiff and heavy, and several of them had a metal spear in their butts so that the weary fisherman could stick the spear into the earth and get a respite from lugging the lumber around. I told the executor that I would not give a nickel for any rod in the collection. Their only value was as curiosities.

Today we have beautiful fly rods, in split bamboo or glass, light, strong, and expertly tapered. They are available in varying sizes and weights from one 6½ feet long of split bamboo and weighing only 2 ounces, with two joints, up to an 11-foot, 3-piece salmon rod weighing 10⅞ ounces of the same material. In glass there is also a wide selection. The range is from a two-piece featherweight, 6 feet long, weighing 2⅛ ounces, up to a salmon and steelhead rod 9 feet long in three pieces.

It is fortunate that with shipments of Tonkin cane having come to a standstill, rodmakers have fiberglass to turn to. Glass rods are really good. They will stand up under severe use better than split bamboo, and have the strength needed to play a heavy and hard-fighting game fish without quitting. Which material is better, split bamboo or glass, is a debatable question. In a rod in the low-priced range, glass is the better buy. For the sportsman who wants the best and is willing to pay for it, to my mind the split bamboo from a first-class maker is unequalled. There is a life and spring to it which gives a little different feel than the glass.

The beginner in fly casting will make no mistake in selecting a rod 8 feet long, weighing 4 ounces, in either two or three pieces. I favor a two-piece rod, feeling that the addition of another ferrule slows up the action a bit. It is as important to the angler to select a rod that fits him as it is to select the proper line for it. It should feel well balanced as you hold it in your hand. It should have the springiness of fine steel. When assembled and you hold it up to your eyes, and slowly revolve it in your hands, the droop at the tip should not be pronounced and should be even. Pass up the rod that does not have this even droop but is irregular and jumpy.

FLY REELS

The fly-rod reel is much less important than is the bait or spinning reel. Its function is merely to pay out or bring in line. Therefore, in comparison with those other types of reels, it need not be expensive. But do not be beguiled into buying one under $5. You can get one that will last for years with ordinary use for about $10.

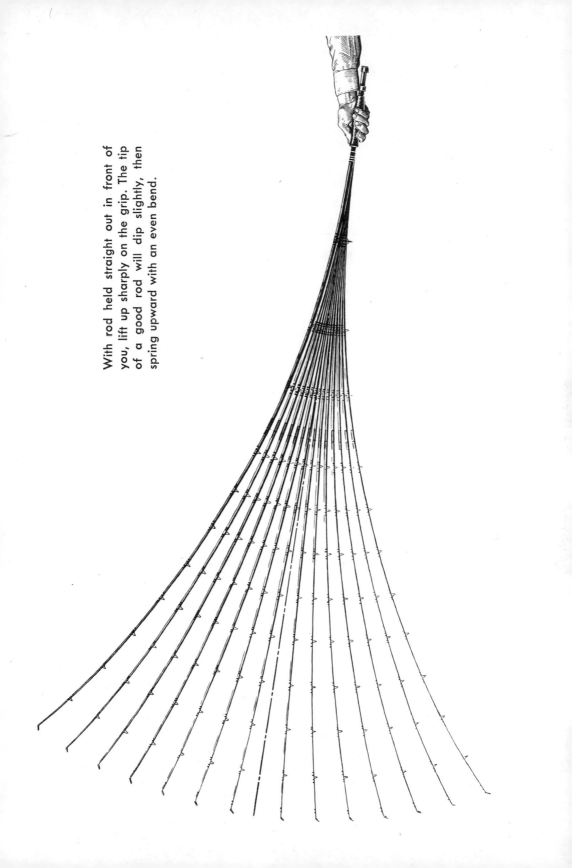

With rod held straight out in front of
you, lift up sharply on the grip. The tip
of a good rod will dip slightly, then
spring upward with an even bend.

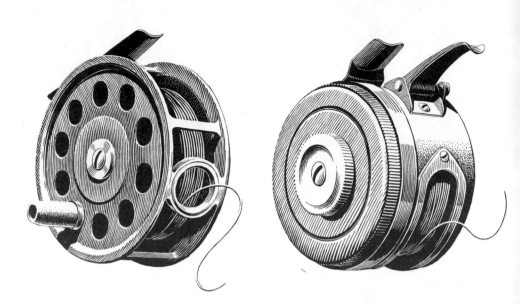

Two basic types of fly reels are the single action (left) and the automatic, which reels in line at fingertip control. When purchasing either type, look for such features as a sturdy frame of rustproof metal, good bearings, and easy accessibility to inside for cleaning and adjustments.

KNOTS

The fly caster must be familiar with the basic fisherman's knots. Using the right knot when tying a fly to a leader, joining two lengths of leader, or tying leader to line often makes the difference between a creeled or a lost fish. The basic knots are the blood knot, perfection loop, barrel knot, turle knot, tucked sheet bend, dropper loop, clinch knot, and figure eight knot. As they are also useful to the bait-casting and spinning fisherman, they are illustrated and explained in a special section beginning on page 307.

LEARNING HOW TO FLY CAST

If a pond, swimming pool, or stream isn't handy for the beginner to practice his casting, a lawn, lane, or gymnasium floor will do. Do not practice with a barbed fly. Use a wire cutter to cut off the point and barb. You will need a fly to develop your casting, as there is a different feel

Pausing at the top of his back cast, with the line extended well behind him, this fly fisherman is about to begin his forward cast. Excess line is coiled loosely in his left hand and will be taken up as the line shoots forward at the completion of the cast. *Garcia Corp.*

and action if fly and leader are missing. Tie a 4- or 5-foot length of nylon leader to your line, then tie the barbless fly to the end of this leader.

The grip on the rod butt is quite important. Do not squeeze the grip. Let it lie easily in your hand. There are two grips which are favored by most fishermen. In the first you grasp the butt with the four fingers and extend the thumb along the top of the cork butt. In the second the thumb does not extend along the cork butt but is curled over the butt and lies on the forefinger. Usually I use the second grip, but when I want to get pin-point accuracy I use the extended thumb grip. Possibly I'm wrong, but it seems to me that I can get a little more accuracy by pointing my thumb at the spot I wish to reach. The butt of the rod lies along the palm of the rod hand, with its end against the bottom of the palm. For many years during the fishing season I have had a callus at the lower left of my right hand where the end of the rod butt rests.

Having gripped the rod butt properly, you are ready to begin your casting. Remember that fly casting requires little strength. It is rod and line that do the work. Your part is to activate them so they will do it properly. You are to start the work, then let them take over. The main

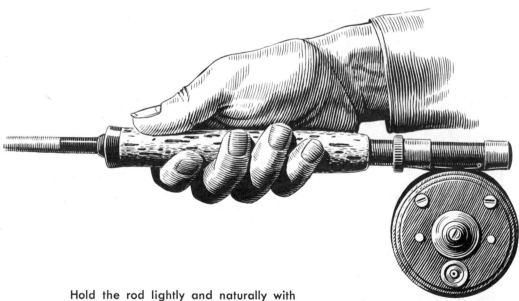

Hold the rod lightly and naturally with thumb along the top, or turned down along the side, whichever you prefer.

instrument that you call upon to do your part is the wrist and not the arm. Should you use strength in your cast, it will be ruined. Your upper casting arm should hang downward, the forearm about parallel to the ground. The rod should be at an angle of about 45 degrees to the ground.

Strip off from the reel from 15 to 20 feet of line and flip it with the rod until it lies fairly straight upon the ground before you. Now you are ready to cast. Raise the rod without jerking it so that the springy tip swings upward a bit, drawing line toward you. Increase the force of your lift so that the line shoots upward and backward, and stop the rod tip when it reaches a position of about 11 o'clock with your forearm now vertical. The cast should begin slowly and gently and be completed with a fast finish. Do not let the forearm come back beyond a vertical position or bend back the wrist. To do so brings back the rod too far, resulting in a low back cast. The line should be kept high on the back cast. A high back cast is the preliminary to a good forward cast. When line and leader hit the water on the back cast it is sure proof of sloppy casting.

Do not start the forward cast at once after completion of the back cast. There is a momentary pause, the length of which depends upon how much line is out. Obviously the more line, the longer that pause. Start the forward cast too soon and there is a crack like the snapping of a whip, and usually the fly has been snapped off. The three steps in a cast—back cast, pause, and forward cast—are about equal in point of time elapsed. Count three slowly and in even tempo. *One* is for the back cast, *two* for the pause before making the forward cast, and *three* is the forward cast. At the end of the back cast there is a slight pull on the tip of the rod which tells you the time has come to make the forward cast. You learn by experience to identify and act upon this pull.

Just as in the case of the back cast, the forward cast is started slowly and accelerates with the forward and downward action of the forearm. Forearm action is stopped when the forearm is parallel with the water and the rod at a slight angle above the horizontal. Then the rod is gently lowered until it is parallel with the water. Stop forward propulsion when leader and fly are about two feet above the water. Then with the gentle lowering of the rod they fall gently upon the water.

False Casts.   The false cast is required in dry-fly fishing to dry the fly between casts and also to determine the distance to a spot on which you wish to place the fly. Line, leader, and fly are kept in the air and not permitted to alight on the water by back casting and forward casting until the desired distance is reached. During this casting, the line is pulled from the

In discussing casts in this book, the author uses the "clock" method of describing positions of arms and rods. All descriptions are based on the assumption that the fisherman is facing toward the reader's right and is holding the rod in his right hand.

reel by the left hand several feet at a time, this slack being taken up by the forward and backward motion of the rod. The rod is stopped on its forward movement when it is at a position of somewhere between 1 and 2 o'clock. When the line straightens out at this position of the rod, the back cast is made. In false casting, as in the regular "business" cast, keep the back cast high.

When you come to a rather short stretch of water which is too shallow and too lacking in cover to support trout, you can wade up through it keeping your false casts going. This is to prevent the need of reeling in the line and getting it out again when you reach more promising water.

Ability to make long casts comes with experience. In most of our trout fishing and on our streams of average size such casts are rarely needed. If you approach carefully and do not silhouette yourself against the sky where the trout can see you, and take your casting position quietly, you can get most of your trout within 40 feet of you, provided your fly, leader, and line drop to the water without a splash. As an aid to gently landing the fly and leader on the water, aim your casts at an imaginary spot about 2 feet above the place where you desire them to fall. The fisherman who drives his casts forward with power and lets line, leader, and fly splash upon the water may catch a fingerling or two but all worthwhile trout will have scooted beneath ledges, rocks, and cut banks.

Together with the ability to make your casts alight gently upon the water, accuracy in placing your casts is desirable. That too comes with practice. The rifleman becomes able to place his bullets in the black circle on the target by practice. Use that same method to attain accuracy with the fly.

If you practice upon a lawn, place upon it a sheet of white paper or a handkerchief. If upon water, a small rock showing above water will do. Take your stand about 30 feet from your target and try to place your fly upon it. Holding the line with your left hand so that several feet of it lie between reel and the first guide, you can control the line you have out. If more line is needed, you can pull it from the reel on either forward or back cast. If less line is required, while the line is in the air on the back cast pull the required footage through the guide nearest the rod hand. With the forefinger of the rod hand, press the line brought in against the rod, and repeat if necessary.

Retrieving the Line.   In wet-fly fishing, retrieving the line after a cast, or shortening it, is best accomplished by the hand-twist method, which enables you to keep a taut line in readiness for a strike. The line is taken with thumb and forefinger of the left hand just below the first guide above the reel and pulled in as far as those fingers will move without moving the whole hand. The other three fingers then reach up and seize the line, bringing it down to be taken in turn by the first two fingers. This is repeated until the running line is brought in as far as is desired.

Roll Cast.   The ordinary forward and backward casts are all that a beginner need learn at the start of his fly fishing. As he gains experience there are other forms of casting which enable him to cope with various problems as they come up. Often the fisherman will find himself facing water that looks productive but where trees, shrubs, or a high bank behind him prevent a back cast. Here the *roll cast* can overcome the handicap. It is an easy cast to learn and a pretty one to watch. Pull from the reel a few feet of line, let it lie on the water and add to it by shaking out with the rod, working it rapidly up and down until you have out 20 to 25 feet. Then with forearm parallel with the water and the rod at an angle of about 45 degrees, bring back the rod inclined slightly to the right until it is at about

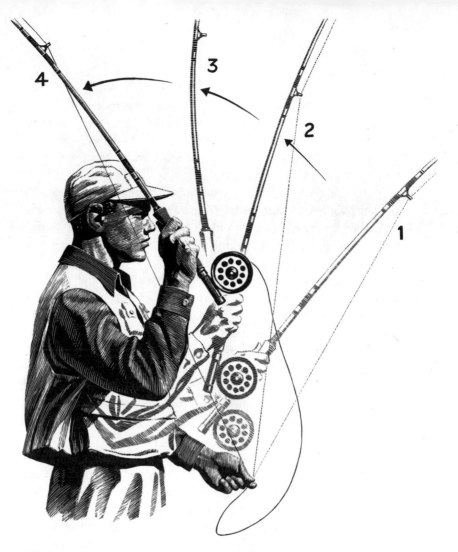

FLY CASTING

Back Cast. 1. Begin pick-up of the line at this point, holding line tight with your left hand to make a clean lift. Allow loop to hang from the hand. 2. Apply full power to the rod, accelerating as it goes up, to throw the line high and clear. 3. Stop the power of the rod when it is at about vertical position. 4. Allow the rod to drift back to this position as the line begins to straighten out behind you. Drawing below shows position of entire line at about step 4.

Forward Cast. 5. Wait with rod in this position for the back cast to nearly straighten out behind, then begin to bring rod forward. 6. Apply full power to the rod, bringing the line forward at accelerated speed. 7. Stop the rod at this point and allow the line to carry forward over the water. 8. Drop the rod slightly in following through, as you release the line from your left hand, allowing it to "shoot" forward through the guides. Drawing below shows entire line near end of forward cast.

ROLL CAST. This cast is used when a back cast isn't possible due to obstructions behind you. 1. Begin the roll cast with about 20 feet of line out in front of you. 2. Raise the rod slowly just past the vertical position to pick up the line and slack. 3. The roll is started by the downward movement of rod. At approximately this point, move the rod sharply forward and down. 4. The line rolls out like a hoop and flattens on the water.

an 11 o'clock position. As you do this the line will be brought in along the water surface and hang from the rod a little back of and to the right of your shoulder. Then move the rod to a 2 o'clock position and then sharply forward and down. The line rolls out like a hoop before you. Of course, in this as in all fly casting, your left hand holds the line between thumb and forefinger between reel and first guide.

Double Haul Cast.   This cast is useful to get distance to your cast when your best ordinary cast would fall short. Suppose you come to a fine pool with smooth surface, too deep to wade and too wide for the usual cast to reach the far side. A fine trout rises close to the bank on the far side. Perhaps you can reach that trout with the double haul. At the start of your back cast you lean forward and with the left hand take the line just below the first guide. As you start the rod into motion for the pick-up from the water, you give a strong pull on the line with your left hand. Then as the rod makes its usual pause before it is started on the forward cast, you raise it as far as you can with outstretched arm, turning to the right, and raising your left hand and arm up with the rod as far as you can reach. As you start the forward cast, turn your body to face the spot at which you are aiming, bring down your left hand holding the line with a vigorous pull, and then release the loose line.

Side Cast.   On about every stream there are stretches where trees extend over the water, giving shelter to the fish, and where the current brings them food. Such water is excellent for trout yet most anglers pass it up because of the danger of fouling. Often it is possible to put a fly be-

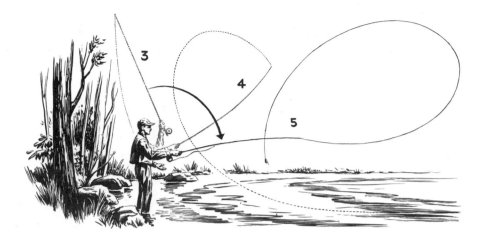

low the tree limbs with the *side cast*. Hold the rod handle with palm turned upward. By pivoting your body you can look in the direction of the back cast to see if you can make it without getting hung up; if all is clear make your back cast with rod held parallel to the water. At the momentary pause between back and forward cast, face front to look at the spot where you want the fly to drop. The forward cast is also made with rod parallel to the water, the forward movement of the rod being stopped before it points at the spot where you wish the fly to touch. Otherwise the fly would swing wide of it.

Grasshopper Cast.   There often are occasions on a stretch of placid water when you see a trout rising at some distance from you. You know that with an ordinary forward cast there is danger of enough water disturbance when leader and fly land on the glassy surface to scare the trout and put it down. This is when a *grasshopper cast* may be effective, to make the fly drop on the water before the leader. Use a high back cast with arm raised high, driving the rod back to an 11 o'clock position. As the line shoots backward, you lower the rod arm to the normal position. Then make the forward cast vigorously. Estimate the distance of the leader's length to the position of the fish and stop your cast abruptly. For instance, if you have on a 9-foot leader, apply forceful wrist and thumb pressure to stop forward movement at that distance from the fish. If made properly, this cast causes fly and leader tip to swing over and touch the water ahead of the body of the leader. Practice this cast until you can execute it properly. It's a good one.

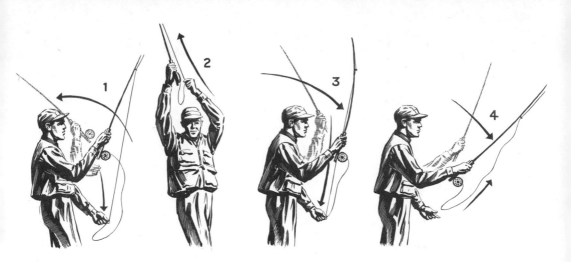

DOUBLE-HAUL CAST is a very vigorous cast to get maximum distance by a "double-pumping" action. 1. Before starting back cast, lean forward and with left hand take the line just below the first guide. As the rod goes into motion for the back cast, give a strong downward pull on the line with your left hand. This accentuates the power in the rod tip, giving it an added starting force. 2. During the momentary pause before the forward cast as the line is going back, raise the rod as far as you can with the outstretched arm, and also raise the left hand as far as you can reach, pivoting body to the right. Pivoting is a natural motion in order to get the left hand close to the reel. 3. As you start the forward cast, turning your body to the front, bring down your left hand and give the line a vigorous pull. 4. Release the loose line in your left hand, allowing it to shoot forward as you complete the cast.

GRASSHOPPER CAST. The purpose of this cast is to flip the fly over and drop it on the water ahead of the leader. 1. Back cast is made with arm held high, driving rod back to the 11 o'clock position. 2. As line in back cast straightens, lower casting arm to normal position. 3. Make the forward cast vigorously. At estimated leader length from fish, stop your cast very abruptly, causing the fly to flip over and drop on the water ahead of the leader.

Mending the Line After a Curve Cast. The need often arises in dry-fly fishing when you wish to cast across a current to reach a trout beyond it. The action of the current on leader or line or both will cause it to drift downstream faster than the fly. Thus there is drag upon the fly, causing it to drown. Rarely will a trout take the fly when this happens. The curve cast plus "mending the line" can prolong the float of the fly. If you are fishing from the left side of the current, you cast a curve to the right in this fashion: Your false cast, or casts, is made using only enough force to keep the line from the water, and with the rod held to one side at an angle of 45 degrees. When you estimate that there is enough line out to reach a spot several feet upstream from the trout you wish to reach, make your "business" cast, and as it is made, turn your rod wrist slowly to the right, pointing the rod tip at the spot you want the fly to drop. The line will turn to the right, and the leader, if the cast is properly executed, will drop the fly at that spot. The current will act upon the upstream curve in the line and carry it downstream. Then with your left hand take up the slack in the line, hold the rod tip close to the water, and flip it upstream, thus mending the line. The rod movement during this maneuver should be rather gentle, the force used being only enough to pick up the downstream belly in the line and move it upstream. Skilled dry-fly men can sometimes do this several times on one cast, thus prolonging the float of the fly. This cast too should be practiced until it can be done effectively. There often is need for it.

3 ABRUPT STOP

MENDING THE LINE. When casting across a current, the line often drifts downstream faster than the fly (1), causing the fly to drown. To prolong the float of the fly, flip the rod tip (2), picking up the downstream belly in the line and moving it upstream without disturbing the fly (3).

Cast in Blocked Area. Sometimes the fly fisherman will come to a stretch of water that is most promising but very difficult to fish. Trees or alders line the banks thickly so it is almost impossible to fish it from either side and, as the stream is narrow and the trees almost meet overhead, a back cast will land the fly among the branches nine times out of ten. Here is the way to lick that problem. Standing in the water, pivot your body so that you face in the direction of the back cast. By facing that way it is easy to make your false casts without getting hung up in the branches. Then, when ready to make your "business" cast, you make your back cast while facing the narrow opening above the stream, pivot, and cast forward into the water you desire to fish.

CHAPTER 6

Bait and Plug Casting

THE INTRODUCTION OF spinning, which made the use of light lures entirely practical, has not abated the popularity of plug and bait casting, nor is it likely to. Plug and bait casting has a field of its own and uses which spinning cannot duplicate, just as spinning can do things which cast ing cannot do. The complete fisherman should be adept in both and be prepared to do either as conditions require.

BAIT-CASTING EQUIPMENT

Bait casting is particularly useful in lake and river fishing for black bass, northern pike, and pickerel. Until recently plug and bait casters favored short casting rods ranging from 4½ to 5½ feet, which were too short to give the play which adds so much to the pleasure of striking and playing a fish. With these rods fishermen could make distance casts, but they were too stiff to give maximum pleasure. A lot of fishermen still prefer them but others have switched to longer and more pliant rods. Glass rods are reasonable and give good service.

Common lure weights run ¼ ounce, ⅓ ounce, ½ ounce, and ⅝ ounce. Rods best suited to these weights, beginning with the ¼ ounce, run 6¼ feet, 6 feet, 5½ feet, and 5 feet. That does not mean that any one of these rods will not work with any of the weight lures mentioned. They will, but best results follow with the lengths and weights described.

In selecting a rod, rig it with line and reel, and tie to the line a ⅝-ounce lure. Thus rigged the rod should have a slight downward bend at the tip. You will know then that the rod, with a fish on, will be sensitive

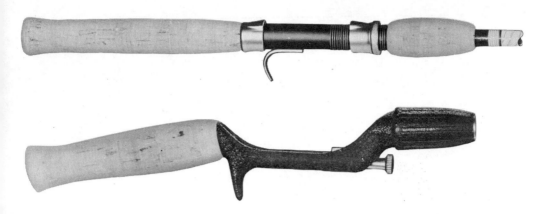

Bait-casting rods may have either a straight or an offset handle. The offset handle permits the caster's thumb to work the spool in a more natural position. *Shakespeare* Co.

to the fight of the fish and not be like an unyielding bean pole. An offset handle on the rod makes casting and spooling easier.

Just as experts prefer rod length adapted to lures of specified weight, so too they like a line fitted to the lure weight. For example, with ¼-ounce lures a line from 7½- to 10-pound test; for ½-ounce lures, 10- to 14-pound-test line; and with ⅝-ounce lures a 14- to 18-pound-test line. The line should be hard-braided and waterproofed, either of silk or nylon. The latter is cheaper and more durable, about 70 cents for 50 yards.

The reel should be quadruple multiplying. With such a reel one turn of the handle turns the spool four times. It also should be level winding, to save you the trouble of spooling the line without guiding it with the thumb.

A cheap plug-casting reel is never completely satisfactory. The fisherman who wants a really good reel, smooth in performance and durable, can get one made by a first-class manufacturer, of aluminum, lightweight, and with bearings of phosphor bronze, for between $25 and $30. Kept clean and oiled it will last a lifetime.

The plug-casting leader is of much less importance than the leader used in fly casting. Fish with sharp teeth, such as pike and pickerel, require a short wire leader. Leaders are sold in tackle stores ready to use, with a loop at one end to which the line is attached and a snap at the other. Get one from 6 to 10 inches long and as light as possible. This is because a heavy leader adversely affects the action of the lure, and the better the action of the lure the more attractive it is to the fish. The wire leader isn't needed if you are fishing for bass. For that fish a 3-foot nylon leader of about 10-pound test is right.

BAIT-CASTING TECHNIQUE

The basic principle in plug and bait casting, and of prime importance in making a good cast, is the position of the reel handle and the relation of the reel to the rod. The reel handle should be up, with the spool at the left of and nearly vertical to the rod. The thumb of the casting hand rests upon the spool and controls the line during the cast, in order to minimize the possibility of that bane of the caster—the backlash.

With the reel set at free spooling position and thumb clamped firmly on the line to prevent it from prematurely running out, hold the rod a little

A good reel for fresh-water bait or plug fishing.

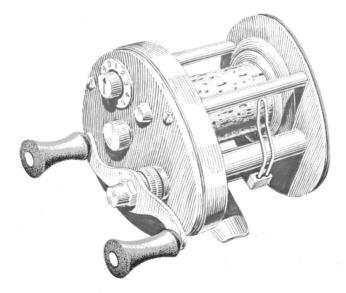

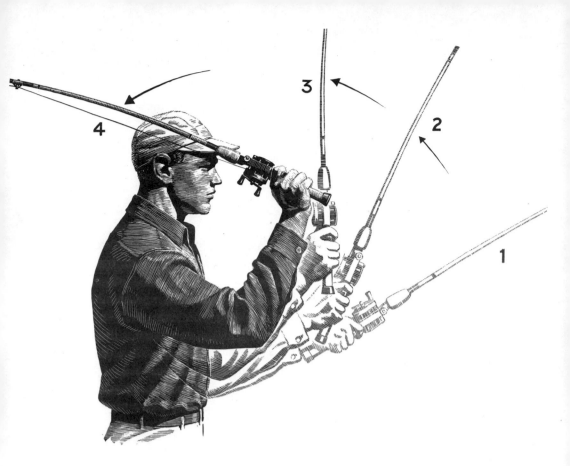

BAIT CASTING

Back Cast (above). 1. Pointing the rod toward the direction you intend to cast, hold it so the reel handles are facing upward and with your thumb clamped on the spool to control the line. 2. Begin lifting the rod with an easy and unforced motion. 3. Power of lift continues until the rod is about in vertical position. 4. Allow the rod to drift back over your shoulder, checking momentum of the lure.

Forward Cast (opposite page). 5. Begin to swing the rod forward with power, thrusting with your arm and shoulder. 6. Release thumb pressure from the spool at this point, allowing the lure and line to come forward. 7. As the forward power stops, follow through and allow the rod to drift to this position. 8. Extend the arm with rod, following the flight of the lure, to lessen the friction of the line through the guides. Increase thumb pressure as the lure loses momentum. 9. As the lure hits the water, press your thumb firmly on the spool to avoid backlash. Then shift the rod to your left hand to free the right hand to wind the reel.

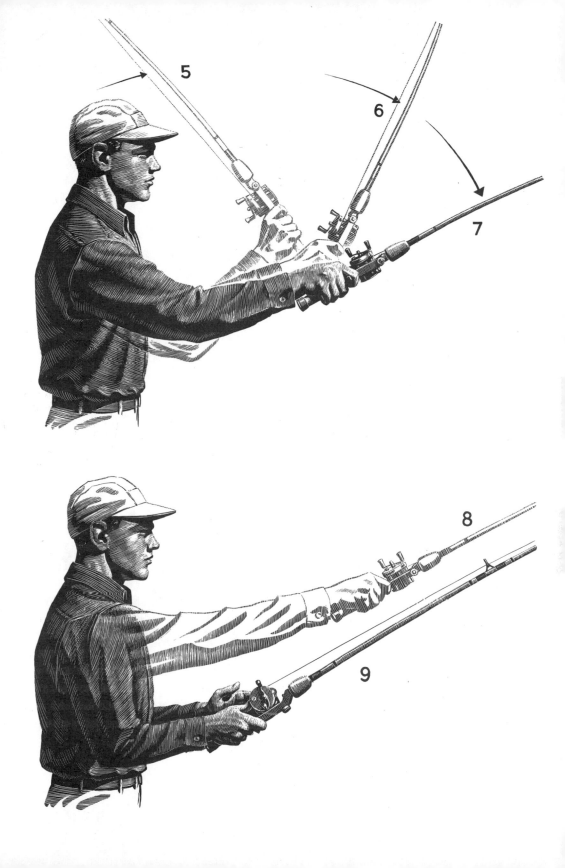

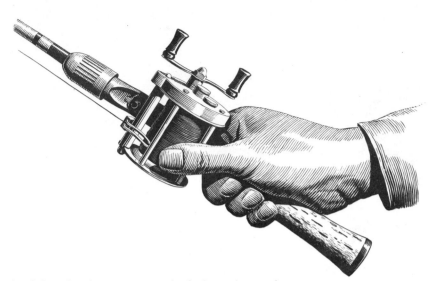

Applying thumb pressure to the bait-casting reel.

above horizontal with the water and pointed at the target, the plug dangling not more than 6 inches from the tip. Then swing it up and back with an easy motion to a position a little behind the shoulder. The tip of the pliant rod will then drop in a curve a little below the horizontal. Your casting hand will be at about the level of the top of your head, and your upper arm nearly vertical. Then swing the rod forward with power, at the same time releasing the thumb pressure on the spool but without losing contact with it. The thumb must always control the line as it shoots out. The rod must always be aimed at the target, and the eyes of the caster fixed upon that target.

As the lure nears its target, the speed of the line loses its momentum. Then increase your thumb pressure progressively, and be ready to jam it down firmly on the spool when the lure hits the water. A backlash is caused when the speed of the fast-revolving spool is greater than that of the outgoing line. So remember the importance of thumb control.

The cast having been completed, with the lure now on the water, shift the rod to the left hand so your right hand will be free to work the reel on retrieve. The beginner should not strive to get distance with his casts until he has learned to make adequate casts under 40 feet.

Recently there have been developed spin-casting reels with fixed spools of the spinning-reel type. These reels have made line control possible with push buttons. Used with monofilament lines they can handle adequately light lures, and they are easier to use than bait-casting reels.

When close to obstructions behind you, such as a high bank or shrubbery which may interfere with your back cast, a backhand cast will solve the difficulty. With rod parallel to the water, reel handle up as always, swing rod back easily, lessening pressure on the reel spool with your thumb. Drive the rod forward, keeping it parallel with the water, clamping the thumb down on the spool at the end of the cast as in the usual forward cast. The sidearm cast is similar except that the rod works in a plane on the right of the body instead of on the left.

Holding the bait-casting rod after shifting it to the left hand for retrieve.

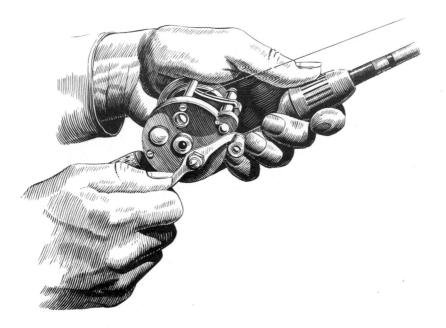

CHAPTER 7

Spinning

Novices, seeing the ease with which spin fishermen get out long casts, the lightness of their·lures, and the freedom from backlashes, are inclined to think that spinning is the do-everything method of fishing.

Spinning does not do everything. It definitely does not supplant fly fishing or bait casting. It occupies a place between those two, and is more or less a connecting link. A good all-round fisherman is adept in all three methods and uses the one he thinks will be most effective on a particular water on a particular day. Each method has some advantages over the others. None of them is perfect, for each has its disadvantages. Each of them gives real pleasure to the fisherman and each of them can result in fine catches. Sometimes one of them will take fish when the others will not.

Spinning is a relative newcomer in North America, having been introduced here from Europe in the late 1930's. Plug and bait casting, a technique devised in the United States about the middle of the last century, was started with the invention of the Milam or Kentucky reel which made bait casting possible by a device permitting a free spool and quick change to a click and drag. Fly fishing dates far back in time to the Greek and Roman periods.

In fly casting, the springiness of the rod drives out line and fly; in bait and plug casting, the weight of the lure, driven by the caster's arm and the rod in unison, gets out the cast. Spinning, however, employs a different type of reel from those used in fly fishing and bait casting. The spinning reel has a fixed spool, and the line comes off it in the same fashion as if you held a spool of cotton by one end and pulled the thread over the other end.

Spinning has these advantages over plug casting: There is no revolving

Spinning permits the angler to make longer casts with very light
lures. Here, a spinning enthusiast fishes for browns and brookies
in Wisconsin's Wolf River. *Wisconsin Conservation Dept.*

spool for the line to overrun and cause a backlash. Because there is no resistance from the reel, and the line itself is very light, considerably longer
casts are possible than in either plug or fly casting. Also, the thin line
makes casting of very light lures possible and is less visible to the fish. Thus
it is possible to catch large fish with spinning tackle, fish that are normally
too wary to be taken in any other way. Finally it is much easier to master
spinning than either fly or plug casting. Practice of an hour or so in a back
yard or field is sufficient enough to familiarize the tyro with its simple prin-
ciples so that he can go fishing and catch fish.

The typical open-face fresh-water spinning reel has a manually operated line pick-up, which must be swung aside to free the line before casting. *Langley Corp.*

The closed-face spinning reel is similar to the open-face in operation, but the working parts are housed under a metal hood and there is no line pick-up to operate. *Shakespeare Co.*

SPINNING TACKLE

Rods. The beginner will make a mistake if he buys the cheapest rod and reel that he can find. They will function, it is true, but good performance means good tackle, and cheap tackle does not hold up as well nor does it give as good performance. You can buy a good rod made of tubular glass for about $20. Select one of 6½ to 7 feet long. Test the rod by whipping it to and fro. You want one with a fast action, one that is neither too soft nor too stiff. Such a rod gives you good play when a fish is on and makes casting a little easier. Hold the rod up to your eye and sight along its length and assure yourself that the droop at the tip is even as you revolve the rod in your hands. Have the salesman hold the rod by the tip and then raise the rod and pull lightly against the resistance. A good rod will then show an even curve all the way from tip to butt.

Reels. Spinning reels are of various types. There are those with pick-ups of full-bail, half-bail, mechanical finger pick-ups, manual pick-ups, some with open- and some with closed-face reels. It is claimed of the closed-face reels that they will handle heavier lines more efficiently than the open-face, and so are better for the bigger game fish such as northern pike and largemouth black bass. Personally I prefer the open-face reel with full-bail pick-up, for the line is in sight all the time and if it gets into any trouble it is easy to spot it and rectify it. You can get a good one for around $25.

The spin-casting reel is mounted on top of an offset-handle casting rod. A thumb-operated lever controls the speed of the outgoing line. *Garcia Corp.*

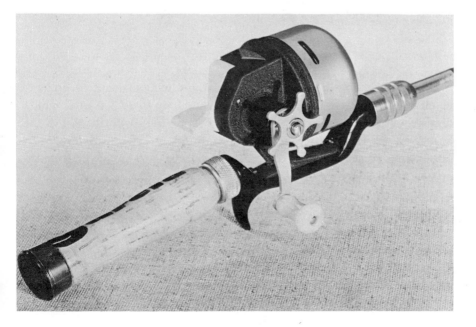

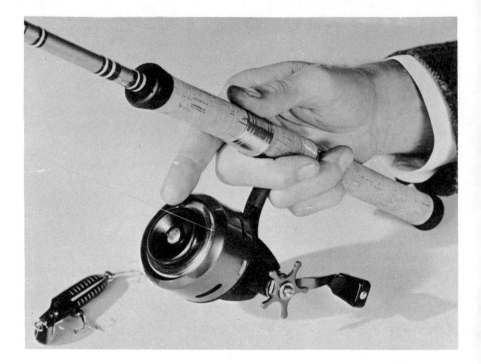

New model reel combines best features of spinning and spin-casting types. A touch of the finger on the spool housing releases the line for casting; turn of the handle automatically picks up the line for retrieve. *Garcia Corp.*

Lines. Spinning lines come of single strand monofilament or braided, in tests of from 1.8 pounds, diameter .0047 inch, up to 19.8 pounds with a diameter of .0185 inch. Prices in 100-yard spools vary with the test of the line, from about $1.35 in the lightest up to $3.40 in the heaviest. Most monofilament lines come off the reel in curlycues, so I prefer the braided line, or one of Stren, the new DuPont product.

CASTING WITH A SPINNING OUTFIT

The proper grip on the open-face spinning reel is to put two fingers on each side of the reel's supporting stem, the thumb extended along the butt, with the forefinger beneath.

Proper grip with an open-face spinning reel. The thumb rests on top of the rod. The reel stem fits between the second and third fingers (some prefer third and fourth). The index finger holds the line by the fleshy part above the first joint. As the rod comes forward, index finger releases line.

Grip with the spin-casting reel is similar to that used with a bait-casting reel. The thumb depresses the control lever during the back cast, thus checking the line, and releases pressure as the rod comes forward.

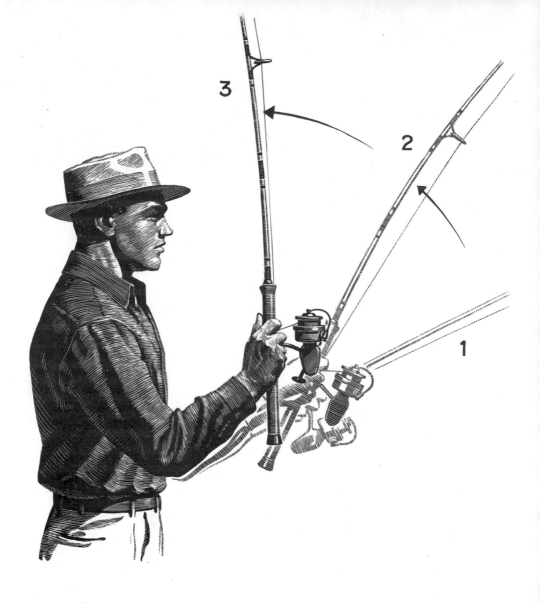

SPINNING WITH AN OPEN-FACE REEL

Back Cast. 1. Begin cast with the rod pointed toward, but slightly above, the target, holding the line with the tip of your forefinger. 2. Lift with an accelerating movement. The lift flexes the rod against the weight of the lure. 3. Stop the rod when it reaches approximately vertical position, allowing the momentum of the lure to flex the rod-tip backward.

Forward Cast. 4. When the lure has reached the farthest point behind you, begin the forward push with a quickly accelerated movement, taking advantage of the rod's springing action. 5. The cast is carried through with a quickly accelerated forward action of the wrist and forearm, and stops at this point. The line is released by the forefinger and the line and lure shoot forward. 6. Follow through by lowering the rod so the tip follows the flight of the lure. Lower your index finger against the spool to control unwinding of the line and prevent possible over-run.

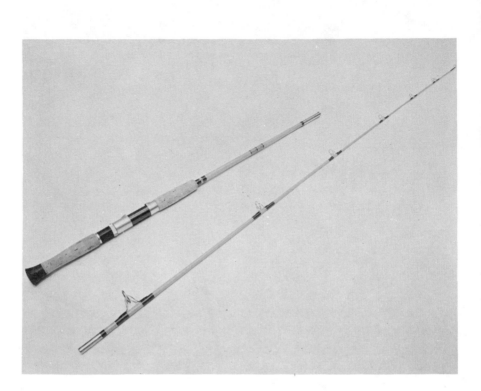

A lightweight two-piece spinning rod of tubular glass construction. Between 6½ and 7 feet is a good length for fresh-water fishing. *Wright & McGill Co.*

To prepare for the cast, the line from the reel should be under the forefinger, which holds it against the rod butt. The left hand then pushes the bail, which holds the line, to one side. This leaves the line free to run off the spool just as soon as the forefinger of the rod hand releases its pressure on the line.

Point your rod at the intended target, the lure hanging about 6 inches below the rod tip. Then, with a quick and firm wrist action, bring back the rod smoothly to a position just a little past 12 o'clock and let it pause there until the weight of the lure swings the rod tip backward. With a smooth and continuous motion, release the line under your forefinger and swing the rod forward to its starting position at about 2 o'clock. As the lure nears its target, stop the progress of the outgoing line by touching the rim of the reel spool with the forefinger.

The sidearm cast is useful when tree branches overhead prevent the usual straightaway cast. This cast starts with the rod forward and parallel to the water and held at an angle a little to the right of the caster. The rod is swung back with a smooth action and then forward with the rod tip aimed at the target at the end of the sweep. The line is freed from the forefinger pressure just before the rod tip completes the arc and points at the target.

The underhand lob is also useful when an overhead cast is impractical because of overhead obstructions. The rod is held low and behind the caster, with tip a little lower than the butt. The lure is swung forward and the rod tip is stopped at a position of about 2 o'clock.

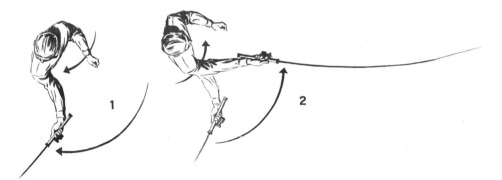

SIDE CAST is used when there is no room overhead and cast must be made low over the water. 1. The entire cast is made with the rod parallel to the water. Holding the rod handle with the palm turned upward, pivot your body so you can look in the direction of your back cast. 2. At the momentary pause between the back and forward cast, face point where you wish the lure to drop, then make the forward cast. Stop the forward movement of the rod before it is in line with the spot on which you wish the lure to land, so line won't swing wide of the mark.

CHAPTER 8

Trolling

TROLLING IS AN indispensable method of fishing, especially for some species of fish at certain seasons of the year. Take for example such game fish as lake trout and landlocked salmon. Shortly after the ice goes out in early spring, for a brief time lake trout, and those landlocks that are lake dwellers, come into shallow water, where they may be caught by casting; but as soon as the sunshine of the lengthening days begins to warm the water, they retreat to the depths, and the one best way to take them is to get down to where they are. The depths at which they lurk may be as shallow as 30 feet, or as deep as 100 feet or more, depending upon the character of the lake. It is necessary to cover a lot of water, and trolling with the proper tackle enables you to do just that.

Trolling has the big advantage of enabling you to fish the most water in the least possible time. If the laws of your state permit trolling from a motor-powered boat, you can operate the boat and troll at the same time. Trolling also enables you when fishing a lake new to you to cover a lot of territory and thus learn the hot spots. And trolling is a leisurely sport which enables you to appreciate the beauties of nature.

Its one disadvantage is that it is slower sport than casting. The caster who places his lure into a pocket among the lily pads where a fish might be lurking gets a thrill akin to that of a golfer who holes a long putt. But the caster is at a loss when the fish are in deep water.

In some lakes even brook trout take to deep water when the surface water gets too warm for their comfort. One August, years ago, I spent the month fishing in a section of Ontario just outside of the Algonquin Provincial Park. I had never been there and was in doubt just what tackle to take with me. I reasoned this way: Those waters, being pretty far north, should be cold all season long; therefore, the trout should be found in water on or near the surface. So I loaded down with fly rods, silk fly lines, fly boxes, and all the rest. I did put in my rod-carrying case a stout 6-foot steel rod. To get some last-moment incidentals I went to my favorite tackle store. The salesman was knowing.

"Where are you going to fish?" he asked. I told him and he shook his head.

"Look here," he said. "You're concentrating on fly tackle. You're likely to find up there that most of the fishing will be down deep in the lakes. That means trolling. Take my advice and be rigged for it."

He sold me a single-action, salt-water trolling reel with side plates 5½ inches in diameter and a narrow spool. The plates were freckled with a number of round openings, and the one on the right side had two handles for winding. The brake was a simple metal band that when pressed with the thumb engaged the plate. It was cheap and effective. He also sold me about 200 yards of copper wire for a trolling line. He explained the copper wire and the reel.

"With a wide-spool reel like your bait-casting reel, when you wind in the wire it's likely to build up unevenly on the spool. That leads to kinking, and kinking means a break. The wire will get down deep where the lake trout are at this season. You may find it necessary to have out 100 yards or more to get down to where the lakers are."

That salesman prevented my trip from being a bust. I didn't have a chance to use my fly rods and tackle. With Archer spinners baited with minnows, I caught plenty of lake trout and also the biggest brookie I have ever taken—5¼ pounds. Trolling with that deep-water rig I caught a lot of other brook trout weighing between 2 and 3 pounds.

In brief, trolling is a fishing method by which you let out a lure behind a slow-moving boat. How slow? About the speed of a leisurely walk. If the boat is rowed, that means that the oarsman should also row at a leisurely pace. Before you prepare to use a gas outboard motor or electric motor, look up the law of the state in which you are fishing: Some states ban trolling from a powered boat.

If you have a friend or guide to do the rowing, the logical place for you to sit in the boat is in the stern, facing the oarsman. If you are trolling from a motorboat, and someone else is operating the motor, sit facing the operator. Then you can watch your line and keep it from fouling the operator, or getting it unpleasantly involved with the propeller.

TROLLING RODS

For fishing shallow to moderately deep water, the conventional bait-casting rod, with a length of 5 to 6 feet, is suitable. Glass is the best available material. Get one with a fairly stiff tip but yet with enough spring to it to give you some play when a fish is on. For such weighty and determined fish as lakers and muskies, you need something stouter. I use a salt-water trolling rod for the big ones, or a surf-casting rod. The trolling rod is of glass, and rated by the dealer as in the 30-pound class. It has a one-piece tip with roller top and a removable butt. The 20-pound class designates a rod designed for use with line of 20-pound test. The surf-casting rod has a tip about 7 feet long, butt section 2 feet long, and weighs about 10 ounces. Both rods can handle the metal line needed in deep trolling for lake trout. Do not use a fly rod for trolling; it is quite certain to get a set.

For trolling in shallow to moderately deep water, a glass bait-casting rod 5 to 6 feet long, with a fairly stiff tip, is adequate for most situations. *James Heddon's Sons.*

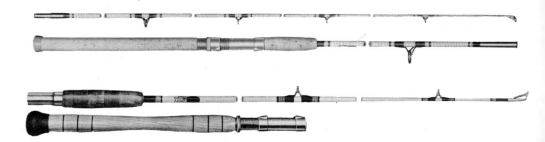

Trolling for lake trout or muskies in deep water with metal line calls for sturdier tackle—a surf-casting rod (top) or a salt-water trolling rod. *Shakespeare Co.*

REEL AND LINE

For the usual type of trolling in water of shallow to medium depth, a conventional bait-casting reel is used, one that can hold about 100 yards of 18-pound-test line, hard-braided nylon preferred. Metal line is not needed in May and June, when the water is still cold enough to keep lakers at a depth of 30 to 40 feet.

Back in the 1940's I was a guest of my friend the late W. B. Tinker, who lived in a town in southern Quebec that sprawled over the boundary line into Vermont. It was the last week in May. We were fishing in Lake Massawippi, a beautiful lake, 9 miles long, lying between Newport, Vermont, and Sherbrooke, Quebec. Tinker had written me, "Don't bother to bring along your rod. I have plenty of tackle."

He handed to me a rod of split bamboo, 7 feet long, holding a reel carrying about 400 feet of linen line. "This rod will get a set if used in trolling," I said. "It already has a set," said Tinker, "but it will give you fine play."

As attractors on my line I tied on two large brass spoons, and for bait Tinker had brought a dozen young suckers 5 to 6 inches long. Tinker sewed one onto my hook. First he killed the sucker, then ran the hook through both its lips, starting from the underside of the lower, then brought the hook up and over to the front, through the upper lip, and back through the lower lip again, thus sewing up the mouth. Next he carried the hook down the sucker's side, inserted it about one-third the distance from mouth to tail, and brought it out again about an inch nearer the tail. Then he ran the hook through the body just above the tail and tightened the gut so that the minnow was shaped into an unaccented curve.

Sewed on in that fashion, the sucker revolved and wobbled in the water. Two swivels on the stout 3-foot leader kept the bait from twisting the line. I let out about 250 feet of line, gauging the distance by counting the marker threads of colored silk. The pull of the spoons and sucker bent the rod, and the tip throbbed like a living thing. That throb told me that the spoons were functioning properly.

With that rig I caught my limit of two lake trout, one weighing exactly 13 pounds, the other 6 pounds. It was a pleasure to fight those fish with that light, 7½-ounce rod and linen line.

But for deep trolling, when the lakers have gone down to 75 feet or more, the metal line is the best bet. Monel metal or lines with a metal core which sink of their own weight are needed. The reel should have a capacity of at least 250 yards, so you turn to a salt-water reel with star drag, or that simple, nonmultiplying reel I used in Ontario. Such a reel, with its narrow spool, is much less likely to kink the line than will the bait-casting reel.

There are several types of metal trolling lines: copper wire, braided or twisted wire lines, monel metal lines, and lines with a lead core. Of these the Monel and lead-core lines are preferable. Copper is harder to handle and is likely to kink, and if you can straighten out a kink in a copper line so it's as good as before, you are a lot defter than I am. Twisted and braided metal lines are subject to twisting when trolled.

When using a hard-braided nylon line in deep trolling, swivels or bead chains should be used in connecting lure to line. To get the line down deep, the triangle rig is good. This consists of a 3-way swivel to one ring of which the running line is attached. To a second ring in the swivel is tied about 5 feet of line of lighter test than the running line, and in turn is tied to a round or oval sinker heavy enough to sink quickly to the bottom. To the third ring of the metal swivel is tied 6 or 7 feet of line of the same test as the running line, and at the end of that another swivel and the lure. This ring permits the sinker to bump along the bottom and slide over most of the bottom rocks, while the lure rides above. If the sinker gets caught on rocks or bottom debris, the weaker length of line to which it is tied will break more readily than the running line, and thus prevent breaking the running line and losing the lure. If fishing for pickerel, northern pike, or muskies—all sharp-toothed fish—it is well to use a wire leader about 10 inches long at the end of the 6-foot length of line preceding the lure; attach the lure to another swivel or bead chain, and that in turn to the wire leader.

LURES

Flash and action are most desirable qualities in trolling spoons or spinners—the flash to attract the fish and the action to provoke it to hit. Wobbling spoons have these qualities. They may be had in all-nickel finish, nickel and copper, all copper, brass, and in color variations. By and large the all-nickel is superior in many lake-trout waters, though the red and white is a proven killer, and should be in every troller's kit. A typical spoon is cupped in shape, and this shape makes it wiggle-woggle through the water.

The June Bug spinner with a minnow has been proven through the years to be the No. 1 attraction for walleyes. As the water resistance is likely to

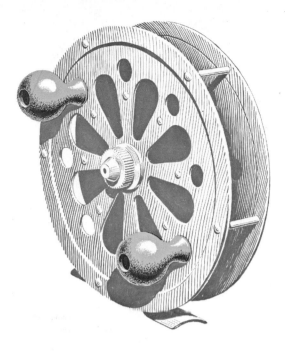

Single-action large-capacity trolling reel (top) or a salt-water reel (below) with star drag is required when deep trolling for lakers.

June Bug spinner with a minnow on the hook is a walleye winner.

pull the hook out if the minnow is hooked only in the mouth, the hook should be run into the minnow's mouth and out a gill, carried back along the minnow's body, and then hooked through the flesh behind the dorsal fin. To prevent line twisting, several swivels should be used on this hook-up. This spinner has a shaft on which the blade is mounted, and is so designed that the blade is always at the same angle to the shaft whatever the speed of the troll. Trolled slowly and deep it really is a walleye winner.

For those sharp-toothed members of the pike family—muskies, northern pike, and pickerel—spoons that revolve on a shaft, such as the June Bug, but with a bunch of feathers concealing the hook, are very good. I have had more success with spoons and spinners that are fluted or dented than with blades that are plain, presumably because their flashing ability is increased. Such spoons come either single or double on the shaft, and the double or tandem spoons work particularly well in deep trolling. Large spoons are needed for large fish such as muskies, northern pike, and lake trout. If they don't work, try adding a sewed-on minnow.

Unlike spinners, which generally are mounted on a shaft, spoons are tied directly to the line at one end, while the hook, or hooks, is at the other. Basically they are of two different types—either wobbling or darting. They are effective not only in trolling but in casting. It is advisable to discover the rate of trolling speed needed to bring out the best action of each type.

As you troll the spoon or spinner, if it is working properly it will transmit a steady throb to the rod, which in turn is felt by the rod hand. If the hooks of the lure pick up weeds, sticks, or some other substance, this steady throb comes to a stop, and you have to retrieve the line to free the hook. Fish will not hit a fouled lure. One of the advantages of lures with hooks hidden by a bunch of feathers is that they are less apt to become fouled in weeds.

When trolling, do not depend entirely on the forward movement of the boat to bring out the action of the lure. Vary the action by raising the rod for a half foot or more, then letting the lure drop back by lowering the rod. Or raise the rod slowly and give it a jerk. As said before, while slow trolling is generally the more effective, if that doesn't work increase the speed of the boat.

Landlocked salmon in early season take a trolled fly beautifully, for then they are in top water. As the fly is light and does not exert anywhere near the same drag on the rod as do spoons, spinners, or minnows, here a stout fly rod may be used with silk or nylon line. In northern New England this type of trolling is the popular early-season method used on these fine fish. Bucktails, streamers, and marabous are the favorites. The most productive flies include the Gray Ghost, Black Ghost, Supervisor, and Edson Tiger, which imitate the smelt on which the salmon feed. Sizes run from No. 4 down to No. 8. Experienced guides in Maine and New Hampshire have advised me that trolling with a rather short line is best, a line that is just long enough to get the fly into the water where the wash of the propeller is dying away. Their argument has been that the wash excites the curiosity of the fish and attracts them to it. There may be something in it, for I have been successful in catching salmon that way.

Feathered spoons are fatal for muskies, northerns, pickerel.
Lures Courtesy of Pfleuger Co.

CHAPTER 9

Hooking, Landing, and Playing Fish

IT IS EXASPERATING for a fly fisherman, after making a good cast, to get a rise and fail to hook the fish. For the bait caster, it is baffling to feel the fish seize the bait, strike hard, and have the bait come free. And in either kind of fishing, it is maddening to hook a fish, play it for a while, and ultimately lose it.

HOW AND WHEN TO STRIKE

When dry-fly fishing for trout, you will find the smaller fish are the quick risers. They are likely to come and go in a flash. Here, the quick strike is needed. Large fish are something else again. They are likely to be slow and deliberate risers. I have seen in clear, slow water a sizable trout come slowly out of hiding and follow the fly for a few feet, sizing it up, then take it in its mouth, turn, and head for the bottom. It is human nature for the novice, seeing the swirl, to become excited and strike hard the moment the trout seems to reach the fly. The correct procedure is to wait until the fish has made its turn and headed for the bottom with the fly. Then, keeping the line taut and raising the rod gently, let the trout virtually hook itself. After taking the fly in its mouth, if the fish feels no resistance, it is sure to turn and head for the bottom. The power of its dive is sufficient to force the barb of the hook into its mouth.

The fly fisherman whose experience has been on trout is quite likely to strike too soon in fishing for Atlantic salmon. It pays to be deliberate here and wait for the salmon to turn after taking the fly. When fishing for trout, you almost invariably strike upward on the rise. But with salmon, strike sidewise, as an upward strike is quite likely to pull the fly out of the fish's mouth. In fact, some salmon fishermen don't strike at all but let the fish hook itself against the taut line as it dives after taking the fly.

The bait fisherman accustomed to getting hard strikes from such fish as pike, pickerel, and bass may go fishless when fishing for steelhead in the far West. These fish are likely to take the bait very gently. As your bait drifts downstream with the sinker bumping along the bottom, that sinker is a telltale. If its bumping stops, while possibly it may be lodged against a rock, strike anyway. It may be that a steelie has taken it.

When fishing with live minnows for bass and members of the pike family, the novice often makes the mistake of striking too soon. These fish can't swallow the bait tail first, for the dorsal fin and flaring gills are in the way. They seize the minnow either at the tail or midbody. A strike then will surely yank the bait out of the fish's mouth. After seizing the minnow, almost invarably the fish will swim off with it. Wait until that run is ended. After making this run the fish will lie still, eject the minnow, then turn it around to swallow it head first. So when you note the strike, let your line flow out freely. When the fish pauses to eject, turn, and swallow the bait, give him time. After gorging it, he will make another run. When he is well started on this run, then sock it to him.

On the other hand, if fishing for bass, with plugs and other artificials, strike at once on the rise. But when plug fishing for members of the pike family, striking is rarely necessary, for these fish hit so hard that they hook themselves. However, when bait fishing for pike, set the hook with force. These fish are hard-mouthed, and a soft strike won't drive the hook home.

CONCENTRATION

Inattention is the cause of many lost strikes. Sometimes you can guess that a rise may be forthcoming—as when you cast skillfully to a persistently rising trout. But you never can be sure. A rise usually comes like a thief in the night, and if you are not alert and concentrated you will react too late. Sometimes when the fishing has been slow, I have been diverted by an oriole or scarlet tanager flying across the stream, or by the sound of an animal in the bushes. Too often a rise from a good fish comes just at that very moment, and my chance has gone forever. I have had rises when I stopped to slap at a mosquito on my face, or when fumbling in my jacket for a match. Trout seem to be psychic in picking such occasions. Concentrating on the lure at all times pays off in increased catches.

In wet-fly or nymph fishing for trout, alertness is essential. Often the fish strikes so gently that it is imperceptible to the rod hand. The fish does not hook itself but ejects the fly immediately on detecting its artificiality. But if you watch intently, you can see the flash of the trout, the shimmering gold or silver of its side as it makes its pass. Strike at the sight of that flash and chances are that you will hook your fish.

When you are trolling, most fish will hook themselves. They see the lure pass and move away from them, and, afraid their prey is escaping, hit it with force.

DULL HOOKS

Hooks become dull through use. When dulled, the points often can penetrate a fish's mouth only with difficulty. Take along a fish-hook sharpening hone, examine the points of your hooks often, and if they are not needle sharp, use that hone.

PLAYING A FISH

The constant, unrelenting pressure of the rod against a fish's runs will exhaust it. Keep the rod tip up and a constant arc in the rod. Don't give any slack line if at all possible. If the fish is powerful, don't risk breaking the rod by having the arc too extreme. Give line grudgingly. The thumb and forefinger of your line hand should be on the line, and you can close them tightly enough to maintain pressure even though the line is going out rapidly. To lessen friction on the line at the first guide above the reel, keep the line hand directly below the guide and in line with it. The thumb and forefinger act as a brake on the running line.

As soon as a fish is hooked, the angler should transfer the rod from the rod hand to the other. Then he is in position to reel in with the hand that has been the rod hand. If you have any slack line in your line hand, hold it tight with the finger of that hand until you have taken it in with the reel.

Trout. Some fly fishermen, when stripping in line, either in casting or playing a fish, hang the coils on their left hand, meanwhile using the thumb or forefinger of the rod hand to press the line against the rod and keep it taut for any strike that may come. Then when casting or paying out line with a fish on, they release these coils one by one as needed. Personally, I don't like those coils on line. I have had too much trouble when releasing them under pressure. In trout fishing with a dry fly, I prefer to strip

Stream fisherman lands a trout with perfect form. He has kept downstream from the fish, his line is taut, rod slightly arced, and he is carefully bringing his struggling quarry within netting range. *Wisconsin Conservation Dept.*

in line when necessary, maintaining control of the line with the forefinger of the rod hand pressed against the line. Allowing the loose line to float past me in the water, I let it out as required, always under the control of the forefinger. Rarely will a trout, even a big one, run many feet, so the floating line is rarely a hazard.

In playing a trout I keep my rod pointed at about 2 o'clock. At that angle the rod not only takes a good arc, but it can quickly be brought farther back in the event the fish runs toward me.

In stream fishing it is important to play the fish upstream from you. Then you have the current aiding you to tire the fish, instead of working against you if the fish gets below you. If you have a heavy fish on and it is strong enough to get below you, as it passes strip off line rapidly and, if possible, take to the bank and run after the fish to get below it. With the letup of pressure on its mouth by reason of the slack, the fish often will

This angler is playing a muskie properly. Keeping his rod high, he prevents the fish from rushing the boat to relieve hook pressure. He will bring battler boatside only when it's thoroughly played out. *Wisconsin Conservation Dept.*

Lower the rod as soon as a fish jumps, giving it a little slack. A heavy fish can break a taut line or tear the hook from its mouth. *Florida State News Bureau.*

stop its downstream run and try to rest in a pocket or small pool in rapids or shallow rifts. The slack line you have released goes on downstream below the fish. The weight of the line plus the force of the current again exerts pressure on the fish's mouth. Just as it sought relief from such pressure when it was above you, so now it seeks to escape by running upstream—which is where you want it.

Playing a trout from above in a rapidly flowing stream too often results in a lost fish, and it may be the best fish of the day. The summer before writing this I lost a fine trout in Vermont's Battenkill in just that way. I kept the fish above me for a while, and then it shot by me downstream. The bank was high, the stream bottom full of rocks, and I judged that taking to the bank or chasing after it in the stream would be impractical. So I played the fish from above. It was on for about five minutes before it broke off. Probably the pressure on the line had worn a hole in its lip, and the hook had fallen out.

Atlantic Salmon. In playing an Atlantic salmon, let it run, though under control. The more the fish runs against the play of the rod, the sooner will it tire and be ready for the net. Exert all the pressure upon it that your tackle will stand. Sometimes the fish wishes to fight in surface water. Then try to get it to go under by easing up a little on the rod. I have lost more salmon hooked and played at the surface than in deep water. Sometimes these fish have strongly wrenched their bodies from side to side. At other times they have jumped and, on returning to the water, have freed themselves from the hook, the line being too taut at the time.

The salmon angler can take heart when his fish runs upstream, knowing that the fish not only is fighting the rod and taut line but the power of the current. Try to keep below the fish and prevent it from turning and racing downstream. Your guide or companion, on seeing a fish attempt a downstream run, should try to turn it back by splashing the water with a landing net or a club. Sometimes hurling a rock ahead of the fish will cause it to retreat.

Try to keep the fish on the move. Should it stop running and rest on the bottom, try to stop its sulking by throwing a rock at it. When it sulks it is resting and getting back its strength. That should be prevented. Sometimes, if the angler plays a salmon too softly, the fish will go into a sulk. Twanging a taut line as if it were a banjo string, or rapping the rod butt with a heavy stick, will jar the fish into action.

If the hooked fish seeks refuge under a ledge or in drowned tree roots at the stream's bank, when pressure is withdrawn often the fish will come out again after a little while, and the battle can be renewed.

It is pretty to see a hooked fish jump, but jumping often helps the fish to escape. Lower the rod as soon as the fish jumps and give it a little slack line. If a heavy fish falls upon a taut line or leader, its weight will break it or tear the hook free. If you have a trophy fish on, when it jumps you can give a powerful sweep to one side with your rod and slam the fish down on its side. Normally it would return to the water head on. One or two such smashes on its side shakes it up and takes the fight out of it. That works well with such fish as black bass or northern pike hooked on plugs, large spoons, or large minnows. Repeated jumps with such weight in the mouth, however, is likely to wear a hole in the jaw through which the hook can slip.

Muskies and Northerns. In playing such weighty fish as muskies and northern pike, try to keep them from the boat until they are licked and ready for the net. These fish may rush to the boat to get relief from the

When landing a fish that is too small to require a gaff, grasp its lower jaw firmly by the thumb and forefinger. This numbs the fish and makes landing it easier. *Florida Fresh Water Fish Comm.*

pressure of the hook. Seek to increase that pressure by applying it in another direction. Raising the rod high in the air will shift pressure by directing it into the air. Jerking the rod to one side may induce the fish to shift its run to that direction.

Lake Trout. Lake trout offer few problems in playing. Except for a brief time in spring when they are in shallow water and you play them as you would a brook trout, they are generally in deep water and hooked on stout rods and heavy metal lines, or an ordinary line weighted with a heavy sinker. They have to fight that weight as well as pressure from the rod. Also, as they are brought up from the depths, there is a radical change in the water pressure. That is enough to leave little fight in them.

LANDING FISH

Most fish will lie on their sides when played out. Muskies may lie belly up when exhausted. That is your signal to bring them in quickly before they have time to recover. If using a landing net, don't shove it at the fish. Anticipate by sinking the net into the water before you, lead the exhausted fish over it, then raise it quickly with the fish inside. It is well to kill the fish at once. While it is still inside the net grasp it from the outside. The cords will help you hold it firmly. If it is an average-sized trout you can insert your thumb and forefinger into the net and grip its upper jaw. Then the jaw can be forced back until the backbone breaks at the neck. Large trout, bass, northern pike, and walleyes can be killed by rapping them sharply at the base of the skull with a closed jackknife, a club or stone.

In landing big fish such as Atlantic salmon or muskies, a gaff is often used. But the gaffing should be done by an experienced hand and not a novice. The latter is almost certain to poke the gaff at the fish or strike at it. This may lose the fish. The gaff should be slid under the fish and the

Two men team up on a fighting walleye. Net man should sink the net into the water, enabling angler to lead the fish over the opening. *Manitoba Dept. of Industry and Commerce.*

gaff point inserted just back of the gills. The fish is then lifted out of the water in a quick and even action.

Some experts who scorn net or gaff seize Atlantic salmon by the small of the tail. Just forward of the tail, the salmon's body tapers down considerably, affording a safe grip, with the fish's wide tail acting as a stop to prevent the hand from sliding off. This is not recommended for the novice.

Smaller fish may also be landed by hand. Grip the fish's lower jaw firmly by thumb and forefinger, inserting the thumb into its mouth. Such a grip seems to numb the fish and render it more docile. A fish may also be landed by inserting the forefinger into the gill, sliding it up as far as it will go, and then clamping down the thumb firmly so as to grip the fish between the forefinger and thumb.

RETURNING FISH

Often the fisherman hooks a game fish which he doesn't wish to keep. It may be too small or out of season. He naturally wants to return it to the water uninjured. The safest and best way to do this is not to handle it but to cut the hook with a pair of fisherman's pliers and let the fish drop to the water. Cut the hook with the fish near the water to lessen the shock of the fall. Or, if you don't have pliers, sever the leader close to the hook with your gut clippers.

Fish, especially the smooth-skinned ones like trout, if handled with dry hands lose some of the protective slime on their bodies, and a destructive fungus is likely to form. If the fish doesn't fall off the hook when the hook is held upright, wet your hands and try to free the barb without squeezing the fish. Hold the fish lightly and try to disengage the barb with the disgorger on your gut clipper. If the fish, when returned to the water, will not stay upright, corral it between your wet hands, hold it upright, and move it gently back and forth to force water through its gills.

PRESERVING YOUR CATCH

Fish will keep in much better condition if dressed soon after being caught. To preserve them for a short time, pluck some grass, wet it, and place it in your wicker creel. Evaporation will keep the fish cool. If, however, you don't expect to cook the fish at once on your return, wipe them dry and wrap them in paper towels. The sooner fish are cooked and eaten after being caught, the better.

CHAPTER 10

The Trouts

THE TROUTS ARE fish of tradition, song, and story. Their beauty of form and color, their gameness, their habitat of cold and pure water, and the tastiness of their flesh have appealed to the imagination of anglers for many centuries. More has been written about them than any other species of fish. Can you ever forget the first trout you caught? You were probably fascinated by its spots and colors, its trim shape. I will never forget my son's first trout. When he was ten years old, I took him fishing with me in northern Vermont. He caught a laker weighing 4½ pounds, and insisted on returning at once to the cottage where he could show the fish to his mother and sister. As I rowed back he held the trout to his breast, hugging it. I'm sure that this adventure is one of his prized memories, too.

The four trouts that have the widest distribution in North America are the brook, rainbow, brown, and cutthroat. The brook trout is the easiest to catch, the rainbow and cutthroat next, and the brown the most difficult. The brook trout was the only one of the four that could be found in the waters of the eastern part of North America when the white man came. Before settlement and the cutting away of the forests, the myriad streams holding this trout were cold, pure, and clear. The removal of the forests inevitably made many streams warmer and above the temperature tolerance of the trout. Add settlements and industrialization, with their pollution of the water, and the result was certain. The brook trout retreated and its range shrunk. Today it is found mostly in wilderness waters or those streams or ponds in the long settled districts that have managed to remain cold and pure. The brown trout, more tolerant of higher water temperatures, has taken over in many eastern streams where once the brook trout was king. The rainbow and cutthroat were the trout of the

106

Four of the most popular trouts (from top): brook, brown, rainbow, and lake. *Ontario Dept. of Lands and Forests.*

Rockies and their range extended to the Pacific Coast. The rainbow has been widely introduced into presumably suitable waters east of the Mississippi River. It often has not succeeded. It has done well in varous streams that enter the Great Lakes, and in some in the northeast, particularly those entering deep, cold lakes of some size. The cutthroat, to the best of my knowledge, has nowhere taken hold east of the Mississippi, and remains strictly a trout of the great mountains of the West, and the streams that eventually enter the Pacific Ocean. What endears these trout to the angler is that, in addition to their beauty, gameness, and tastiness, they all take the artificial fly as well as bait.

BROOK TROUT

The brook trout is scientifically known by the name of *Salvelinus fontinalis,* which means the "salmonlike fish of the springs." It is also called squaretail in northern New England, Eastern brook trout, speckled trout, native trout, mountain trout, and speckles. Its range extends from northern Georgia to Labrador and west to Saskatchewan. It also is found in northern Alabama and South Carolina, and westward into Minnesota and Iowa, the only states west of the Mississippi where it is indigenous. It has been introduced into the Mountain states, and from California north into British Columbia. For example, in 1959 I found it thriving in beaver ponds in the Kaniksu National Forest in the state of Washington.

The brook trout's color varies depending upon the water in which it lives. I have caught them in amber-colored streams where the water was

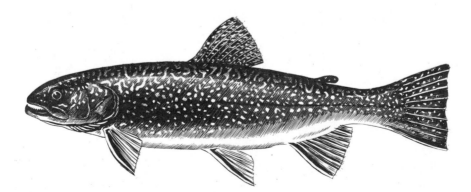

Brook Trout

shaded and the trout were very dark. In more open waters such as a meadow brook they may be almost silvery. The brook trout has a square tail. The back is mottled and there are red spots on its sides. Its fins are white-edged and the lower fins red. Its scales are so tiny as to escape the casual glance and appear to be just skin. It feeds primarily on insects, both aquatic and terrestrial, crustaceans, other fishes, and mollusks. Scientifically it is not a true trout but a char to which family the lake trout and Dolly Varden both belong.

The water that the brook trout inhabits must have a suitable temperature, rarely going above 70 degrees in the hottest weather of the year, and the water also must be well aerated. Therefore, in a stream a considerable current is required or else tributaries with good flow or entering springs. In a lake or pond the water must be cooled and to some extent aerated by streams or bottom springs. The ideal brook-trout stream has a gravel bottom, water that is not too deep, a moderate current broken by rocks, rapids, and small waterfalls to give needed aeration, ample pools that will provide winter refuge, eddies, adequate natural food supply, and overhanging cover from trees and bushes to afford shade and protection from such birds as kingfishers, herons, and fishhawks.

The brook trout spawns in the fall, when summer temperatures have passed and the water has cooled. It goes upstream to shallower water where there are suitable spawning redds of gravel. I once saw these trout spawning in a small stream in the Province of Quebec. The stream there was about a foot deep, and the bottom of gravel that was almost white, being quartzlike in character. Lying flat on my stomach, I peered through a fringe of tall grass and weeds. The females, identified by their smaller heads, made a sort of nest by using their noses and tails to fan away the gravel and make a depression in the stream bed. Each female was accompanied by a male, identified by the hooked underjaw at that season. When the female had finished making a depression to her satisfaction, the male rubbed against her, seeming considerably excited. As she emitted her eggs, the male fertilized them with his milt. Then the female covered the eggs with gravel, again using her nose and tail. I noted that the pair would go through the same routine on another nest.

At first spawning, the female brookies may deposit anywhere from 150 to 250 eggs, the number depending upon the physical condition of the fish, whether fat or gaunt. Older females may lay up to 2,500.

As a game fish the brookie is not the spectacular fighter the rainbow is, rarely jumping on the hook, preferring to bore down into the depths. It takes the dry fly quite well but not quite so readily as the brown trout. In the smaller streams this trout may be adult at 5 inches and in such streams a 7- or 8-inch fish is about the maximum. Usually, in streams a little larger, the fisherman's creel will hold brookies ranging from 7 to 10 inches, the average size being about 8 inches. The record fish of this species weighed 14 pounds, 8 ounces, and was caught in Ontario's Nipigon River in 1916.

BROWN TROUT

The North American fisherman may well be grateful that when deforestation and settlement rendered many former brook-trout streams unfitted for the brookie, the brown trout was here to take over. This fish, introduced from Europe in the 1880's, tolerates water several degrees warmer than the brookie will, and has kept trout fishing alive in many streams now

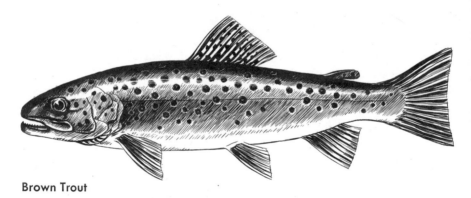

Brown Trout

unsuited to the native trout. Southern New England, New York, New Jersey, Pennsylvania, and Maryland, for example, now depend largely upon this trout as the chief support of their trout fishing. Two separate strains of this species have been introduced, one from Germany known variously as the Von Behr or German trout, and the other from a Scottish lake and still called the Loch Leven out in the West. But interbreeding both in the hatcheries and in the streams has wiped out any distinguishing marks between the two, which fundamentally were of the same species. Brown trout now are widely distributed over the United States, and to some extent in Canada.

The brown trout is more scaly than either the brookie or the rainbow. On its sides are red spots surrounded by light rings. Its color varies with

These modest brook trout, all between 7 and 10 inches, will make up in taste for what they lack in size. *Quebec News Bureau.*

the water in which it is found, and may be a muddy brown or a bright golden brown. The scientists know it as *Salmo trutta*. The largest on record weighed 39½ pounds and was caught in Loch Awe, Scotland, in 1866.

Overfishing may soon exterminate brookies or rainbows in smaller streams that are not regularly stocked, but fishing pressure will probably never threaten the brown trout with extinction. This fish is much more wary than either of the others, and should remain indefinitely if the water remains unpolluted.

The Provo River in Utah is stocked yearly with heavy plants of rainbows and a much smaller number of brownies, yet at the end of the season the brown trout far outnumber the rainbows. A stream survey was made of a water reported to be fished out. The survey crew collected 87 brown trout from only 175 yards of stream and 52 were of legal size. This is the explanation: The rainbows that were stocked in that stream were more active in the search for food, ranged more widely, and fed during daylight hours. This fish likes fast water where the fisherman is less visible, and will strike at about anything that comes along which looks edible. The brown trout prefer less lively water with more cover. The larger ones in particular do most of their feeding at night. They hide under cut banks, overhanging bushes and trees, under logs and shelving rocks. They find spots that suit their requirements and are likely to stay there. Also, the brownie spawns in the fall when the spawning redds are much less likely to be washed out by floods.

The brownie is a favorite with the dry-fly fisherman. In sizes up to 15 or 16 inches it feeds actively on the surface, and is a strong and stubborn fighter. Where the water has a good food supply it puts on weight rapidly and fish of 7 or 8 pounds are not uncommon. The larger fish are mostly flesh eaters, preying on minnows and smaller trout. When you come to a pool or eddy that fairly screams trout but yields nothing, it is quite likely, if it is a brown-trout stream, that a lunker has taken over and the smaller fish find it healthy to keep out. I remember such a pool in a Pennsylvania stream. There is a right-angle pool in the little river where the current hits a shelving rock on the far side, and turns on itself to make a foam-flecked eddy. I could never get a rise in that pool. One late evening I learned why. I was returning after a day on the stream to the farmhouse where I was stopping and remembered that pool. Now was the time to try it out. There was just enough light in the sky so that by holding a big White Miller above me I was able with much fumbling to tie it to the end of my leader. I risked a cast with it. It landed at the edge of a floating foam patch and the rod was almost torn from my grasp. A whopper had taken the fly, and the strike was so fierce it broke my leader.

RAINBOW TROUT

The rainbow trout (*Salmo gairdnerii*) once was native to the Pacific Coast from Southern California up into Alaska, but its beauty, gameness, and high quality as a food fish resulted in its being introduced into many waters across the continent. It has gone into England, Germany, France, Japan, Ceylon, Chile, Argentina, and New Zealand, and in some of these countries is providing fabulous fishing. Among its many good qualities is its ability to thrive in waters a little warmer than those tolerated by the brook trout, provided they are fast-flowing and well aerated. It is my favorite among the trouts. It rises very well to the fly and large specimens are more likely to be taken on artificial flies than are large brown trout. Also, it is a more spectacular fighter and is likely to make a number of jumps. It is easier to catch than the brown trout and only slightly less so than the brook trout.

The rainbow feeds upon insects, crustaceans, worms, and smaller fishes. It is caught not only with dry and wet flies but also by bait casting, trolling, spinning, and still-fishing. It is liberally speckled with small black spots on the back and tail which extend below the median line for a short distance. Along its sides is the birthmark of its species—a broad band of color varying from a pink flush to bright red, depending upon the water

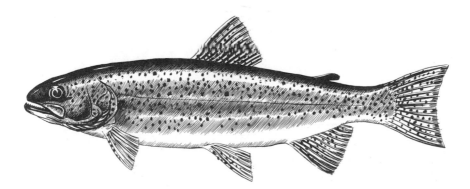

Rainbow Trout

Rainbow trout fatten during their stay in lake. Witness these 6-pound lunkers displayed by young anglers on the shore of Lake William, Manitoba. *Manitoba Dept. of Industry and Commerce.*

in which it lives. Where there is access to salt water or a large body of fresh water, it likes to run down into it, but it will return to the stream to spawn, usually in early spring. There is some evidence, however, that in certain waters rainbows tend to spawn at a later time.

This descent to the sea or to large lakes has resulted in distinct spawning runs in the Esopus in New York State, which empties into the big

Ashokan Reservoir; in Catherine Creek, which is a feeder of Seneca Lake, one of the larger Finger Lakes in New York; and in the rainbow streams of northern Michigan, Wisconsin, and Minnesota. The young rainbows usually stay in such streams until they are about 6 to 9 inches long. Then they run down into the big water where they put on weight rapidly, returning to the streams of their birth when weighing from 2 to 5 pounds.

Dams, so often cursed by fishermen for destroying valuable fisheries, have proved a boon in some of the southern states. The tailwaters of some of the big dams in Arkansas, Tennessee, Alabama, and Georgia now provide fine rainbow fishing. Rivers that once were too warm to suit the rainbow have become cold for miles because it is not surface water that flows from the dams but the bottom water, which is considerably colder. Also, this cold water becomes well aerated by the force of its discharge. The largest rainbow trout of authentic record to be caught on rod and line weighed 37 pounds and was taken in Lake Pend Oreille, Idaho, in 1947.

CUTTHROAT TROUT

The cutthroat trout (*Salmo clarki*) is a handsome fish, liberally spattered with black spots that are even found on its jaws and belly. The tail and fins also are spotted. Along its sides is the same rosy stripe that the rainbow has. Though this fish is considerably more spotted than the rainbow, its chief mark of distinction is the red slash at its throat, from which it gets its name. Like many other of our fishes it has various local names, including black-spotted trout, native trout, and Colorado trout. It

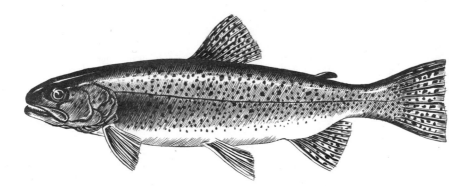

Cutthroat Trout

Winter steelheads often call for bait or spoon fishing. Angler took
this 6-pounder from Oregon's Sandy River. *Oregon Game Comm.*

is peculiarly a fish of the West, being abundant in the Rocky Mountain and Pacific Coast states, ranging from California up through British Columbia into Alaska. Its habits and food are the same as those of the rainbow. It rises readily to the fly and is active when hooked. The largest of record in sport fishing weighed 41 pounds and was caught in Pyramid Lake, Nevada, in 1925.

STEELHEAD

The magnificent steelhead trout is simply a rainbow that has acquired a liking for salt water, and the scientists have dubbed it *Salmo gairdnerii,* the same as the rainbow. The steelhead is to the rivers of the Pacific Coast what the Atlantic salmon is to the Northeast, a terrific and spectacular fighter which reaches heavy weight in some waters. Originally native to rivers from Southern California up into British Columbia, it has been introduced into suitable waters of several of the Great Lakes states and some eastern states. To maintain its identity as a migratory fish it needs access to large bodies of water like the Great Lakes. Otherwise it soon reverts to the rainbow type. Silvery when fresh from the ocean, after a stay in the river in which it spawns, the flush along its sides deepens. The time of its return to the river from the sea varies; in some rivers the runs may be in spring and summer; but most runs are in late fall and early winter.

To show how the time of the biggest runs varies from river to river, we give herewith the months of the best steelhead fishing in the state of Washington. The schedule is based upon two typical winter seasons of 1957-58 and 1958-59. Where the best months vary for the same river the earlier winter is named first.

The rivers follow; Skagit–March; Green–January; Humptulips–January; Cowlitz–March, December; Puyallup–January; Columbia—January, December; Snake–December; Chehalis–January, December; Snohomish–January, December; Samish–January, December; Nisqually–March; Toutle–March, February; Lewis–December, January; Naselle–January; Willapa–January; Elochman–January, December; Pilchuk–December; Soleduck, January, March; Satsop–February, March; Washougal–December; Skykomish–February, March; Nooksack–March, January; and Dungeness–January, April.

Each of the above rivers yielded steelhead catches ranging in the thousands up to an estimated total of 14,803 in the Skagit. Next highest in yields were the Green with an estimated total of 9,914 and the Hump-tulips with 8,501. The months of the best runs are determined largely by the head of water in the river. Steelheads, like the Atlantic salmon, are prone to wait for a good flow before entering.

Winter steelheads do not rise to the fly as well as the summer steelheads. For that reason most fishermen prefer bait or spoon fishing. A good rod for this fishing is one 8½ to 9½ ounces, either of split bamboo or glass. A line to fit such a rod would be a GAF line with 150 yards of 15-pound-test backing. For fly fishing the tried and true Atlantic salmon flies do very well, also the Umpqua, Gray Hackle with yellow body, and Mickey Finn bucktail. The flies should be of heavy wire in sizes No. 4 and No. 6.

In bait fishing, as you need to get the bait down near bottom, use the long, slender type of sinker known as the "pencil," which, because of its shape, is not as apt to get caught on bottom rocks, and if it should is more readily freed. The sinker may be tied to the leader loop with about 6 inches of stout thread. Then, should you get snagged, the thread can be broken easily, and only the sinker will be lost. If the water is high and colored, the leader can be only 6 feet long and of lower test than the line. If the water is low and clear, use a longer leader—9 feet and tapered to 6-pound test is about right. If the water is high and colored, the hook should be about a 1/0 when using an egg cluster, or a No. 6 if low and clear.

There are two popular ways of fastening an egg cluster, or "strawberry," to the hook. In the first, run the leader tip through the eye of the hook and fasten it at the beginning of the bend, leaving a loop in it between the eye of the hook and the knot large enough to slip in the egg cluster. Then pull tight on the leader, thus jamming the cluster against the shank of the hook. To prepare the eggs for the hook, snip off with a sharp knife a group of eggs from the skein about 1 inch long, first halving the skein longitudinally.

In the second method, cut a piece of the roe approximately the size of a walnut, and cover loosely with a piece of cheesecloth. The "strawberry" can be tied to the eye of the hook with a very thin wire.

The winter steelheads will mostly be found in the less turbulent water close to the ledges, rocks, submerged logs, or heaps of drift. After their journey from the ocean, they seek to evade strong currents and rest in less broken water. Cover a glide carefully, beginning at its head, casting across stream, and lengthening your casts until you are reaching the far side. Then move down several feet and repeat. Let your sinker bump along bottom. The way a steelhead takes the bait is almost as tricky as the way other trout take an artificial nymph. The take is usually gentle, almost imperceptible. If your line seems to pause, strike at once. It may be a steelhead or possibly the sinker has lodged against a rock or snag. Where use of salmon eggs is legal, they are sold in most tackle stores, usually in a small jar of preservative. Among artificials the Cherry Bobber has enjoyed considerable success. Shiny nickel spinners, in sizes 1 to 3, also are good.

Spinning for these fish is also productive and has the added advantage of enabling you to reach water that would be impossible with a fly rod. This is a decided benefit in fishing those big brawling rivers of the West Coast. Trolling in the lower stretches of these rivers with flashing spinners and wobblers is effective, as is bait casting with wobbling spoons.

The best time to use artificial flies on summer steelheads is in the months of July, August, and September. Water temperature here is important, for the fish rise best to the fly when the temperature is somewhere between 50 and 65 degrees. Summer steelheads show their preference for the colder water by gathering at or near the mouths of the colder, spring-fed entering streams. Dry flies do well if tied not with feathers but with hair such as caribou, polar bear, and bucktail. Bucktail and streamer flies with gaudy patterns do well.

Good spots in which to find summer steelheads are in deep water, pools, and smooth, fast-flowing runs with underwater ledges. Cast the fly across and a little upstream, letting it drift down, raising and lowering the rod. Work underwater rocks, covering the water above them, to each side, and below. Put the fly so it will drift along the edges of the ledges. A steelhead often will seek rest from the current by getting behind a rock that splits the current. If your unweighted wet fly doesn't do business, try putting on enough lead to take it down into the depths. On a bright, sunshiny day, the fish are likely to lie near bottom, so you must use enough lead on your leader to get the fly down where they are. These fish are fast, powerful, and make long runs, which means that it is imperative to have plenty of backing on your fly line.

In fishing the wet fly, quarter your casts downstream and follow the fly with the rod tip. When the fly reaches the end of its drift, do as you do in wet-fly fishing for other trout. Pause for several moments, then retrieve with little twitches, and follow by letting the fly drop back. At the end of the drift, when the fly swings around in an arc, be doubly watchful, for that is when the most strikes come.

The record steelhead caught with rod and line weighed 37 pounds and was taken in Lake Pend Oreille, Idaho, in 1947. The Kispiox River in British Columbia yielded one almost as large, a splendid specimen of 36 pounds.

In California the best steelhead rivers are the Klamath, Trinity, Eel, Ten Mile, Noyo, Garcia, and Gualala, which give both summer and winter fishing.

Oregon's best rivers are the famous Rogue, Umpqua, and Willamette, which have runs in both fall and spring. In that state also are the Nehalem, Nestucca, Alsea, Sixes, McKenzie, and Deschutes.

In British Columbia are some very fine steelhead rivers which include the Campbell on Vancouver Island; the Oyster, Puntledge, and Qualicum. That province boasts one of the greatest, the Kispiox. The Vancouver Island steelhead rivers have both summer and winter runs. Strangely enough it is the rivers on the west coast of the island that have the summer runs, while those on the east coast have only winter runs. These runs start late in December and taper off in early March. The west coast runs begin in June and last until early October. Should you plan to visit that province for the steelhead fishing, avoid disappointment by writing the British Columbia Game Commission in Victoria, state the time of your visit, and ask just what rivers they can recommend at that time.

LAKE TROUT

The lake trout (*Salvelinus namaycush*) reaches the top weights of all our trouts. It is a creature of the cold, deep northern lakes from New

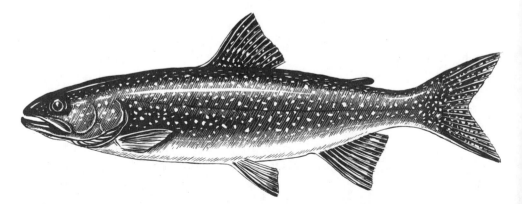

Lake Trout

Brunswick west through the northern states and Canada to Vancouver Island and northward into Alaska. Regionally it is known as Mackinaw trout, Great Lakes trout, salmon trout, and laker. In Maine you hear of it as togue. Generally its color is gray, almost black or of a pale shade, depending upon the water in which it is found. It has many almost round pale spots. It is a hearty feeder and eats about everything in the way of flesh that its habitat affords—smelt, minnows, eels, and smaller fishes of all kinds. Formerly the commercial lake-trout fishery of the Great Lakes was important, but in recent years has been practically wiped out by the predations of lamprey eels. It is said that the commercial fishermen in the past have taken lakers up to 125 pounds, but the record of the species caught with rod and line weighed 63 pounds, 2 ounces, and it was taken from Lake Superior in 1952. The average fish of this species, however, weighs probably not more than 4 or 5 pounds.

The laker's mouth is large, its teeth prominent, and its tail is forked. While cold, deep lakes are its natural habitat, not all such lakes will do for this fish, for the depths must be well oxygenated. That is the principal reason why stocking has failed in a number of instances in waters that seemingly were well suited to the fish. As a table fish it rates high; its flesh is flaky and rich.

For the best lake-trout fishing in the United States the angler should go to northern New England, New York, Michigan, Wisconsin, and Minnesota, though this fish is now established in some western lakes.

In the spring, after the ice has left the lakes, the laker goes into shallow water and for about two weeks stays there feeding. At that time it will rise to the artificial fly, and I have had some rare sport with it using a Royal Coachman dry fly No. 8 and No. 10, a 10-foot fly rod, and a 9-foot leader tapered to 2X. The fish that I have taken have averaged 2½ to 4 pounds, though at least once I caught a 5-pounder. When these trout are caught on fly tackle in shallow water they put up a pretty fight, equal to that of a brook trout of the same weight. None of the fish I caught jumped; rather, they put up a dogged fight and tended to bore to the bottom.

Taking these fish in deep water where they have retreated after the surface water has warmed a little is quite a different matter. To get down where they are, a Monel metal line or one with a metal core is needed. The fish have to fight the weight of the line and suffer the change in water pressure as they are brought to the upper layers. Thus they usually appear to be logy. Trolling is the best way to catch them when they are in the depths. A fly rod should not be used, for the weight of the line plus the

Largest of the trouts, the laker may occasionally reach such huge proportions as this 51-pound, 4-ounce giant, dragged from Gods Lake, Manitoba. *Manitoba Dept. of Industry and Commerce.*

weight of the lure is sure to put a set in the rod. If the fish run large, a stiff bait-casting rod, or what is known as a boat rod, is required. An ordinary reel will not handle a metal-core line well and a solid metal line even worse, for the metal comes onto it in too small a circumference. Get a reel specially designed for deep-water trolling. There is one with an extra-large winding arbor which will bring in a solid metal line such as Monel without kinking, and will hold up to 200 yards or more of such line. There is another which looks like a standard type but is so made that it will hold 100 yards of lead-center line. This line is made of braided nylon with a lead core which handles like an ordinary line, yet sinks well, and will not kink or abrade rod guides. Also, this special line is marked at intervals of 10 yards so that when the fisherman gets a strike he can tell at what depth the fish is lying.

Favorite lures for lake-trout anglers are large nickel or copper spoons and wobblers. The lead-core or solid metal line will take the lure to the bottom. When it hits bottom, raise it so it swims several feet above. Should you feel it bumping along bottom, be quick to raise it to prevent fouling. If you attach the lure to a short nylon leader of about 10-pound test, then if you get hung up and can't get the lure free, a good strong pull will break the leader and save your rod. Another good lure for trolling is a minnow 4 or 5 inches long, rigged with a couple of swivels. Trolling should be done at slow speed, about three miles an hour. Some states ban trolling from a motorboat, so consult the state laws before you use a motor to drive your boat.

Trolling with an ordinary waterproofed silk or nylon bait-casting line also can be fruitful. Unlike the lead-core or metal line, this type requires the use of a sinker. Tying a two-way swivel to the end of the line, attach a 4-foot nylon leader to one eye of the swivel, and a heavy sinker to the other end. To the other eye of the swivel attach a 6-foot, 10-pound-test nylon leader to which the lure is tied. The sinker should bump along the bottom, while the lure rides above bottom for several feet. If large bottom rocks threaten to foul the lure, attach a bobber large enough to float the lure between lure and swivel.

Like the brook trout, the laker is a fall spawner. It spawns beginning in late September and may continue into December. Spawning takes place on gravel or rocky bottom, sometimes in water only 6 feet deep.

DOLLY VARDEN

The Dolly Varden (*Salvelinus malma*) is probably the least respected member of the trout family, and its voracity is responsible. It gorges on the eggs and young of other trout, and will take almost any flesh bait, as well as the artificial fly. It has a number of aliases, among them salmon trout, bull trout, Western charr, Malma, and Oregon charr. It is abundant in Alaska and British Columbia, and is found in the Columbia River basin to Idaho and Montana. Its range is nowhere but in the Pacific drainage.

In shape and color it resembles its cousin, the brook trout. Some of these fish have dark yellow or orange spots on their sides, but they are absent in others. Where these spots are present they are as large as the fish's eye. The back has similar spots, but they are smaller. The general color is olive. The record for the species is 32 pounds, and that fish was taken in Lake Pend Oreille in Idaho.

Where found in streams, the Dolly Varden takes the artificial fly well and gives pretty good sport. The bait fisherman need not be choosy about his baits. Minnows, worms, strips of flesh cut from a fish's side, a piece of liver, or salmon eggs where legal—all will do.

GOLDEN TROUT

The most beautiful of all the trouts, and in my opinion the most beautiful of all fishes, is the golden trout (*Salmo agua-bonita*). It is olive above, with golden sides and belly and with parr marks similar to those that distinguish the young brook trout. Along its sides is a broad scarlet band. It is native to Volcano Creek and the South Fork of the Kern River in California, but it has been introduced into other suitable waters in several western states. This fish seems to be suited only to waters at altitudes of about 10,000 feet or more. Its food is chiefly insects and it takes the artificial fly very well. The average size of those caught by the angler is rather small, usually not over 1 pound. The record for the species, caught in Cook's Lake, Wyoming, in 1948, weighed 11 pounds.

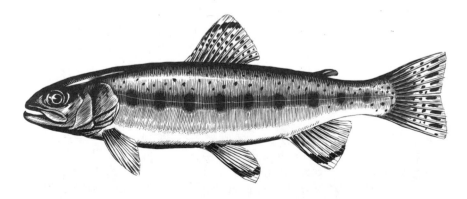

Golden Trout

CHAPTER 11

The 100 Best Trout Streams in the United States

IN THE ISSUE of May, 1959, *Outdoor Life* rendered a great service to the fishermen of the country. It published a list of the 100 best trout streams in the United States. This list was compiled by its angling editor, Wynn Davis, from his own wide experience and the results from 450 letters sent to leading experts—guides, anglers, camp operators, and owners of famous tackle shops—asking for a list of the best trout streams they had fished in the United States. The streams had to meet the following requirements: Excellent trout fishing, accessibility from at least one highway or passable road, within easy drive of good accommodations, food, campsite, and tackle shop, and at prices the average man can afford. The streams must also be open to public fishing, have a good supply of natural food, have good pools and one or more great days during the season with big fly hatches, spawning runs or other conditions offering excellent fishing. Also, they should be well stocked and large enough to stand considerable fishing pressure. The names received were checked and rechecked.

The list is so useful and so unique that it is reproduced here. I personally have fished a number of these waters and from my experiences on them believe they are indeed well chosen.

NEW ENGLAND AREA

Maine
MOOSE RIVER—Tops for big brookies, beautiful canoe water.
ST. JOHN RIVER—Excellent brook trout. Hard to reach.
ALLAGASH RIVER—Excellent brook trout. Hard to reach.
KENNEBEC RIVER SYSTEM—Excellent rainbow, good brook trout.

New Hampshire

UPPER CONNECTICUT (also Vermont)—Big rainbows, also browns. Fly fishing only. Beautiful water.

AMMONOOSUC—Brook trout.

SWIFT DIAMOND—Brook trout.

SACO (also Maine)—Rainbows, brookies.

ANDROSCOGGIN—Excellent rainbow, good brookies.

WILD—Brook trout.

Vermont

BATTENKILL (also New York)—Top brown-trout river in New England, also some rainbows and brooks. Classic water.

WHITE—Rainbows, browns in Bethel-Sharon area, some brookies in headwaters. Wonderful water. Best in fall.

WEST—Rainbows, browns from Dummerston to Jamaica. Some brookies above.

NULHEGAN—Rainbows, excellent brookies upstream. Drains Vermont's largest unpopulated area. Wonderful water.

MIDDLE ATLANTIC AREA

New York

AUSABLE—Top brown-trout water in state and area. Some rainbow.

SALMON—Beautiful brown, rainbow water. Some brook upper reaches.

WEST CANADA—Brown, rainbow.

BEAVERKILL SYSTEM—Classic dry-fly water; brown, rainbow, brook.

ESOPUS CREEK—Big brawling river when gates are open. Spring rainbow run, also brown, some brook.

OSWEGATCHIE—Brown, rainbow, brook.

Pennsylvania

YELLOW BREECHES—Big browns, rainbows, now top trout river in state.

KETTLE CREEK—Excellent brown, fair rainbow, some brook. Fine water.

PINE CREEK—Brown, rainbow, heavily stocked.

BRODHEADS CREEK—Once one of best brown-trout rivers in nation. Now suffering from flood damage. Heavily stocked, should recuperate.

PENNS CREEK—Fine river for big browns, rainbows.

LACKAWAXEN—Famous brown, rainbow water.

West Virginia

WILLIAMS—Best of all-round trout stream in state for brown, rainbow, brook.

CRANBERRY—Excellent brook, rainbow.

SOUTH CENTRAL AREA

Arkansas
  WHITE—Below Bull Shoals for 68 miles.
  NORFOLK—Below Norfolk Lake.
Tennessee
  OBEY—Below Dale Hollow.
  LITTLE TENNESSEE (also North Carolina)
  FRENCH BROAD—Below Douglas Reservoir.

NORTH CENTRAL AREA

Michigan
  HURON (upper Michigan)—Tops for pre-season rainbows.
  TWO-HEARTED (upper Michigan)—Rainbow, brown, some brook.
  BOARDMAN (lower Michigan)—World-famed brown-trout water. Big fish.
  PLATTE (lower Michigan)—Becoming one of state's best brown-trout waters.
  CARP (Upper Michigan)—Rainbow, brown, some brook.
  AU SABLE (lower Michigan)—Brown, some rainbow.
Wisconsin
  BRULE—Best in state. Exciting rainbow runs spring, fall.
  TOMORROW (Portage County)—Excellent brook, good brown, rainbow.
  MECAN (Waushara County)—Brown.

MOUNTAIN STATES AREA

Colorado
  GUNNISON (including Taylor)—One of top rainbow, brown-trout rivers in nation.
  CRYSTAL (Glenwood Springs area)—Excellent small river full of wonderful trout. Ideal for tourists, beginners.
  WHITE (upper reaches)—Excellent rainbow, good brown, fair brook.
  RIO GRANDE (upper reaches)—Rainbow, brown, some brook.
Montana
  MADISON (also Wyoming)—Brown, rainbow, cutthroat, golden, brook.
  BITTERROOT (above Hamilton)—Rainbow, cutthroat, brown.
  KOOTENAI (Libby area)—Fly caster's dream, but hard to reach. Rainbow, Dolly Varden.

GALLATIN—Brown, cutthroat, brook.

YELLOWSTONE (also Wyoming)—Rainbow, cutthroat, brook till mid-summer.

JEFFERSON—Brown, rainbow. Some brook, cutthroat, grayling.

SUN (Great Falls area)—Great brook, grayling. Also rainbow.

MISSOURI (Three Forks area)—Lots of big browns, also rainbow, also cutthroat. Some grayling.

SMITH (near White Sulphur Springs)—Excellent trout fishing.

STILLWATER—Excellent trout fishing.

BIG HOLE—Brook, cutthroat, brown.

BEAVERHEAD—Brook, brown, heavily fished.

Wyoming

FIREHOLE—Brown, rainbow, brook.

GIBBON—Brown.

POWDER (also Montana)—Rainbow, brown.

BIG HORN (also Montana)—Brook, brown, rainbow.

GREEN—Rainbow.

NORTH PLATTE—Big fish, rainbow, brown.

SWEETWATER—Excellent river.

Idaho

BIG WOOD—Rainbow, big fish.

BIG LOST—Rainbow, big fish.

SNAKE (also Wyoming)—Big rainbow.

COEUR D'ALENE—Rainbow.

ST. JOE—Brown, rainbow.

SALMON—Excellent rainbow, good steelhead.

Nevada

TRUCKEE (also California)—One of the best brown-trout rivers in this general area. Also excellent rainbow, good cutthroat.

PACIFIC COAST AREA

California

KLAMATH (also Oregon)—Summer, winter steelhead, rainbow, brown.

EEL—Big steelhead.

RUSSIAN—Steelhead.

TRINITY—Steelhead.

TUOLUMNE—Excellent rainbow, good brown, fair brook.

AMERICAN—Fair steelhead.

PIT—Excellent rainbow, some brown.

RUBICON—Rainbow, brown, brook.

FEATHER—Excellent rainbow, some brown, brook.

Oregon

DESCHUTES SYSTEM—Excellent brown, rainbow, summer steelhead, brook trout in headwaters.

UMPQUA—Excellent summer, winter steelhead, good cutthroat, brown, fair rainbow.

JOHN DAY—Excellent rainbow, good steelhead. (Best water is in Indian reservation. Permit required.)

ROGUE—Steelhead, rainbow, fair Eastern brook, cutthroat far upriver.

WILLIAMSON—Fine rainbow fishing, big fish.

WILLAMETTE—Rainbow, steelhead, fair cutthroat in headwaters.

SILETZ—Steelhead, cutthroat.

MC KENZIE—Excellent rainbow. Wonderful water.

Washington

SKAGIT—Big winter steelhead, cutthroat, summer rainbow. King-sized fish.

YAKIMA—Rainbow, brown, summer steelhead.

GREEN—Winter steelhead, sea-run cutthroat. Rainbows all summer.

COWLITZ—Winter steelhead, small rainbow, cutthroat.

PUYALLUP—Winter steelhead, rainbow, cutthroat all summer. Big fish.

SKYKOMISH—Winter steelhead, cutthroat, small rainbow all summer.

HUMPTULIPS—Winter steelhead.

QUEETS—Winter steelhead, cutthroat, Dolly Varden.

KALAMA—Winter steelhead, rainbow, cutthroat all summer.

CHEHALIS—Winter steelhead.

CHAPTER 12

Dry-Fly Fishing

SINCE THEODORE GORDON, the famous New York fisherman, pioneered in the Catskills with the dry fly in 1890, using flies tied in England, the cult of the dry fly has grown mightily among those who clearly see that much of the pleasure in trout fishing does not come from the size of the catch, but from the skillful use of light tackle which is pleasurable to handle.

The principle of dry-fly fishing is easy to understand. The fly is to float and imitate the adult form of insects that have passed through the various phases of their life cycle, and have emerged from the water as winged adults. These insects may pause on the top of the water and become trout food or, after mating in the air, touch the water repeatedly while in the act of depositing their eggs. Then, too, they become trout food, and the female's frequent dapping of the water is likely to stir the trout into a feeding orgy. Later, after the mating and egg laying, both male and female insects die, and their lifeless bodies floating on the water are also taken eagerly. Then there are the terrestrial flies that often are blown upon the water and also make trout food. There also are land insects such as butterflies, moths, and damsel flies which often touch the water when in flight, and they too become trout food.

It is obvious then that the dry fly becomes most effective when there are flies upon the water to bring up the fish from the depths. Unfortunately, on many of our streams large fly hatches are not common, and there are few if any fly flights before the water temperature rises to 55 degrees or more. The best hatches come when water temperatures range from about 58 to 65 degrees. Thus the early season is not productive for the dry-fly

130

fisherman. The water is too high and cold. Both trout and aquatic insects hug the bottom. The bait and spinning fishermen get the catches.

FLY HATCHES

There has been a change in the fly hatches on many of our eastern streams during the past twenty-five years. Today's hatches on various waters are noticeably smaller, in part due to Nature and in part to Man. Deforestation has caused rapid run-offs in late winter and spring. The roots of forest trees once held the melted snow of winter and heavy rains of spring so that they did not come down in one big rush but more in the form of gradual release. The early spring run-offs have tremendous power. Large boulders are moved. Stream bottoms are scoured and spawning beds removed or covered deep with gravel or silt. Insect life suffers. Recall how the streams that you fish become greatly changed from year to year. Pools that were good holders of trout have disappeared and new ones formed. What once were fine pothole stretches have become wide, shallow, and choked with sand and gravel.

I remember a stream in Delaware County, New York, which was a tributary to a river. For a half-mile before it entered the river it flowed through a meadow where herds of dairy cattle pastured contentedly. About fifteen years ago a flood changed the course of the stream. Now its entry into the river is about a half-mile below its former mouth. The meadow has been ruined. It is covered with rocks brought down by the flood, and instead of one swift-flowing stream, there are a number of small and shallow brooks where only small chub lurk. The water in the meadow formerly was icy cold. Now spread out and shallow, divided into several streams, it has become too warm to support trout, especially since the alders that once bordered it have been swept away.

Man has taken a hand in this stream damage. It is reported that the Highway Department of New York State has often dredged gravel out of the beds of fine trout streams in order to make road repairs. Doubtless this has happened in other states. Thus we see a state conservation department trying to preserve and improve trout streams while another department of the same state is severely damaging them.

This has a bearing on the dry-fly man. Insects require suitable and undamaged stream beds while in their various larval stages. The fewer there are of such suitable stream beds, the fewer insect hatches. The fewer flights of flies, the less often will trout be brought to the top, and the less successful will be the dry-fly angler. However, wherever there are trout, dry-fly fishing has its place as the most appealing of all forms of fishing. Add to this fact that brown trout take flies on the surface more readily than either brookies or rainbows, that many eastern streams are now exclusively brown-trout waters, and the dry-fly man has plenty of justification for his sport.

However, it should be remembered that aquatic insects spend most of their lives under water, and that the largest percentage of insect life upon which brown trout feed is in its underwater form. For better catches, study the water to learn on what forms of insects the trout are feeding. If they seem to be working under the surface—as shown by flashes made by the fish as they bulge the surface water, breaking it only with their tails—the chances are that they are feeding on nymphs or the early forms of the insect life. In that case switch to nymph or wet-fly fishing. It will be more productive. If the flies are hatching in top water, and the trout are taking them there, stick to the dry fly, for then it will get you more fish and give you much more fun. Test the water temperature with your thermometer and you will probably find its temperature to be above 55 degrees. You will find the best insect hatches when the water temperature is between 60 and 67 degrees, and if the beginner dry-fly fisherman does not want to be discouraged in the early stages of his sport, he will do well to wait until the water is within that band of temperatures. Then the trout no longer stick to the depths where the water has been more to their liking. They spread out into the shallower water of riffles and pothole rapids where insect life is most abundant. Most deep pools have shallower water at the tail, below which are usually riffles and rapids. Approach such water with the utmost caution. It is likely to hold some good fish. It requires a more cautious approach than the broken water below since such disturbed water tends to make the fisherman less conspicuous. I've taken brown trout in riffles and rapids from a pothole not more than 10 feet from me.

THE DRY FLY

In fishing dry flies, select only those that are tied on thin wire. Heavy wire defeats the purpose of the dry fly, which is to float. The hackles are highly important. They must be stiff to hold up the fly properly. I like to test a dry fly by dropping it upon the glass showcase of the sporting goods store. If it has a good bounce when it hits the glass, it passes the test. Or place the fly upright on the case to see if the hackles support it so the body of the fly is clear of the glass or table surface. Also, good dry-fly hackles feel stiff and brittle to the finger touch. Reject a fly that does not stand up straight but leans to one side. Such a fly will not float upright on the water but lie upon its side.

Flies that are on the colorful side usually are not as attractive to brown trout as those of more subdued colors such as smoky blue, ginger, grizzly, shades of brown, and black. There are times when winged flies do not pay off but when flies that are all hackle, like the palmers, do well. These palmer-tied flies do not look much like any type of natural fly, but they float well if tied with good hackles, and I suppose that the fish may take them for caterpillars. The Brown Bivisible is a good example of this. It is a fine floater, easy to see on the water, and one of the best of all patterns.

There are times in dry-fly fishing when you are lucky enough to be on the stream when there is a good hatch of flies. I know dedicated dry-fly men who have made arrangement with boardinghouse proprietors or hotel men in the valley of New York's famous Beaverkill to be wired collect when the coffin fly or May fly hatch is on the water. It looks easy to make a fine catch when you see how the trout are rising, and that there are far more fish in the stream than you ever suspected. But often the number of fish you catch will disappoint you. It may be that the fly pattern you have on is too large. Switch to one that in size and general color looks like those in the hatch. Sometimes this will work and you may take several fine fish before your casting puts them down. Then there often are occasions when the trout that are feeding greedily will refuse your fly even though it closely resembles the natural in color and size. Then if you change the fly and put on a larger one quite different in appearance from the one on the water, often it will be taken. It stands to reason that when there is a big flight of natural flies your pattern, good copy of the natural that it is, is in competition with hundreds of the living insects and so is unnoticed.

FISHING THE DRY FLY

Dry-fly fishing is done upstream. Try to fish such a fly downstream and it soon drowns. You cast upstream, picking the water so that the fly will float down toward you without drag. Drag, that bane of the dry-fly angler, results when the line or leader, or both, moves downstream faster than the fly and drags it under the surface. As the fly floats down toward you, use your left hand to strip in line and be ready to strike when there is a rise. When the fly comes within a short cast of you, make your back cast and keep line and fly in the air while you make several false casts to dry them before again casting to the water.

Cast to water that is most likely to hold a trout—deep little potholes in riffles and rapids; where two currents come together below an island or big boulder; glassy glides of some depth; just off a current where there is some depth; piles of driftwood near enough to a good current so that a trout sheltering there has food coming right to its door; and undercut banks. A trout wants shelter from its enemies. It wants that shelter to be close to possible food so that it can get it without undue exposure.

Remember that trout, like deer, are quick to detect motion. Be slow in your movements. Where you are exposed, as on the bank and without a wooded background, keep low. When wading, use care how you place your feet upon the stream bottom so that you will not be displacing or rattling stones. Water is a good conductor of sound and trout are quick to take alarm.

As you wade in rough and heavy water, be sure of the footing of your advancing foot before you take your weight off the other. Sometimes when I have seen the rise of a good fish and have tried to get within casting distance, I have neglected to do this and trusted to chance. This has resulted in various mishaps. Sometimes I have placed my forward foot on a rocking underwater stone, resulting in a spill or wild maneuvers to keep my balance. Sometimes my forward foot has gotten jammed between two rocks. Do this in heavy water and you break out with goose pimples. Though it is rather awkward to carry, when there is rough wading and a strong current I like to use a wading staff.

In approaching water that appears to be tricky wading, look for water near shore that is out of the main current and relatively shallow. If you do not see water of that type, take to shore. It is most unpleasant on a chilly day to get a ducking in water that is the next thing to liquid ice. I well remember an experience I once had on the Pequest in New Jersey. It was in early May and the air was cold and the water much colder, high and colored. I came to a pool where to take to the bank meant climbing a steep little ridge, handicapped with waders that would bind at the knee, or else trying to force my way through a thick growth of bushes. I chose what I thought was easier, to wade through that cloudy water in a pool of unknown depth. I took several cautious steps, then brought my forward foot down on the slanting side of a big, unseen rock, slippery with mud brought down by the rains. I put my weight upon that forward foot and slid helplessly down the side of the rock and completely into and under deep water. My waders were heavy and filled with water. I could not get to my feet and practically crawled under water to the shore. My heart was pounding from the chill and I was gasping for breath.

In England, where dry-fly fishing was developed long before it was tried in this country, the favored method is to prowl along a stream until a rise is seen. Then the fisherman stalks that rise with great care and seeks to cast the fly above the trout so the fly will float down over it and provoke a rise. The expert makes his casts so that the fly and not the leader is presented to the fish.

Casting "to the rise" rather than "fishing the water" would be impractical most of the time in North America. The American practice is to cast the fly over any promising water, whether a natural rise is seen or not. Natural rises, except during a hatch, are not too common, and to wait until a rise is seen would greatly limit the chance of a catch. Trout in favored locations can often be persuaded to rise to the artificial dry fly if it is properly presented to them even though there is no natural hatch upon the water.

Types of Water.   In fishing dry flies it makes a difference upon what sort of water you make your casts. Very fast water, with no patches of relatively smooth-surfaced potholes such as you find in riffles, is not good water for the dry-fly man. Brown trout do not like such water, and if rainbows are present, it is well to leave them to the bait or wet-fly fisherman. Furthermore, on such water the dry fly drowns so quickly that it is ineffective. But shallow riffles with rocks appearing above the surface usually will have pockets above or below the rocks where the water is relatively smooth. Trout love such pockets. Here they can lie, with a fast current on each side of them to bring down food. They can dart out from the pothole, seize a morsel of food and retreat to their shelter. Study such a riffle before you fish it and locate these pockets.

Dry-fly fishing is mostly done by casting upstream, so approach the riffle from the lower end. Taking your position at its foot and fanning out your casts, reach all promising potholes. Broken water makes you less visible to the fish, so do not try for distance but make your casts relatively short, say from 15 to 25 feet. After you have exhausted the possibilities of potholes easily reached from that spot, advance several feet with caution. If you frighten a fish near you, it will shoot upstream and may alarm the fish farther up.

Not only noise but your shadow upon the water will scare trout and spoil your fishing. If the sun is shining, seek casting positions where your shadow is not on your fishing water. The advantage of making short casts is that you can better control the float of the fly and its appearance upon the water.

Flies fished on broken water are less visible to your eyes than those upon calmer and more glassy surfaces. This is because of the varying lights on such water caused by reflection from different surfaces. Here is one place where you can put on a large fly, say a No. 8 or 10, and find it effective. Some excellent dry-fly patterns such as the Irresistible and Gold-ribbed Hare's Ear are almost impossible for me to see on such riffles. The Coachman and Royal Coachman, with their white wings, can easily be followed by the eye in such pothole fishing. When fishing with the dry fly, you have to be able to follow its float or you will miss many rises.

In riffles such as described above there not only are potholes but stretches of fast-moving water with relatively smooth surface. Do not neglect such stretches. Riffles are the pantries of trout, and they may range all over them in search of nymphs and other food.

Above a riffle there usually is a pool. It may be long, somewhat shallow, and with slow-moving current, or again it may be deep and short in length. Here are the hardest-fished places on a stream. Many fishermen will fish only them, moving from one to another, and neglecting the riffles.

I know a long, still pool on the Willowemoc that, with the exception of its head, where the current is well broken by rocks, is almost impossible to fish throughout its length except at night. The bed is mostly gravel, its surface is almost as smooth as that of a millpond, and the stream bottom is almost as free of sheltering rocks as an asphalt road. Yet there are plenty of trout in that pool throughout its length. They find shelter under the banks. You can't fish it from the banks, which are thick with alders and other trees. As you wade it, your wading sends ahead of you waves of water to warn the fish. Having been frustrated in fishing it many times, I finally got to leaving the stream at the foot of the pool and walking up to its head where there was a good chance of getting a fish or two. One May morning I came to this pool and to save a scramble up a rather steep little bank, waded into the foot of the pool. Too late I saw the darting shadowy forms of trout, some of them sizable, shoot up the pool ahead of me. They had been cruising there for food.

The foot of a pool, just before the water speeds up into a riffle, is a good feeding place for trout, especially in early morning and at dusk. It must be reached and fished with caution. The water there is shallow, the trout feel exposed to their enemies, and are doubly wary. If there is cover on the bank at this spot, it is well to sneak up to it, keeping low, and to make your casts from the shelter of a bush or tree. The water being glassy and shallow, the leader should be long, and tapered to a test of not more than 1–2 pounds. Make your first cast as good as possible, for it may be that the one cast is all the trout there will stand before being scared witless.

If such bank cover is not present, be prepared to practically grovel. Crouch as low as you can. You want to get as close as is feasible, for at the lower lip of the pool the water speeds up to join the rapids below. Thus it is almost imperative to make the cast so that no part of the line and very little of the leader falls upon the water affected by that speed-up of the current. That means a short cast. If there is a bank high enough to act as your background, take advantage of it. If there is nothing like that which you can use to your advantage, try casting from a low crouch at the head of the rapids just below the foot of the pool.

The relatively quiet water above the lip of a pool can be good fishing. It has this great handicap: The wading fisherman telegraphs his approach by the waves he has made. If the fisherman has reason to believe that the middle portion of the pool between its lip and its head has trout, he can wade as carefully as possible, moving slowly, until he reaches the spot he has selected as a stand, and then stop and be patient and still for as long as 10 or 15 minutes. By that time the trout may have forgotten the waves and start to rise again. Don't be impatient if you see a fine trout rising at the very head of a long pool. There may be a half-dozen good fish between you and it. Cover all the water carefully with your casts before you cast to that fish. On that quiet water you will need at least a 9-foot leader, and a 12-footer is better, tapered down to 4X or even 5X. The leader should sink, the line float. Treat the leader with a sinking solution, and treat the line with dressing to keep it on the surface.

There is a current in every trout-stream pool, even though the pool is so long as to make the current imperceptible. If the slow float of your fly does not attract a trout, try making it quiver or flutter on the water. A gentle movement of the rod-hand wrist or rapping the rod with the line hand can do this.

On the placid water of a pool, the large fly, which may be useful in broken water, usually is not as effective as small flies such as No. 14 and smaller. In still-water fishing, you should make as little disturbance upon the water surface as possible, and the large fly, at home in broken water, makes too much fuss on glassy water. Furthermore, large flies do not cast well on the long hair-point leader required for still-water fishing. The man who slashes the calm water when he lifts the fly from it to make a back cast may catch an unsophisticated, freshly stocked hatchery fish, but the wild trout will leave his fly strictly alone.

The type of water that gives me the most pleasure to fish is the glassy glide. Here the water has a depth of perhaps 18 inches or more and moves with considerable speed without being broken. The fly is in sight all the time and gives a good float. Trout like that kind of water. Fishing upstream as you should, cast from an angle, shortening line as the fly comes nearer, and paying it out after it passes. If you hook a trout in the lower stretch of such water, try to keep it from running above to frighten other trout that may be in that run. Sometimes such a piece of water is good for several fish. In casting from an angle it is possible to keep the leader from passing over the trout before the fly, and that is highly desirable.

There is another type of run that is difficult to fish with the dry fly but is likely to yield fish if you can avoid drag when casting. This kind of run moves at good speed but has counter currents and underwater conditions that cause little swirling eddies and boils on top of the water. The eddies catch the fly and quickly drown it unless you can read the water and avoid them. Such water usually means a short float and quick action to lift the line and leader from the water as soon as drag can be detected. Sometimes it is possible to prolong the float by "mending the line," as described in the chapter on fly casting.

CURVE CASTS

Sometimes a glide has twisting currents or eddies, with water moving at different speeds, which makes dry-fly fishing tricky since preventing drag is difficult. The line is likely to land on a spot where the current is swifter than where the fly falls. The current will pull the line downstream ahead of the fly. Here a curve cast is needed.

There are two kinds of curve casts—right and left. The curve to the left is made by holding the rod well out from the side, slightly above the horizontal, and casting to a point upstream above the spot where you want the fly to land. As the line is about to land on the forward cast, pull the rod tip back a little. Properly done, this gives some slack line to the cast, and the line will curve to the left and land above the fly, permitting a longer float.

Throwing a curve to the right will also prevent drag and can be used when you see a rise across current from you and there is a high bank or thick shrubs and trees behind you which would spoil your back cast. In such a situation, face the fish and, holding the rod parallel to the water, make your false casts up- and downstream, making the casts just fast enough to keep line and leader from hitting the water. When you see that you have enough line in the air to reach the rising fish, on the forward cast turn your wrist slowly to the right so that the rod points at an imaginary spot several feet above the place where you saw the rise. This swings the rod tip over, moving the line to the right, and lands leader and fly on that imaginary spot, giving enough float, without drag, to take the fly down over the fish.

SLACK-LINE CASTS

A slack-line cast is useful when you have to cast across currents of varying speeds in order to reach a trout rising beyond them. It is usually done by checking an ordinary forward cast just before its completion, and then quickly pushing the rod forward as though it had not been checked. Another way is to cast as usual but without giving the rod enough drive to straighten out the line. The line then drops in small snakelike curves upon the water.

DRY-FLY PATTERNS

What are good dry-fly patterns all over the trout range? Here are my favorites, suited to conditions usually met during the season from coast to coast. The list does not include all good patterns or flies that are local favorites, but it is quite unnecessary to load up your fly boxes with more flies than you can use. In fishing any water new to you, it is well to inquire locally what flies are the most popular among the good fishermen.

Adams. Yellow body, a mixture of brown and gray. Sizes 8, 12, 16.

Blue Dun. The blue-gray hackles have about the same color effect as that of many insects which hatch along a stream. A fine pattern but difficult to see on the water in some conditions of light. Sizes 12, 14, 18.

Black Gnat. Some type of black fly is needed and this pattern has been good over many years. Sizes 12, 14, 16, 20.

Brown Bivisible. This fly was the innovation of that masterful angler, the late Edward R. Hewitt. The white hackle tied in at the head makes the fly visible even under trying light conditions. A large fly in this pattern often works on large trout at dusk. Sizes 8, 10, 12.

Badger Bivisible. A good floater and good color pattern. Sizes 8, 10, 14.

Ginger Quill. One of the indispensable flies wherever you do your fishing. Another fly tried and true over the years. Sizes 10, 12, 14, 16.

Hair-wing Royal Coachman. Better than the Fanwing Royal. Floats better, visible in almost any light and on any type of water. Brookies, rainbows, cutthroats, and brownies all fall for it. I use it more than any pattern in my fly boxes. Sizes 8, 10, 12, 16.

Dark Hendrickson. The hackles and tail color are important in this pattern. They should be a dark smoky-blue. Sizes 10, 12, 14, 16.

Irresistible. A grand fly, good floater because of the clipped bucktail hair body. It's fine east, west, north, and south. Only fault, hard to see on water in dim light and under overcast skies. Sizes 10, 12, 14. On the Madison River in Montana I used this pattern in a No. 8, and it worked well.

Multicolor Variant. A splendid pattern with fat and stubby little wings, and a gold body. A favorite with me on trout that are hard to raise. Sizes 10, 12, 14, 16.

Quill Gordon. A grand all-purpose fly, and probably the best all-round fly in the list. Fault—hard to see on the water when the light is poor. Sizes 10, 12, 14, 16.

The Spiders—Badger, Brown, Ginger, Honey. Good floaters with the fly resting lightly on its hackles. When trout are hard to get to rise, a Spider often will change their minds. Only fault is that sometimes it's difficult to hook the fish on one of them. Sizes 12, 14, 18.

Gray Wulff. One of those deer-hair patterns that make fine floaters. I'm sold on them.

CHAPTER 13

Fishing Wet Flies

THE FIRST FLY fishing I did was with wet flies. At that time dry flies and dry-fly fishing were practically unknown in North America. True, we read something about that method in English books and fishing magazines, but if we gave it a thought we assumed that it was something adapted only to English chalk streams and entirely unsuited to the rushing waters so characteristic of our North American trout brooks and rivers. Most of our anglers in those days would cast across and downstream, using a leader with two or three wet flies, and skip them across the water with fast jerks. Strangely enough this method would take fish, though the action of the flies was quite unlike that of any natural insects, or of the nymphs upon which trout so largely feed. Perhaps these fast-skipping flies excited the trout's curiosity or anger. Perhaps they mistook them for minnows making a fast getaway. At any rate there were relatively few wet-fly fishermen then who could rate as experts. Those who could make fine catches with the wet fly did so on waters that had little fishing pressure as compared to today. When we read in the books and magazines of that era of the typical catches of brook trout, they seem fabulous.

But today even the brook trout, native to the stream, always hungry and easier to catch than either the brown or the rainbow, has learned some caution from the constant pounding with bait and fly of its home waters, and, except in true wilderness lakes and streams, requires something more than flies skipping wildly across the water to provoke a rise. Hatchery trout are something else again. In the hatchery tanks, they were fed by men who stood in plain sight and scooped out ladles of food to them at feeding time. Thus they have associated the sight of man with food, and the angler on the bank or in the stream excites no fear. Before they learn that man the feeder and man the fisherman are quite dissimilar, most of them have been caught. It takes little skill to catch fresh-stocked hatchery trout. The rainbow is a little more wary, while the brownie has caution bred right into him. As so many of our streams now have brown trout, the wet-fly fisherman must exercise skill and caution to be successful.

Fishing a wet fly takes more skill than fishing a dry fly. It takes almost as much skill as nymph fishing which so completely separates the master from the tyro. The wet fly has this advantage over the dry fly—it can be fished near the bottom where the trout often lie. The dry fly has this advantage, and it's a big one—the rise can be seen and tells the fisherman when to strike.

From the start of the season until the water becomes low and clear in midseason and late season, the wet fly is better than the dry. To use the dry fly in early season, when the water is high and turbid, is almost always a waste of time. The water then is not only colored but colder than the trout likes. It is true that the trout is a cold-water fish, but in water colder than 50 degrees it does little feeding and is not completely comfortable. So it lies close to the bottom where the temperature may be a degree or two higher and the current less strong.

Wet-fly fishing properly begins when the water temperature is between 50 and 55 degrees. After the water temperature rises to between 55 and 65 degrees, aquatic flies are hatching and the dry-fly fisherman comes into his own. In water under 50 degrees, as it is early in the season, the bait fisherman is the man who has fish to show to his friends.

CASTING THE WET FLY

Rarely have I been very successful in taking trout with the wet fly when making long casts. The trouble has not been with lack of hits so much as trouble in knowing when I had one. There will come a slight pause in the progress of the line, and by the time I have made my strike the fish often has gone about other business. In my experience, casts somewhere between 20 and 40 feet are the fish-getters, and this is especially true when you are fishing those productive stretches of pothole water which are almost flat but have a fast current and are sprinkled with a lot of rocks and boulders. The current in such water is checked by underwater rocks. It has gouged out the bottom of those rocks and made deep little pockets. Trout love such water, for here nymphs and other underwater life are more abundant than anywhere else in the stream. The current often will dislodge such creatures from under the rocks where they cling, making them easy prey for the trout.

I recall such a riffle in the Willowemoc of New York. There was a large flat-topped rock that emerged a few inches above water at a normal stage. The current hit that rock and bounced back for about a foot. I had always thought the downstream side of that rock, where the water was about 18 inches deep, to be the logical place for a trout to lie. Fishing upstream with the dry fly, I would always cast to right or left of the rock, letting the current take the fly down along the edge of the pothole behind the rock. But I never had a rise there. One day I casually cast my dry fly just at the rim of the water boil above the rock where the current recoiled from the contact. Much to my surprise a fine fish made a pass at the fly, but the current was too swift, the fly swept by, and drag followed. I tried that trout several times, raised it again, but always missed hooking it.

Then I got wise and changed tactics. I changed reels and put on one with a sinking line, tied on a No. 10 Black Gnat, soaked it well with mud, clamped on a small split shot, and let the current take it to the spot where the trout was lying. He took it. I saw the boil he made as he rose, and was ready. It was a brownie that measured 13 inches. I have taken several other trout from that same spot, which seems to be a favorite lie for a fish. Stepping into it, I found a hole nearly knee deep.

PLAYING THE WET FLY

I have found that letting the wet fly drift along naturally on a sunken leader and sinking line is generally the most productive method. First, cast upstream at an angle of about 45 degrees and let the fly drift along to the end of its arc. During this drift keep your rod tip pointed at the fly and following it through its entire course. The pull of the current upon the line will bring the fly, at the end of its drift, to a point directly below the rod tip. Then retrieve the fly about an arm's length by raising the rod, and permit it to drift back to where it was before the retrieve. Repeat this several times.

The hot spot of the drift will be just where the fly has ended its natural drift, and the swing across current has started. This may be because an investigating trout has followed the fly along its drift, sees it apparently escaping, and seizes it before it can get away.

The next most likely place to get a hit is where the fly has reached the end of its course and remains stationary for a moment, and when you make several short retrieves as mentioned above. If the straight retrieve of arm's length does not provoke a hit, vary it with little twitches and drop backs. At this point do not lift the fly from the water to make another cast. A slow hand-twist retrieve which brings back the line to within a few feet of you will sometimes be effective.

If the water you have been fishing does not bring a hit, though it looks fishy, perhaps the fly has not gone deep enough. If the current there is not too strong, you often can get the fly deeper by pulling out more line from your reel with your left hand, then releasing it. If that does not work, put a small split shot on the leader about a foot above the fly. What you want to do is to get that fly down close to bottom where the trout are lying.

In the method of fly fishing which we have just described, you cast across current and let the fly drift down. There is a second method which also is good. Again you cast upstream so that the fly drops into the current, either the main one or a lesser one, and let the fly be swept down by the current, taking in line as it comes nearer and letting it out again as it passes you, keeping the line almost taut but not quite, the object being not to interfere with the drift of the fly but to be ready to tighten if a trout rises to it. When the fly reaches the end of its drift, let it pause there for a moment, then gently raise and lower the rod tip several times to give the fly a quivering action. Then retrieve slowly with the hand-twist action until the fly is a short cast from you. Repeat, being careful not to slash the water as you lift the fly for another cast. Watch the leader. If it twitches, strike.

MULTIPLE FLY RIGS

The question always arises whether to use a single fly on the tip of the leader, or one or two other flies tied on the droppers. The advantage of using more than one fly is that if different patterns are used, you can tell the type of fly that is most effective on that day. Also, an additional fly or two hanging from the droppers often has an alluring action in the drift unlike that of the end fly. Using, let us say, a dropper fly, it will swirl around on the surface or near it, and often attract fish that refuse the tail fly. I've had the experience in fishing three flies when every fish caught was taken on just one of the three patterns. A disadvantage of using more than one fly is that there is the possibility of getting hung up on overhead branches or snagged in the water.

When you fish a cast of three flies, it is good strategy to select for a top fly a pattern that is easily seen to tell you when you have a strike. My favorite for this is a No. 10 Coachman. For the tail fly I like the Black Gnat in size No. 8, and for the middle fly a No. 10 Light Cahill. If these do not work, I choose from among such patterns as the Gold-ribbed Hare's Ear, Quill Gordon, Dark Cahill, Ginger Quill, March Brown, Royal Coachman, and Campbell's Fancy. The Royal Coachman like the Coachman makes a good top fly for it is also easily seen because of its white wings. When you see that top fly twitch, make your strike at once. Also, the top fly often will dance on the top of the water like an insect laying its eggs, and its action can be irresistible to a hungry trout.

When the drift method does not work, as a last resort try working the flies with fast jerks, always seeking to have the tail fly deep in the water. The tail fly sinks better if it is tied on a hook of heavy wire, and here the size of the hook also helps. A No. 8 or even No. 6 for this reason makes a good tail fly. Such wet flies are the reverse of the dry fly. In the latter a fly tied on light wire is desirable for then it will float better.

A mistake many fishermen make when fishing a deep pool or a deep slow-moving run is to start the retrieve before the tail fly has sunk far enough. Make your cast, then wait until you are quite sure the tail fly has sunk so that it is near the bottom. Control your impatience and give the fly time to get down deep toward the bottom. Then make quick twitches of the rod as you raise it. After several of these, let the fly sink again. As the fly sinks, there is a short period when your line is slack. As a hit often comes when the fly is sinking, be ready to strike with authority if the leader twitches or you see the flash of a fish in the water.

Remember that in early season the flats in a stream, such as you find in meadows, where the water is exposed to the sun all day, have warmer water than in the pools and deep runs, and so will attract the fish. That also is true of riffles, where the water usually is shallow and which also are exposed to the sun. In deep pools the water is likely to be several degrees warmer at the bottom than on the surface. Trout there will rarely rise to flies several feet above them, but will take a well-submerged fly that comes near them.

For wet-fly fishing in spring, when the water ranges from 50 to 55 degrees and is likely to be high and cloudy, a leader 7½ feet long and tapered to 1X is about right. If, on the other hand, the water is clear, a leader 9 feet long with a finer taper such as 2X or 3X is better.

It is well to experiment, not only in working and retrieving the flies, but also with the depth at which the tail fly is submerged. Trout may feed at different levels. When you have found that fishing at a certain depth is effective, then stick to that depth until it no longer works. In water that is almost sure to hold fish, such as where two currents converge below a large boulder or island, an undercut bank, a log or a heap of driftwood close to a current that will bring food, if you don't get a touch somewhere between the surface and bottom, you may well come to the conclusion that (1) the trout aren't feeding; or (2) a change in fly patterns or method of fishing is in order. In fishing such promising water make each cast carefully, for a sloppy cast will scare the trout and cause them to refuse any lure. Also, plan your approach with care. Look over the water and study it, so that you may select a casting position where you can't be seen by the trout. Reach that position without rattling stones underfoot. Stalk it as though your life depended upon being unseen. If fishing from the bank, keep a bush or tree between you and the promising stretch of water. The very first and most important rule in trout fishing is to *keep out of sight and to avoid sound*.

NIGHT FISHING

On hard-fished streams, particularly those with a good population of brown trout, big trout are very wary and do most of their feeding at night when practically all fishermen have quit for the day. When I say "night" I don't mean twilight or that period of darkness which directly follows, but the time from midnight until the first flush of dawn.

That lesson was taught me years ago. It was in June, my favorite month for fly fishing in the East. All day I had been fishing a small river in Pennsylvania that held only brown trout, beginning directly after an early breakfast. Conditions seemed to be favorable. The rhododendrons were in blossom and made patches of pink and white in the woods, and there were a few flies on the water. I fished dry flies exclusively with only fair success. I kept at it until dark when I was more than a mile upstream. When I quit I had a half-dozen trout of disappointing size, for the largest was only 10½ inches and most of them were around 9 inches. That was a pretty scant reward for a fishing day that had begun at 7:30 in the morning, and had continued until 10 in the evening.

I walked back toward the farmhouse where I was staying, keeping to the woods until I reached a stretch where there was no light from the starlit sky to guide me, and I began to stumble and fall. Then I took to the stream where a little light was reflected from the sky, and while the wading was very rough and slippery, at least I could see, though faintly, where I was going.

I came to a deep pool and stopped in surprise. It sounded as though bathers were in it. There were many splashes, and I could see flashes of white made by rising trout. That pool was perhaps the biggest and hardest fished of any on the river. It was a natural. It fairly shrieked trout. I had fished it carefully on my way up that morning and hadn't had a rise, though I had approached it with care and felt sure of getting a good trout or two from it. These rises were not from fingerlings but from heavy fish, and they came from the tail of the pool right up to its head.

I assembled my rod with difficulty, largely from feel. When I had taken it down at the end of fishing, I had not cut the fly from the leader but had coiled it and placed it in my leader wallet. The fly was a large Coachman, about a No. 8, which I had tied on at dusk the better to see it on the water. Now, with heart pounding, I circled the pool and made my first cast. As the fly touched the water, there came a boil and I hooked the fish. It was a big one. As it felt the hook it raced upstream and then came back on the other side of a submerged rock. The leader came back to me cut in two. My fishing was over for it was too dark to take another leader and tie on another fly.

Night fishing with wet flies can be highly exciting. The darkness hides you from the trout. I have felt them bump my legs as I stood in water above my knees. They have lost their daytime caution. They are on the feed. They accept the darkness as a protective shield. Night-flying insects are plentiful and furnish a diet rich in protein. And the fishermen who have stirred up the water during the day have gone. During the daytime, one missed strike from a rising brown trout will put it down, and it will not rise again. But at night, when you miss a hit, that same trout is quite willing to strike again at that same fly.

The night fisherman must study the water in the daytime, note the logical hiding place for a large trout, and locate the spot from which it is best for him to cast. He should familiarize himself with the stream bottom between the selected spot and the point of his approach. If there are sizable rocks on the bottom in the path of his approach, he should study them so that he can go around them and not stumble over them. It will help him in his night wading to take with him a stout wading stick or staff so that he can carefully feel ahead with it and be able to plot his course without mishap.

Selecting a place where big brownies lie is not too difficult. All of us have fished most promising water without success, yet our stream knowledge has told us that a trout must be there. The chances are good that a lunker has taken up residence there and has kept out all other trout. Such places include deep pools; sharp bends in the stream where the current has washed out a hole under the bank and there is considerable depth; large sunken logs where the current has gouged out the bottom and made a deep pocket; underwater ledges; and large boulders under which the current has washed a hole.

Don't use a flashlight in fishing your chosen spot. Should you need some light in changing flies, do so well back from the stream where the light will be unnoticed. The temptation will be strong to use a light in wading to the position selected. Don't.

Night fishing means short-line fishing. Long casts will get you little or nothing. Keep line and leader taut. The leader should be stout and at least 10-pound test. As soon as the flies land upon the water, put them into slow motion. Twitch the flies across the surface and when the rise comes, sock the fish hard. The flies should be large, the hooks heavy, and the points needle sharp.

The wet flies for this nocturnal sport should be big and bushy. Black is the best color, dark brown the next. Their size makes you think they are suited only to bass fishing. Use No. 4's and select from among the Black Gnat, Black Hackle, Blue Dun, March Brown, Black Woolly Worm, and Brown Hackle. In daytime fishing a lot of hackle is often a handicap. At night it is an asset.

A word of warning. In several states, such as New Jersey, legal trout fishing is limited to stated hours between dawn and dark. Before doing any nighttime fishing be sure that you are within the law.

STREAMERS AND BUCKTAILS

Streamers and bucktails are forms of wet flies and strong medicine for large trout. The usual wet and dry flies in theory are supposed to imitate natural insects in the adult winged form or in the underwater stages of their development. But streamers and bucktails are designed to represent minnows or the young of game fishes. As the food of the larger trout is largely of this type, these imitations can be very effective when properly fished. The larger trout don't attack minnows gingerly. They realize that the minnow can be a fast swimmer when danger threatens and can scoot under a rock, into weeds or sunken brush, and escape. So big trout, seeing what they take to be a minnow, don't fool around but take it with a rush, and so are more easily hooked than when they take an ordinary wet fly.

Among landlocked salmon fishermen, the streamer is a favorite, and those patterns which imitate the smelt—the salmon's favorite food—are excellent. Landlocks are a deep-water fish after the surface water warms in late spring. But while the water is under 50 degrees they feed close to the surface and then give fine sport on patterns that imitate smelt. These patterns include the Gray Ghost, Black Ghost, and Supervisor. These and other streamer patterns are trolled behind a rather fast-moving boat. I have done that kind of fishing in May on the First Connecticut Lake in northern New Hampshire. The fish I've caught were not lunkers, averaging about 2½ pounds, but they put up a pretty fight, jumping, tugging, and boring. Best results came when the water was rather rough. When it was glassy, there was little success. To keep the streamer from skipping across the surface of the water, my guide clamped several split shot upon the leader, which sunk the streamer some inches below the surface.

During this period in early spring when the top water is still cold, I have made regulation casts from the shore with the same streamer patterns. The landlocks seemed to be feeding among the rocks near shore, and attacked the streamers ferociously.

The larger trout also take streamers and bucktails eagerly on occasion. The best time to fish for them is early in the season, when the water is likely to be high and colored. In such water I have had little luck in fishing the top water with these big lures. Put on enough split shot to sink the fly, then make it move through the water with little twitches, imitating the way many minnows swim. Fish across stream and let the current take the fly down. At the end of the drift, start the twitches, and work the fly back and forth in an arc. Brook trout require slower speed in working the fly than do rainbows, which are more often taken when the movement of the fly is rather fast. Vary the fly action until you find the proper speed to induce rainbow strikes. Both brook trout and rainbows like streamer patterns that are light colored, of gray and white, and red and white.

On the other hand the wary brownie prefers patterns that are more subdued, of brown, brown and white, and black and white. It also likes these colors in bucktails. The Muddler Minnow, a relatively new pattern, is excellent for big brownies as well as large rainbows. This is a versatile fly. It is bushy and can be fished either wet or dry. If using it as a dry fly it should be anointed with oil. Then the fish take it for a large insect. When submerged it resembles a large nymph. It also can be drawn swiftly across the surface and when thus fished is often effective.

A streamer fly that is not used as much as it should be is the Marabou. When wet it looks too slender and skinny to be of any use, but it often works when others don't.

CHAPTER 14

Nymph Fishing for Trout

FLY FISHING FOR trout falls into four groups—dry-fly, wet-fly, bucktail and streamer, and nymph. While each method at times proves successful, I am convinced that in the long run, over the whole season, and taking into consideration the varying stages of water levels, weather, and water and air temperatures, nymph fishing is the most effective method for taking trout. Wet-fly fishing comes next, and this, it seems reasonable to assume, is because trout take that form of fly for a nymph.

Dry-fly fishing appeals to me as the sportiest and the most fun. You see the rise of the trout as it comes at the fly; there is a splash, a bulge, or a slight depression at the surface. When you fish the wet fly you may see the flash of the trout under water and strike as soon as you see it. More often you feel a slight tug, and your strike is too late, for the trout that hit the fly hard and hook themselves are in the minority. In nymph fishing the signal that the trout has come to the fly is so slight, so unaccompanied by any visible warning, that until you have by experience, to some extent by intuition, solved the art, you have a feeling of almost complete frustration.

It isn't difficult to understand why nymph fishing can bring in more and larger trout than any other method of fly fishing. The big hatches of flies once so common on many of our streams, particularly in the East, are not what they used to be. Once many of these streams were heavily forested along their banks, and the spring run-off was retarded and less violent because rain and melting snow sank into the root-filled soil, much of it to be retained, with the surplus retarded in its flow to the streams. With the forest gone and the ground bare there is little to hold back the water, and floods often become the rule. These floods have scoured stream bottoms,

151

moved boulders, filled pools once offering winter refuge for the trout, and destroyed insect life. Insect hatches bring up the trout from the depths to feed at the surface and make life happy for the dry-fly fisherman. When they are lacking in quantity and variety, it makes the trout more dependent upon bottom food. So the skilled nymph fisherman is successful since he fishes where the fish are feeding.

Biologists say that nymphs are very rich in protein, and that they make up the most important part of a trout's diet. Aquatic insects may go through a number of different stages before they take to the surface and rise into the air as the perfect, winged adult insects. They favor the fast-water stretches of the streams, and particularly the riffles. That is why so often the fisherman will find the best fishing in the riffles rather than in the pools.

Most nymphs are rather dark colored, having brown backs and yellow or grayish-white bellies. Most of them are small so that a No. 14 hook makes the best all-round size to use. The larger nymphs, such as the stone fly, are in the minority. Most nymphs are flat-backed. To determine whether to use a large or small artificial nymph, turn over several rocks on the stream bottom and examine the nymphs sheltered there. Or better yet, if you have caught a trout open it up and examine the stomach contents. If the nymphs therein are small, match the size with your artificial. If large, go to a larger size. During the daytime nymphs are likely to be inactive, clinging to their stone refuges, but in the evening they may swim about a little. Thus the evening feeding carnival of the trout is likely to be mostly due to the fact that nymphs have become easier to take.

A long leader, tapered to no larger than 3X, is the minimum for nymph fishing, with a taper of 4X or 5X even better. A 12-footer will get you more fish than even a 9-footer. As the movement of the artificial nymph through the water must be slow, to imitate the movement of the natural insect, more time is given the trout to inspect it carefully and reject it if he has reason to suspect it. Cast across stream and let the nymph drift naturally with the current. At the end of the float do as you do in wet-fly fishing, pulling it in slowly, then letting it drift back. Watch carefully. If the leader stops its drift, raise the rod quickly. It may be a trout or it may be a snag, or the fly may have lodged on a rock. It will help you a lot if you put something on the leader to act as a float and tell you about where the leader is, and if the nymph is doing business for you. I like to tie a white-wing fly like a Coachman or Royal Coachman to the leader loop where it is tied to the line. Using a 4X leader tippet about 8 inches long, tie it to the leader loop with a clinch knot. Run the end of the tippet through the leader loop, bring it back on itself, wrap around the end of the tippet over the main strand about four times, then take the end and pass it through the loop you made with it at the leader loop and jam tight, cutting off the surplus at the end. When the fly on that tippet wiggles or stops, raise the rod.

If the riffle is quite deep and the unweighted nymph gets no response, try a split shot on the leader, 8 or 10 inches above it.

For water that is relatively quiet, such as in a deep pool or on a lake, try greasing part of your leader with line dressing to make it float. Leave the lower end untreated for a distance of several feet above the fly. Your object is to make that nymph submerge while the rest of the leader floats. It helps to rub the lower end of the leader with leader soak. If you have none, it is well to carry a tube of toothpaste in your pocket. The toothpaste, rubbed on that part of the leader, will help it to sink. A split shot on the leader is inadvisable here since it makes casting more difficult and also makes more commotion when it hits the water, and in nymph fishing particularly the utmost caution is necessary. You must avoid alarming the trout. It is best when fishing these deep pools to cast upstream.

As the natural nymph has an unhurried movement, the trout knows that it will not dart away like a minnow. The trout takes its time, is slow and deliberate, and when it takes the artificial is quick to realize that it is inedible, and spits it out. Sometimes you will see the flash of the fish as it turns in the water to take the nymph. More often the only indication that the nymph has been taken is the momentary pause of the floating leader. You have to be watchful all the time and quick in your response.

Fish the nymph at the edge of a current. Here it is that trout lurk to nab food brought to them by the water. Let the fly drift around underwater rocks and emergent boulders where the trout love to lurk. Watersoaked logs and heaps of debris close to the current are good, as are cut banks. Pockets in fast water are excellent.

If you want to bait-fish, the larvae of the caddis fly are good bait. You'll find them on the bottom of quiet pools. Trout feed greedily upon them. They are encased in little bundles of what appear to be sticks or coarse straws. Peel off the outer casing and you will find a yellowish worm inside. This is the caddis-fly larva. The case in which the worm is found may be distinguished from similar debris found at the bottom as they are open at one end. The casings are of varying appearance. In addition to sticks or strawlike material, they also may be of tiny pebbles, sand, leaves, or bark, according to the type of stream. The casings seem to be gummed together by some sort of mucilaginous secretion of the nymph. The trout gobble them, casings and all. That is why when you examine the stomach of a trout you often will find it full of a muddy mess. Don't use this natural bait without assuring yourself that it is legal in the state in which you are fishing. For instance, New York forbids the taking of bait from trout streams.

For this type of nymph fishing, use a short-shank thin wire hook, about No. 12 or 14. Run the barb of the hook through the head of the worm. Put enough weight on the leader with split shot to let the worm roll along the bottom or a short distance above it.

Don't try to cast when you are using this natural bait, for it is soft and comes easily off the hook. Use a sidewise or underarm swing. Watch that leader carefully just as you do when using an artificial nymph. If the leader hesitates in its drift, strike at once.

CHAPTER 15

Early Season Trout

WE HAVE TO face the facts. Dry flies in early season, when the water is high, colored, and cold, are a waste of time. Wet flies fished near the bottom and just off the main current may get you some fish; nymphs, properly fished, are better than either the dry or wet flies, as are bucktails and streamers. But the prize early-season lure for trout is the faithful angleworm, a small and lively minnow, or the toothsome and protein-loaded shrimp.

WET FLIES

If, surprisingly, the stream you select for your early-season fishing is only a little higher than normal and not much colored, wet flies fished near bottom with a sinking line and leader treated with leader soak should get you some fish. On brown-trout waters such sober patterns as the Black Gnat, Black Prince, and Gold-ribbed Hare's Ear do well. Where brookies and rainbows are present try the more colorful Coachman, Royal Coachman, and Grizzly King.

You will find most eastern start-of-the-season fishermen gathered at the larger pools, packed elbow to elbow. They know that the state hatchery men have probably dumped trout into such waters. I have seen the recently stocked trout lying near the bottom in schools like suckers. If they were not fed before release they are easy prey. The chaps standing in the water or lining the banks in full sight of the fish yank them out one after another. On the other hand, if the trout were stocked some days in advance of the season's opening, they are likely to be scattered, as are the holdovers from previous seasons. The holdovers have acquired a measure of caution from experience, and give better sport than the logy hatchery fish not yet accustomed to freedom. The thing to do is to find out where the trout are.

A water thermometer is a great help in telling you where the trout are likely to be. In water as cold as it normally is in early season, say at 50 degrees or lower, the bottom levels of a stream's pools usually are a little warmer than the top water. Trout are not likely to be active or feeding in the higher levels and probably will be lying on pool bottoms, or in deep pockets to be found before or behind boulders, under cut banks where there is depth, or in deep pockets the current has gouged out of the bottom of sunken logs. It is quite unlikely that you will find them in a strong current. Seek quieter water, rather deep and near enough to a current that will bring the trout food. They dart out after it and then retire to their stations.

LIVE BAIT

In water as cold as 50 degrees, worms, minnows, or shrimp fished close to bottom in deep quiet water will get you fish. Don't work your bait. Let it take a natural drift and follow its progress with the tip of your rod. I have often seen a bait fisherman working his bait just as he would a plug when after bass, jerking it to and fro, the bait near the surface or skipping over the top. Occasionally, a hatchery brook trout or rainbow will fall for such a method of fishing, but a wild or holdover trout knows instinctively that a worm washed from the bank and adrift in the stream does not act that way and will refuse it.

To give a natural drift to the worm you must avoid drag. Drag is caused by the pull of the line when the worm has been stopped in its drift by the tautness of the line. You have swung the worm upstream from you and let it drift toward you and past you, meanwhile stripping in the line to have it under control should a fish take the bait. Then, as it passes you, the line should be released little by little so there is no check in its progress to set up drag. The easiest way to do this is to coil the line in your left hand as the worm drifts toward you, and then as it passes release the line as needed. If the line does not slip through the guides of the rod fast enough, you can help it do so by swinging the rod tip from side to side.

If your leader, which should be 6 to 7½ feet long and of 2- or 3-pound test, has been treated with leader soak, the worm should sink to the bottom.

The worm will bump along the bottom and now and then lodge against a rock or some underwater obstruction. In that case, raise your rod to let the worm continue its drift. Should the stopping of the drift be caused by a trout taking the worm, your fingers which are letting out line will be sensitive enough to get the feeling of life at the end of the line. Sometimes a trout that is not very hungry will take the worm gently in its lips without gorging it, nibbling at it as though to enjoy its savor. To strike at such a time means a lost fish, so when you feel such a gentle nibble, it is better to wait until the trout moves off with it, giving it line for a short time, and then make your strike. A vigorous taking of the worm means that the trout has it in its mouth, so strike at once.

If the trout, after taking the worm, swims upstream with it, that will put a pronounced downstream curve in the line. Should you strike while there is this curve in the line, there is a good chance of losing the fish, for you will be striking against that curve in the line rather than against the mouth of the fish. Before striking, take in enough line so your strike will be on a line that is almost taut between the fish and you.

We have been considering situations where, though the water is high and the current strong, a heavy worm such as a nightcrawler at the end of a short leader treated with leader soak can be fished close to or on the bottom. If the worm does not sink far enough, you should put on enough split shot to get it down. That may take some experimentation. It is better first to put on one light shot and see how that works. Then, if needed, add another. Too much weight in split shot may prevent the natural drift which is so desirable in worm fishing. Should you find this to be so, let the worm rest on the bottom, then at intervals lift the rod enough to take it off the bottom, move it forward a few inches, and repeat. The worm should be lively and fresh and so hooked that there are two free ends to wiggle and squirm and attract the fish. If the worm becomes mangled, replace it with a fresh and lively one. A good size hook for this fishing is a No. 8.

One test of water temperature is not enough. Within a mile on one stream you may get several different readings, and find water several degrees warmer than your first spot. There are relatively shallow riffles where the stream is wider which are exposed to the warming influence of the sun. There are stretches where a small brook comes in with sufficient water to affect the stream you are fishing for some distance below the junction. A stream in early season is likely to have warmer water where it flows through open fields and meadows. Your object, then, is to locate suitable resting spots for the trout where they are out of the current yet near enough to seize any food that drifts down in it.

An undermined bank where the water has some depth is an ideal spot for a large trout. If the water is only slightly colored, the trout can see the fisherman much better than when it is running so stained that you can't see anything six inches below the surface.

In large streams holding lunker trout, it is worthwhile to try minnows, for large trout are flesh eaters and gorge many small fish. In stream-fishing with minnows you don't have to use live minnows, for the best way of hooking them involves killing them anyway. I like a tandem-hook rig: two hooks mounted on gut, the upper one an inch or two above the lower, one hook with bend pointed up, the other with bend pointed down. The minnow can be hooked through the head with the upper hook, and at the base of the tail with the other. The leader should be attached to a 3-way swivel which is tied to the line. To the third eye of the swivel, tie a length of leader material about 18 inches long to which attach a sinker heavy enough to sink to the bottom. If the sinker is a long, slim pencil type of even diameter, it stands a better chance of not getting caught on rocks or debris. Sometimes it helps in hooking the minnow to put enough curve in its body so it will wobble and spin in the water.

Another good way to rig a minnow is to use a double minnow hook with the shank pointed at the eye end. Run the shank through the minnow from vent to mouth, then tie it to your leader, or line if you're spinning. The minnow then rests between the two hooks down at the tail. Cast so that the current will take your sinker gently to the bottom and along it, then retrieve with abrupt short jerks.

NYMPHS

Should you find a good riffle, with water a little higher in temperature than in the deep pools, here is a good spot to try an artificial nymph. Riffles are trout pantries, for here are the largest populations of natural nymphs. The current dislodges some of these little creatures, and they are carried downstream to be picked up eagerly by trout which have done little feeding all winter and need to put on flesh. Nymphs are much richer in food value than minnows and most natural baits. Try drifting a nymph above, to each side, and below rocks in the riffle, using methods explained in detail in the chapter on nymph fishing. The results will often surprise you. Nymph fishing is difficult, but the art can be acquired, and the size of trout taken on such a lure is often above the average for the stream.

STREAMERS AND BUCKTAILS

Streamers and bucktails were originally designed to imitate minnows and often are very effective in the high and colored water of early spring. Cast across stream and let the current take the fly downstream. As the fly nears the end of its drift, it will cut across current. As it comes to a stop, retrieve it with short, fast jerks which will overcome the weight of the split shot or sinker and bring the fly nearer the surface.

Don't overlook your spinning outfit as a good bet for this early-season fishing. It is versatile, for with it you can use a minnow bait, a spoon, a weighted fly, or a worm.

THE FOLLOWING SIXTEEN pages contain accurate, full-color paintings of dry flies, wet flies, nymphs, streamers and bucktails to help the reader visualize those described by the author in the text. The flies were selected and prepared by Jim Deren, proprietor of "The Angler's Roost" tackle shop in New York City, and were painted by G. Don Ray, well-known wildlife artist and ardent fisherman. They are printed here with the permission of H. J. Noll, copyright owner of *Guide to Trout Flies,* in which they originally appeared.

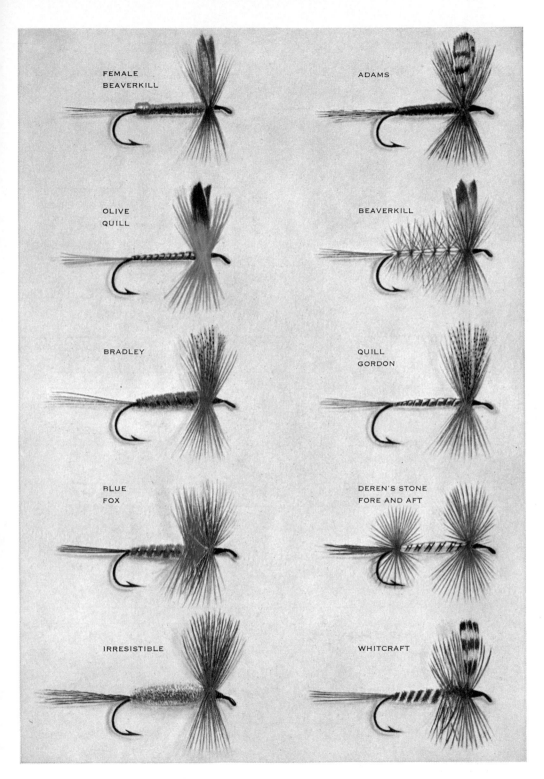

FEMALE
BEAVERKILL

ADAMS

OLIVE
QUILL

BEAVERKILL

BRADLEY

QUILL
GORDON

BLUE
FOX

DEREN'S STONE
FORE AND AFT

IRRESISTIBLE

WHITCRAFT

Dry Flies—Plate 1

SKUES

WHITE
WULFF

TUPS

GRAY
WULFF

RED
QUILL

LITTLE
MARRYAT

HUNT'S
TEAGLE BEE

WOOLLY
WORM

MARCH
BROWN

GOLD-RIBBED
HARE'S EAR

Dry Flies—Plate 2

PINK
LADY

DEREN'S
FOX

BROWN
BIVISIBLE

BLACK
GNAT

BADGER BIVISIBLE
SPIDER

LIGHT
IRRESISTIBLE

LIGHT
HENDRICKSON

LIGHT
CAHILL

CHOCOLATE
DUN

HOPPER
FLY

Dry Flies—Plate 3

PETRIE'S
GREEN EGG SACK

GYRO FLIGHT'S
FANCY

FAN-WING
COACHMAN

COCKY
VARIANT

ANT

GREEN
DRAKE

FIFTY
DEGREES

SPENT-WING BROWN DRAKE

GRAY
FOX

DARK BLUE
SEDGE

Dry Flies—Plate 4

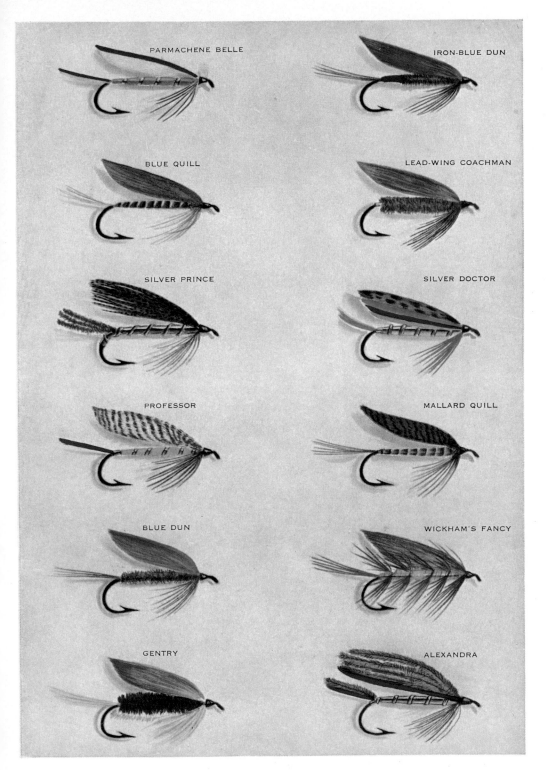

Wet Flies—Plate 5

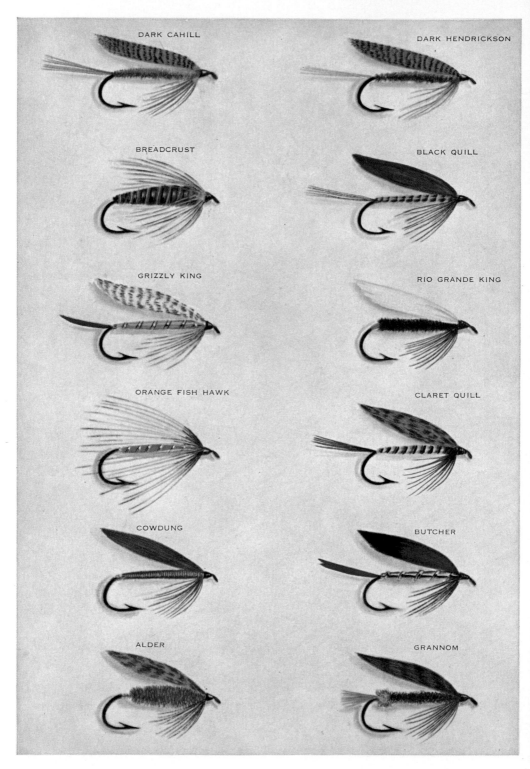

DARK CAHILL

DARK HENDRICKSON

BREADCRUST

BLACK QUILL

GRIZZLY KING

RIO GRANDE KING

ORANGE FISH HAWK

CLARET QUILL

COWDUNG

BUTCHER

ALDER

GRANNOM

Wet Flies—Plate 6

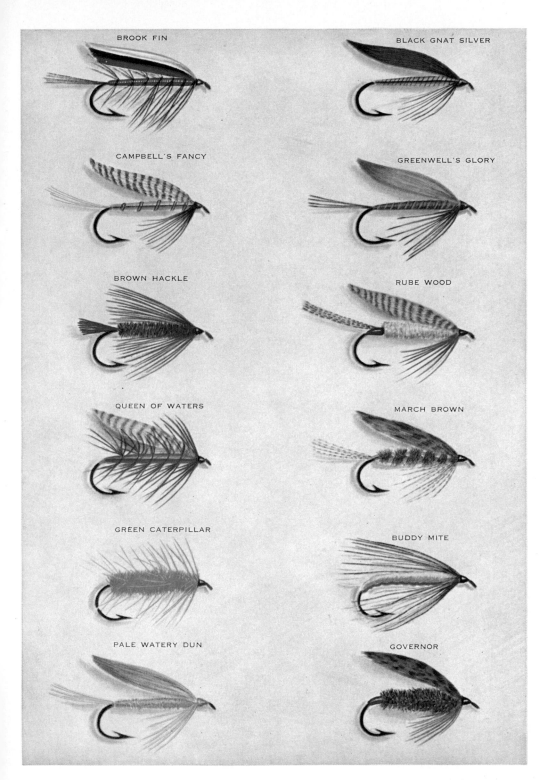

BROOK FIN

BLACK GNAT SILVER

CAMPBELL'S FANCY

GREENWELL'S GLORY

BROWN HACKLE

RUBE WOOD

QUEEN OF WATERS

MARCH BROWN

GREEN CATERPILLAR

BUDDY MITE

PALE WATERY DUN

GOVERNOR

Wet Flies—Plate 7

HARE'S EAR

MONTREAL

RED IBIS

YELLOW SALLY

MONTREAL
WHITE TIP

BLACK PRINCE

WHIRLING
BLUE DUN

SPRUCE

GOLDEN DEMON

GINGER QUILL

COACHMAN

CREAM CAHILL

Wet Flies—Plate 8

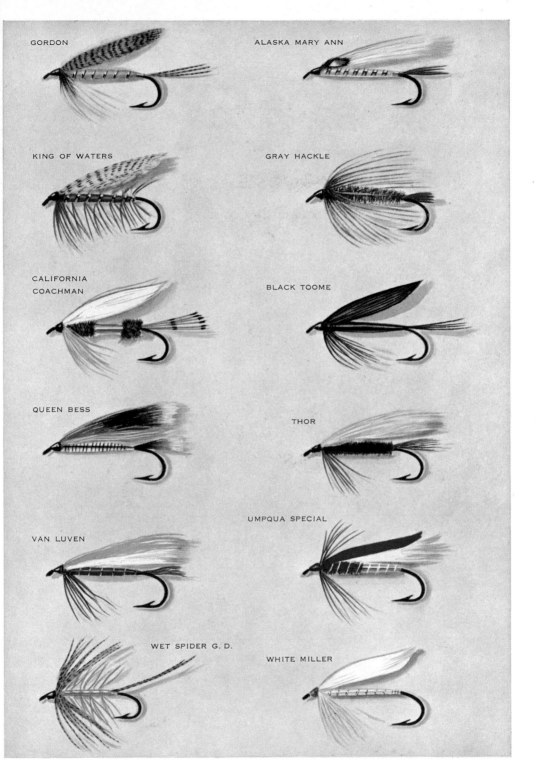

GORDON

ALASKA MARY ANN

KING OF WATERS

GRAY HACKLE

CALIFORNIA
COACHMAN

BLACK TOOME

QUEEN BESS

THOR

UMPQUA SPECIAL

VAN LUVEN

WET SPIDER G. D.

WHITE MILLER

Wet Flies—Plate 9

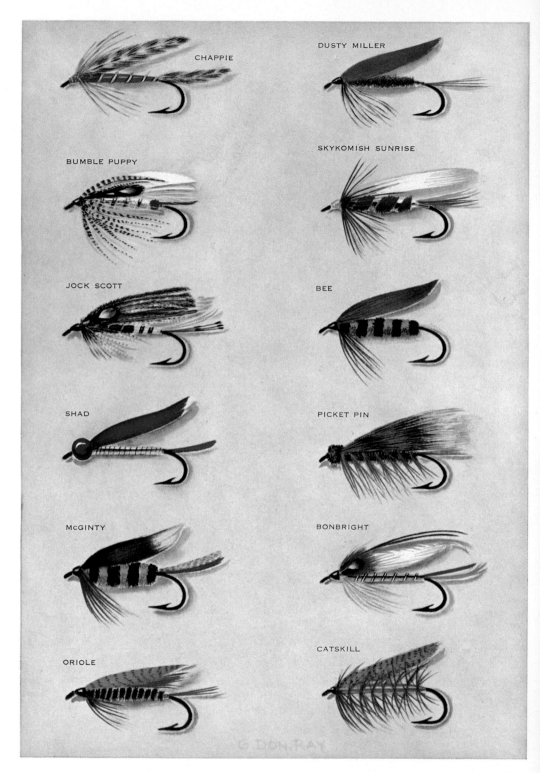

CHAPPIE

DUSTY MILLER

BUMBLE PUPPY

SKYKOMISH SUNRISE

JOCK SCOTT

BEE

SHAD

PICKET PIN

McGINTY

BONBRIGHT

ORIOLE

CATSKILL

G. DON RAY

Wet Flies—Plate 10

DARK HENDRICKSON

GREEN CADDIS

LIGHT CAHILL

MARCH BROWN

ROCHE'S MAY FLY

ROCHE'S DRAGONFLY

BAILEY'S MOSSBACK

GREEN DRAKE

GRAY FOX

DEVASTATOR

Nymphs—Plate 11

DEREN'S HARDBACK

HENDRICKSON

LITTLE MARRYAT

LEAD-WING COACHMAN

DARK CADDIS

HELLGRAMITE

QUILL GORDON

STONE-FLY CREEPER

ROCHE'S STONE FLY

COLLINS' HARDBACK

Nymphs—Plate 12

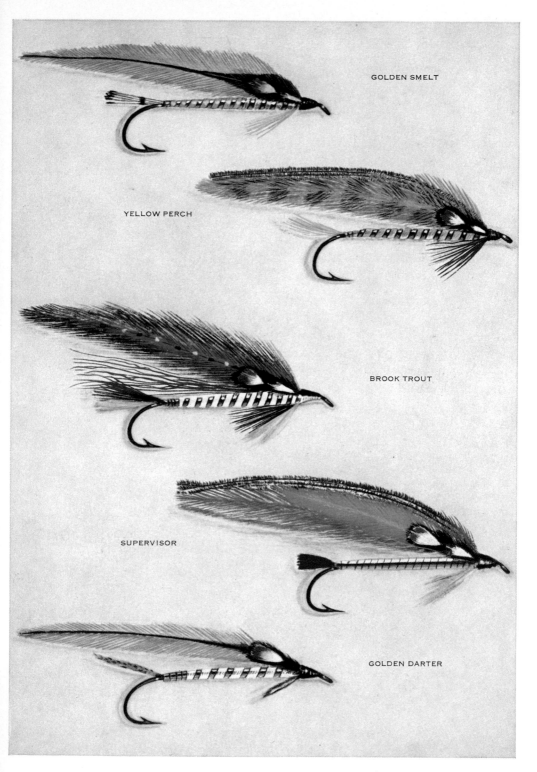

GOLDEN SMELT

YELLOW PERCH

BROOK TROUT

SUPERVISOR

GOLDEN DARTER

Streamers—Plate 13

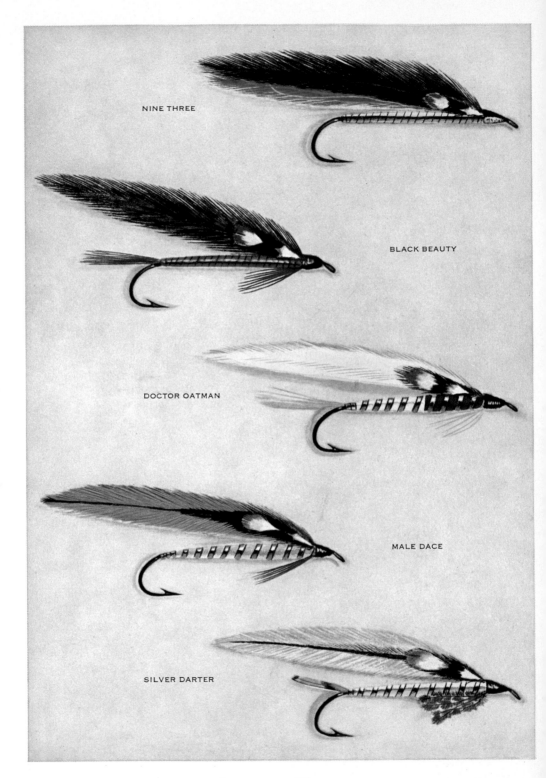

NINE THREE

BLACK BEAUTY

DOCTOR OATMAN

MALE DACE

SILVER DARTER

Streamers—Plate 14

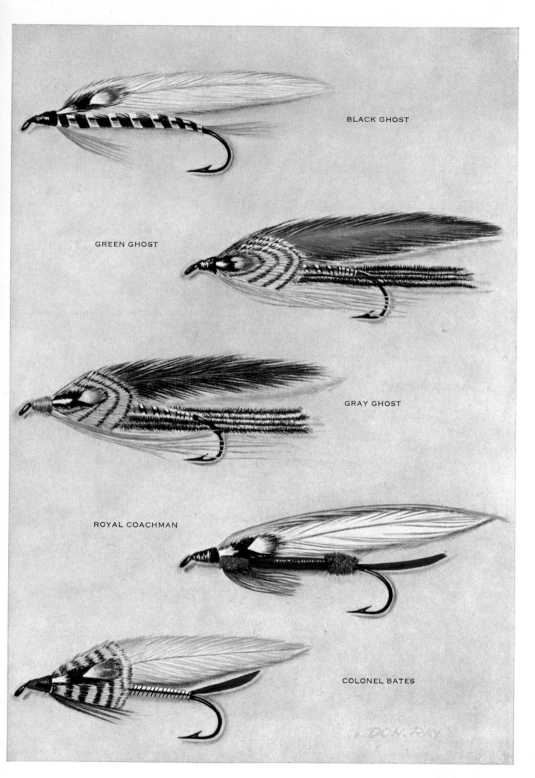

BLACK GHOST

GREEN GHOST

GRAY GHOST

ROYAL COACHMAN

COLONEL BATES

Streamers—Plate 15

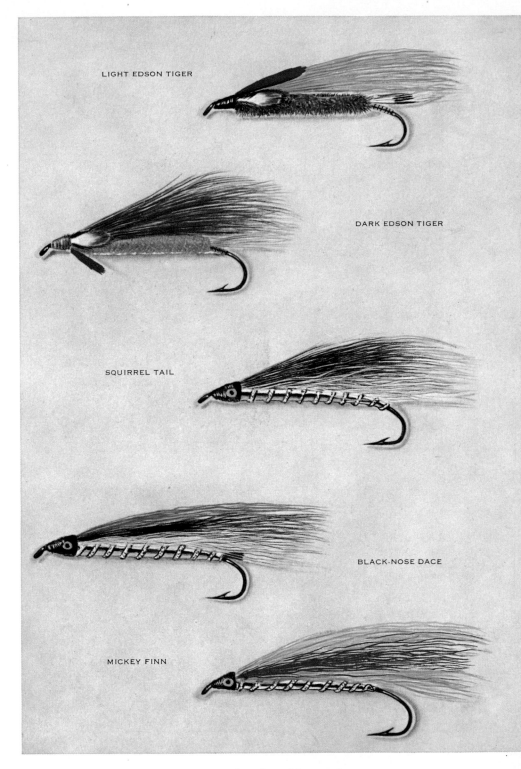

LIGHT EDSON TIGER

DARK EDSON TIGER

SQUIRREL TAIL

BLACK-NOSE DACE

MICKEY FINN

Bucktails—Plate 16

Trout Fishing in Brooks

MOST OF US begin our trout fishing as boys, and in a brook. These small streams have a charm all their own. They are intimate. The fisherman rarely finds in them a current strong enough to make safe footing a problem or water so deep as to require waders. This is hip-boot fishing. The angler can easily reach with a fly or worm any spot that looks like a good lie for trout, and the fishing water is so confined that such spots are readily observed. For that reason the brooks require less skill than the larger waters.

Often the brooks are not stocked by the state, which prefers to plant its hatchery trout in the larger streams which not only have more natural food in them but also are fished harder. Thus the trout in the brooks are spawned there and are truly wild. These fish are vulnerable to the predations of mink, raccoons, water snakes, kingfishers, and sometime herons. The water in which they live is limited and confined. Unlike the fish in the larger streams, they have no wide avenues of escape. They have so many enemies that they have to be wary to survive. So usually they hide under cut banks, rocks, the limbs of overhanging bushes or trees, or where a patch of grass or ferns leans over the water. There they lie in wait, watching for morsels of food to be brought down by the current. When such appear, they dart out, seize the food, and speedily return to their hiding place.

It follows, then, that the fisherman should be careful to remain unseen and unheard. He should keep low, hide behind boulders or brush, and avoid any body motion except necessary movements of arm and wrist when casting. While trout do not have ears in the sense we know them,

The rocky, fast-flowing mountain brook provides enjoyable fishing but, owing to limited food supply, rarely holds big trout. *Ontario Dept. of Lands & Forests.*

they have a median line which is highly sensitive to vibrations caused by noisy wading or walking along the banks.

Trout brooks generally fall into two categories: stony mountain brooks and meadow brooks. The typical mountain brook is spring-fed, cold, rocky, and fast-flowing. It descends from the heights in a series of steps, the water cascading from one pool to another. There are relatively few flat stretches or gravelly runs. There are many big rocks and boulders. Natural food is relatively scarce in such streams and the poverty of the food supply is easily seen in the fact that a trout of 5 or 6 inches in such water may be adult and a spawner. Those brooks rarely hold a trophy trout. The usual size of those caught runs from those under legal size up to the exceptional 10-incher. Where the brook is tributary to a trout river, large or small, there are times in summer or fall when larger trout, seeking colder water, will run up into the lower stretches of the brook, particularly if it has pools of a size and depth to afford them suitable cover.

The typical meadow brook flows slower than the mountain brook. It usually is thickly bordered by alders or bushes and has occasional placid pools. The soil through which it flows is much richer than the scanty acid soil of a mountainside, and so is a much better producer of food. Freshets wash worms in the water. Grasshoppers, crickets, and such insect life as is common in a meadow fall into the brook. The alders and brush along the banks attract flying insects which can drop into the water, and there may be hatches of aquatic insects to tempt the trout into rising. The hill brooks rarely have a good insect hatch. So the meadow brook may yield some good fish.

As it is important for the fisherman to keep out of sight, both types of brooks are best fished upstream. Trout cannot see a fisherman who advances directly behind them. That angler who fishes upstream, keeps out of sight, and walks or wades with the greatest caution, will outfish the heedless fisherman two to one.

The mountain stream usually doesn't afford opportunity to cast in the accepted sense. It is best to keep a short line, which with 2 or 3 feet of leader is not more than 7 feet long. The fly or bait is swung out underhand rather than overhand and the water covered in that way.

A meadow brook, on the other hand, may have stretches where the usual casts can be made. On both types of water there are often occasions when it is advisable to crawl on one's stomach in order to keep out of sight of the fish. Where the cover on the stream banks is sufficiently high and thick, the fisherman may walk upright. Otherwise he should stoop

The author fishing a tributary of the Madison River in Montana, a typical slow-moving meadow brook with good insect hatches and no overhanging foliage to restrict casting. *Bill Browning.*

An angler must exercise caution when approaching a clear, shallow brook.
Stalk the water quietly and crouch as low as possible when making your cast.
Tom McNally.

as low as he can. When fishing upstream, look ahead, and if the bank cover is thin or absent, walk well back from the water, making a detour to your next stand.

Pick your positions so that if there is sunshine, your shadow will not fall upon the water. This often means switching from one side of the brook to the other. Trout are highly sensitive to shadows, particularly if they are moving. I have stood hidden on the bank of a pool and seen several trout out in the open awaiting food to be brought to them by the current. I have seen these fish scatter wildly when a crow or a hawk flew overhead and cast its shadow on the water. A split second after a shadow passed, not a trout remained in sight. They had fled to cut banks or under rocks. I have also experimented by shaking a bush, with the same result. Windy weather, I have found, is generally unfavorable for trout fishing, and I suspect that the movement of tree limbs and overhanging bushes is at least partially responsible.

The standby of the brook fisherman is the worm. It is too bad that the run of brook fishermen use the conventional barbed hook and worm bait. In the mountain brooks there are many little trout, and as native food is scarce they take the worm eagerly and engorge it so deeply that even if restored to the water they eventually die. I remember once meeting a man on such a brook who complained that though he had caught at least twenty-five trout he had been able to creel only five. He was worm fishing with a barbed hook. How many of the little fellows he had "thrown back" survived? When I fish a mountain brook, it usually is with flies. When I take to worms I either pinch down the barb of the hook with my fisherman's pliers, or else use the manufactured barbless hook.

It may be objected that there is little to hold the worm on a barbless hook. That is true and there will be a certain loss of some bait. But there are two types of worming hooks that offer some degree of security. The first one is the split-shank hook which has sharp points on the shank of the hook over which the worm can be pushed; the second is the tandem hook. The tandem hook consists of two hooks joined together on a length of gut, the lower with the bend directed down, the upper one about an inch above the lower with the bend directed up. Put on the hook so that it pierces the worm about 1 inch from one end, which might be called the head and the other hook through the worm at about 1 inch from the tail, leaving a little loop in the worm, and the bottom end dangling.

The best time to fish a mountain stream after the usual early spring run-off is after a heavy rain when the water is high. Then the trout are on

A very difficult spot to fish on a mountain brook. The heavy over-growth limits casting and the fallen logs spell possible snags. The fly or bait must be swung out underhand, using only about 7 feet of line. *Ontario Dept. of Lands and Forests.*

the feed, eager to seize the rations brought down by the rain. Water that under ordinary conditions has seemed fishless now surprisingly yields trout. Rapid runs, the glides that in bigger streams offer so much promise to the dry-fly fisherman, and broken water out of the main current and of fair depth—these are the waters to fish. The water right under the miniature waterfalls is not very productive. If worm fishing, it is better not to let the worm sink to the bottom. Hold the rod so that the worm glides along about six inches below the surface, and keep the rod tip following the bait as it travels along. Don't try to give action to the worm and don't try to hurry it along. Let the natural drift be the only motion.

In these small streams, with much overhanging cover, particularly good spots for the fish are under the low-lying cover given by bushes or alders. In such places side and switch casts are most useful to get the bait or fly under the cover. The side cast is made by holding the rod close to the water and parallel to it, the rod hand palm upward on the butt. While any great accuracy is difficult with this cast, it can get the lure about where you want it. The switch cast depends upon the resiliency of the rod. If a split shot is on your leader, hold the shot by the thumb and finger and pull against the rod tip which then acts as a bow, the lure then functioning as an arrow. Releasing the grasp on the leader, the spring of the rod casts the lure in the desired direction. Here too the rod should be held near the water and parallel to it. An adaptation of the roll cast is also useful here. Leaving the fly or bait in the water, the rod is raised, tilted to one side, then brought over with some force in the direction toward which you want the lure to go.

Brook trout and rainbows take bait with more dash and less caution than brown trout. Mountain brooks in the eastern part of North America generally are brook trout streams; in the West the rainbow is the typical fish. Both of these trouts are greedy takers when the water is high after a rain, and there is little doubt when they take the worm. The rod jerks and telegraphs the bite to the fisherman. The brown trout is likely to be different. You may see the leader hesitate in its course downstream, twitch or change its course a little, or there may be a faint pull on the rod tip. To strike at this time may lose you a fish. Shove the rod forward a little to give some slack line, and follow the fish's direction with the rod tip. Mentally count five slowly. Then give the trout the works. A shorter time is advisable in high water.

Striking the fish when fishing either with bait or wet fly is better done by twitching the rod either to right or left and not upward as is the usual way. An upward strike may jerk fly or bait out of the fish's mouth.

In fly fishing handling the strike is different. My favorite wet flies for brooks are the Coachman and Royal Coachman. When they don't work I tie on a Black Gnat. The first two patterns have white wings which are quite visible in the water. When I see a fish flash in the water near the fly, I strike, and the trout usually is hooked. Sometimes you will feel a faint twitch on the line held in the hand, or see the rod tip curve slightly. Then strike at once. Or the line may straighten out. Here again strike at once.

If the trout jumps clear of the water, lower the rod tip at once almost to the water. Otherwise the fish may fall upon the leader and either tear the hook loose or break the leader. Should you happen to hook a large fish that is hard to handle in the confined waters of a brook, where snags and sharp-edged rocks are a hazard, and where you don't have the freedom of movement that you have in larger waters, get it into a current, try and keep the trout's open mouth just above the water level so that the current will pour water into it. That quickly takes the fight out of the fish.

The meadow stream, having quieter water than the mountain brook, is often fishable with a dry fly. It is important to have the fly drop to the water with the least possible disturbance. Perhaps you have seen a rising trout. Do not aim your cast at the spot where was the rise, and where the water rings are now spreading outward. Direct your cast at a spot about three feet above the location of the rise, aiming it at an imaginary location in the air and about two feet above the water. As the line shoots forward, the forward motion of the rod is stopped at about the 2 o'clock position, then lowered a little.

Here follow two anecdotes which illustrate the different types of fishing offered by the mountain and meadow brooks. I was in New England for a weekend of fishing a pretty good trout river. The night I arrived there was a series of heavy thunderstorms. The next morning the river was a muddy boiling torrent and unfishable. My map showed a tributary brook coming down from the hills. I asked the boss of the small country hotel where I was stopping how best to reach it. He told me of an abandoned road that paralleled the brook. "Used to be farms back there in the hills and the r'od served them," he said. "But the farms were deserted one by one, so the town let the r'od go to pot. It's pretty well grown up but I guess you can make it. It's sure to be better by a whole lot than to go up the brook. That's such a mess of boulders and rocks that even a 'coon would have trouble in going up it."

The road indeed was "grown up." It was thick with young trees and saplings but you could follow its course as it lay between two ancient stone walls, gray with lichens. Now and again I passed a cellar hole, almost invariably marked by big lilac bushes. There also were old apple trees, most of them with dead and dying limbs. The live growth was gay with blossoms, and an occasional breeze brought down a shower of petals.

I saw only one house that was still standing and it stood forlornly with broken windows and a wide-open front door. Behind stood a barn, with swaybacked roof, and leaning at such an angle that it looked likely to fall at the first stiff wind. I walked over to take a closer look at this scene of desolation, and passing a thick patch of briars was startled almost witless when a whitetail doe bolted out of it with a *whoosh* and bounded away with white tail erect.

The road builders had chosen a route over the hill rather than along the brook which was too rocky and in a ravine so narrow that a lot of excavating would have had to be done. Finally I came to a spot where once the road passed over a bridge. The bridge was gone, a few rotting beams that had tumbled into the brook being all that was left. I had walked for about two miles, so I decided to begin my fishing there.

The brook tumbled down the ravine in a series of steps, each step marked by a small waterfall with a pool beneath. I tied a No. 12 wet Coachman to a 3-foot, 3X leader, pinched down the barb, and began my fishing. I stalked each pool by hiding behind a boulder if one was high enough, and where it was only 3 or 4 feet high I reached it in a crouch. Having taken my position, selected in advance, I swung out the fly, let it drift down just off the current, then covered the rest of the pool on both sides. These upper pools were rarely more than 8 or 10 feet long, 5 or 6 feet wide, and perhaps a couple of feet deep. I took one or more pretty little brookies out of each pool, not one more than 6 inches long, and the barbless hook let me restore each one gently to the water without injury.

A half hour passed before I got one that I could keep with a clear conscience. It was 9 inches long, pretty near tops for a brook of that character. Then I came to a place that required a change in tactics. It was a bench much wider than those I had passed, being about 50 feet long. Its banks were free from any growth, consisting of a solid ledge with no soil to support plant life except a few ferns growing in crannies in the rock. But I saw that by standing in the water at the foot of the pool, I could reach readily any part of it. I detoured well back from the pool to reach the spot I had selected. Then I began to make casts that fanned out until

I had covered the lower water. Then I lengthened my casts so I could progressively reach every part of the pool. Here was the deepest water I had found, perhaps 4 feet at the head. I had gotten halfway up the pool when I saw a flash in the water underneath the Coachman and soon I had creeled a 10-incher. Soon afterwards I caught another of about the same size. Now my casts were reaching close to the hot spots, the relatively slack water off the main current and where the water was deepest. About 5 feet below the waterfall at the head there was an eddy with patches of foam circling lazily around. I put my fly at the intake of the current feeding the eddy and let it drift along the circling course of the eddy. I saw the water become agitated and struck. The resistance told me I had something bigger and bulkier than the fish I had been taking. The fish didn't jump but continually tried to bore to the bottom to get under a rock. I kept the line taut because you can take no liberties whatever with a barbless hook and a slack line means a lost trout. When finally I had the fish in my net, it proved to be a brookie 12¼ inches long. It was a male as evidenced by its hooked and rather ugly lower jaw. The female brookie is a much handsomer fish than the male.

I ended up my day's fishing with eight nice fish, and had restored to the brook about twice as many. I had caught them, first, because the stream was high with the rains of the night before, secondly, because at no time had I exposed myself to the fish, and thirdly, I had been most careful in my approach, catfooting as I walked, and when doing any wading using the same caution wherever I placed my feet.

In Annapolis County, Nova Scotia, I once fished a typical meadow stream. I had to walk to it for four miles over a heavy sandy road. I fished down it with wet fly with poor results until I came to a bridge over another road. I was about to quit, for the day was bright, sunny, and rather hot, and my creel only held several 8- and 9-inch brookies. Below the bridge was the longest and deepest pool I had seen that day. The left bank was thick with alders; the right bank had a fringe of uncut grass about 2 feet high along its edge where the mowing machine had left it. The field had been gleaned, and the farmer and his helper were raking and pitching hay in the field beyond. There was a glare from the sun on the water so I couldn't look into its depths. The pool was flattish and about 100 feet long. A cloud passed over the sun and in its shadow I could now see into the water. I noticed a number of dark objects lying motionless on the bottom and thought they were sticks. But a grasshopper alighted on the water and one of the "sticks" came to life, shot upwards, and grabbed the insect.

I lost no time and crawled through the two fences, approached the farmer, and asked his permission to fish on his property. He was friendly and readily gave permission.

"Don't think you'll do much," he said. "Pretty bright and hot. Time to fish it is in spring when there's more water and it's cooler."

I thanked him, went back to the harvested field, lay down my rod, and went to work. As I scuffled through the grass stubble, I flushed one of those hoppers with a coat of light green. I hurled myself at him with outstretched hat and caged him. Then carefully feeling under the hat I finally captured him. I took a long-shank fly that was scantily dressed, removed as much of the dressing as I could with gut cutter and thumbnail, and impaled the grasshopper by inserting the hook at the hopper's head, then ran it through the body and out at the tail. Tying the hook to the leader I made my stalk of the pool by crawling on hands and knees to the bank edging of grass. I didn't cast but held out the rod so that the grasshopper touched the water with no part of the leader showing. I jiggled the rod tip a bit so that the hopper was given a little movement. Splash! A lusty trout came up and grabbed the hopper. I didn't play that trout for I wanted others of that school I had seen from the bridge. I hooked it and derricked it out with one sweeping motion. "B'gorry, he's got a trout!" I heard the farmer say.

With my trout secure, I crawled back from the brook and sought another hopper. It took some doing but before long I had another and continued my fishing. I got three trout from 11 to 13 inches before one that I had hooked broke loose as I yanked it into the air and fell with a resounding splash, causing the rest of the trout to flee to shelter. They had been out in the open to feed on the grasshoppers and crickets which, disturbed by the haying operations, had fallen into the water. My method of fishing, known as "dapping," is often very effective in summer if the fisherman stays concealed.

CHAPTER 17

Lake and Pond Trout Fishing

THE TROUT FISHERMAN who goes to a lake or pond which he never has fished, but which he knows has brookies, rainbows, cutthroats, or brownies, is likely to feel pretty much at a loss. Here is a broad expanse of water, but where shall he fish? The chances are that unless it is early morning or near dusk he will see no rises to tell him where the fish are. Then he is likely to "chuck and chance it" and trust to luck. This can prove to be rather frustrating.

EARLY SEASON FISHING

Early in the season the trout in lakes and ponds may be in shallow water where it is warmer and there is a better chance of finding food. Try the coves, off beds of water weeds, or off bars handy to deeper water. You can locate such bars by using a plumb line with depths marked off on it by bits of colored yarn tied at intervals of 6 feet. Then, anchor your boat or canoe within casting distance of the bar and fish this water. Or, if bait fishing, make a closer approach and swing your bait toward the bar, using a bobber to hold the bait just off bottom.

When the water temperature reaches from 55 to 60 degrees, brook trout get hungry and give good sport. It takes a bit warmer water with temperatures, say, from 57 to 70 degrees to put rainbows and browns on the feed.

Early in the season a dry fly is pretty ineffective. Use wet flies in sizes from 8 to 12, choosing such patterns as Grizzly King, Coachman, Royal Coachman, Black Gnat, Campbell's Fancy, and Dark Cahill if the lake holds rainbows and cutthroats, adding the Parmachene Belle if brookies

189

are present. Also, early in the season bucktails and streamers such as the Gray Ghost, Edson Tiger, Black Ghost, Supervisor, and Mickey Finn are effective, particularly in trolling.

After each cast, retrieve with the hand-twist method, so aptly named by Ray Bergman. This is a most effective retrieve. If you are right-handed, after making the cast grasp the line between thumb and forefinger of the left hand, and pull the line in as far as possible without drawing the hand backward. Then raise the other three fingers and pull in the line with them as far as you can, again without drawing the hand backward. You

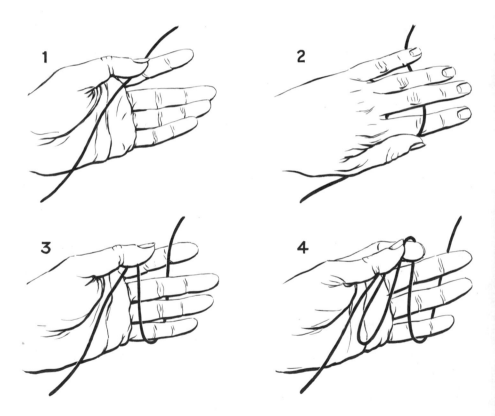

Hand-twist retrieve: Grasp line between thumb and forefinger (1), then turn hand over (2) and catch line with remaining three fingers; turn hand upward again (3), drawing line in and catching next section of line between forefinger and thumb (4), repeating process until line is retrieved.

will find that your thumb and forefinger are now in position to grab the line above that which has been brought in by the three fingers. You repeat this until you have brought in enough line to make another forward cast.

Try a slow and steady retrieve at first. Repeat the method until you are satisfied that the slow retrieve is not the winning ticket for that particular stretch of water on that particular day. Then quicken the retrieve. You will find that sometimes a slow retrieve is the best, and that at other times a retrieve made just as fast as you can do it is what the trout want.

Not only is it well to vary the speed of the retrieve, but also the depth at which you fish the flies. At first, after making the cast and the wet flies are still on the surface, begin the retrieve at once. If this method proves successful, stick to it. If it doesn't, then let your fly or flies sink a little before retrieving. If that doesn't work, then anoint your leader with a soak preparation, and let the fly go down close to the bottom. At such a time I like to switch reels and put on the rod one loaded with a Dacron line. At all times fly fishing will be better if the water is ruffled with a light breeze. When there is a stiff wind and the lake has whitecaps, rarely is the fishing good. I recall a visit to Anahim Lake in British Columbia, famed for its big rainbows. When the four of us got there, the lake appeared to be in good order, with a surface-ruffling breeze. While we were unloading outboard motor and duffel from the truck, the wind suddenly freshened and by the time we launched the boat there were whitecaps and sizable waves. Despite the rough water, we trolled, took to partly sheltered coves, and cast and cast. There was not a rise to any fly, yet the lake was loaded with trout.

If, after fishing at various depths, varying the speed of retrieves and changing the fly patterns, you don't get a touch from a trout, move on and try another stretch of water. If you have been cautious in your approach and have avoided noise or undue splashing in your casting, either there are no trout in that piece of water or else they are very unwilling.

WARM WEATHER TROUT

When the water warms with the coming of summer, use your water thermometer. Look for the cooler water which all the trouts love. You will find colder water where a feeder stream comes in, bringing water cooled by springs, and aerated by rapids. In the warmer season the trout hang around the mouths of such streams, which not only bring colder water but also much food. Don't make the mistake of paddling or rowing right into this fresher water, but lay off it within casting distance and cast into it. In such places trout will take a dry fly, while the wet fly is especially effective if fished at varying depths and retrieved with the hand-twist method.

Even in the heat of summer, trout will often rise to the dry fly in certain favored areas, and early in the morning and at dusk. There is great pleasure in fishing at such times. In early morning the air has been freshened and cooled by the night. Mist curls from the water. The bird songs of spring have been stilled, but there are chatterings and stray notes that tell the birds are still around. The lake or pond is likely to be deserted and for once you have it to yourself. The quiet will be repeated at dusk. Then other fishermen will have left for the evening meal. Crickets will join in a subdued chorus, and bullfrogs will hit bass notes as they become vocal at the close of day. Water that seemed dead and troutless during the heat of the day will often be dimpled with rising trout which have come in from the cooler depths to feed upon flies which become more numerous at these times of the day. At such times a dry fly will work very well.

I was fishing a lake in Washington state in August, 1957, when the trout were dimpling the water. I found that casting over a rise, then letting the fly stay motionless for a moment or two, and then giving it a quivering motion by vibrating my rod hand gently, pausing again for several moments, then slowly retrieving, was very effective on rainbows. This also has worked well on other lakes in that state, and has gotten me some nice brookies in Maine ponds. On the other hand, on lakes in central British Columbia when rainbows were rising well on the surface, while my dry fly did take some fish, a wet fly fished several inches under the surface did a lot better. On a brook-trout lake in northern Vermont, the most effective method I found was to cast a bushy dry fly and as soon as it landed on the water start a steady slow retrieve. It is well to experiment to find the method that works best on a particular water at that particular time. What works beautifully on one day may prove to be a lamentable dud on another. Game fishes do not follow set patterns in taking a lure.

In the Northeast most of the trout lakes, or "ponds," as they usually are called, are on the small side. That makes it easier to locate the trout. In one Maine pond, when I was there in August, the fish were hard to find. I located about eight places where the water temperature was several degrees cooler than in the rest of the lake. By lining up from shore to shore in two directions at right angles to each other, using a prominent tree, the tip of a point, a big boulder, or a camp on shore, and putting my

On large lakes, trolling a silver spoon with a spinning rod is often effective, as this angler with rainbow in tow will testify. He is fishing on Lime Lake, Michigan. *Michigan Conservation Dept.*

findings down in a memorandum book, I was able to visit these cold pockets again and again and catch trout. The cooler water was doubtless due to springs entering from the bottom. That these springs had considerable flow was attested by the fact that while the only stream entering the lake was nothing but a trickle, the outlet was a brook with considerable flow.

TROLLING

On the larger trout lakes, if you don't know just where the trout are lying, trolling slowly is probably the best way to learn the water and get you some fish. Here again you have to find by experiment at what depth to fish. Bucktails and streamers are good for this. In early season such flies may be trolled at the surface or near the surface. As the water warms up, split shot or sinkers or a sinking line are needed to get the fly down. Also, a bait-casting or spinning rod trolling a silver spoon or wobbler is effective. Don't use a valued bamboo fly rod for spoon trolling as it is almost certain to get a set.

BEAVER PONDS

Many beaver ponds hold goodly numbers of trout. In the East they are likely to be brookies, and in the West either rainbows or eastern brook trout, with the latter in the majority. Rainbows generally like faster water than is found in such ponds. On the other hand, brookies are likely to get along beautifully in such water and become self-sustaining.

There is a difference of opinion among fishermen and state technicians as to whether beavers are an asset or a nuisance on a trout stream. Many eastern fishermen condemn the beaver because the dams he builds expose an appreciable amount of water surface to the warming sun, and often make the water of the stream too warm to support trout below the dam. Beavers also cause considerable siltation, and the bottom of a beaver-made pond gets cluttered up with tree branches, twigs, and other vegetable refuse. On the other hand, beavers in the mountains of the West act as water conservationists. Their dams are useful in storing water and slow up the swift and damaging current at the time of spring run-offs or later torrential rains. Whether the busy dam builders are a sportsman's aid or a destructive influence depends upon the type of stream and where located.

Personally, I like beaver ponds. Sometimes they give the most dependable fishing in their areas. Those that I have fished in both East and West have held brook trout only. In most of them I have tried both wet and dry flies, and almost invariably have found wet flies the best. Usually I have had better success when I fished as deeply as possible without getting down deep enough to get fouled on the bottom. As beaver ponds usually are shallow, that means getting the wet fly down about a foot or two under the surface by treating it and a foot or two of the leader end with leader soak. I have lost a lot of flies in this fishing but the trout caught has made it worth while. The usual run of brookies in such ponds is from 8 or 9 inches up to an occasional lunker of 12 to 14 inches. These brookies almost invariably have been heavy for their length. I once caught a 14-incher with a belly so deep that it almost had the shape of a black bass and weighed 1½ pounds. My favorite patterns for this beaver-pond fishing are Black Gnat, Coachman, Grizzly King, and Royal Coachman in sizes 10 and 12.

The worst of this fishing is that often it is difficult to get off a good cast. Probably there will be alders to foul your back cast. The pond bottom is too mucky and filled with snags to wade, and you are apt to stand in muddy ooze in the open or else on the dam itself, which may require a balancing act for you to keep your footing. I have fallen off of one and I can assure you it's no fun. Also you may have to endure hosts of biting insects like mosquitoes and "no-seeums." So carry a good insect repellent with you.

Even a small beaver pond can show an astonishing number of brook trout. For instance, in July of 1960 I spent my fishing vacation at Ben Sheffield's dude ranch in Montana, near the Madison River. I had been fishing the Madison River all day, and after supper Ben offered to show me some small beaver ponds on the small brook running through his ranch that flows down through the foothills and eventually empties into Ennis Lake. So I got my fly rod, and with my friend Bill Browning of the Montana Chamber of Commerce got into Ben's truck. He took us on a roadless ride and within ten minutes he stopped the truck and pointed a finger.

"There's the easiest one to fish," he said. "The others are too thick with alders."

I doubt that pond covered more than half an acre. It lay in a hollow between two hills. The side toward us was open and the water that was open enough to cast into was not more than 30 by 10 feet. It was early dusk and the water was broken by a dozen rises in that limited area. I put on a Coachman and cast into that open water. Result—a brookie between 11 and 12 inches long and fat as butter. I took about a dozen fish out of that pocket of water and returned to the water those that were uninjured. While I was doing this, there were many splashes from trout rising in unreachable water.

When I quit, I said to Ben, "I guess I've taken about all the trout that open patch of water can stand to lose."

"I don't think so," said Ben. "Lots of trout in there and it's a good thing to take some out. The rest will have more to eat."

It was indeed surprising to find such fat and well-conditioned trout in so small a body of water. The stream feeding the pond is small and can't bring down much food. The bottoms of those ponds must have many underwater creatures that trout love to eat, as well as the flies that fall upon the water, for each trout caught was deep of body and brightly colored. And that has been true of about every beaver pond that I have fished.

Washington has done a fine job of lake rehabilitation, poisoning the trash fish which infested many lakes, and stocking them with trout. These restored lakes are yielding the fishermen tons of fine trout. In the Midwest, Wisconsin and Michigan also have done considerable work along that line, and in the East, Massachusetts has been notably successful in its trout lake efforts. Opportunities for good lake and pond trout fishing are definitely on the upswing.

CHAPTER 18

The Smallmouth Bass

THAT THE SMALLMOUTH bass is one of our finest game fishes need not be argued. Anyone who has tangled with one of them, thrilled to its frantic runs and occasional jumps, seen its speed as it runs with the lure, and battled its strength as it bored and resisted the curving rod, will stoutly maintain that no finer game fish of its size exists anywhere. Here is a stubborn fighter, strong and unyielding.

Known scientifically as *Micropterus dolomieui,* the smallmouth today has a wide distribution, far exceeding its original range, for its good qualities are responsible for its having been stocked in many waters to which it was not native. Originally its range was only in southern Canada, the Great Lakes area, the Ohio, and Upper Mississippi River areas. Now it thrives in most of the states. In some sections it was stocked in waters that better had been left to trout, for it is a fish eater and preys upon young fish of that type. The average smallmouth caught with rod and line weighs from 1 to 2 pounds. The record for the species weighed 11 pounds, 15 ounces and was caught in Dale Hollow Lake in Kentucky in 1955.

Today the smallmouth gives fine fishing over a wide range that includes the Great Lakes and St. Lawrence River areas, the Upper Mississippi, the Ohio and Tennessee River systems, New England south to Florida, and on the West Coast from California to British Columbia.

Like the trout it prefers clear and cool streams and rocky lakes. It is not often found in the smaller trout streams but I have caught it on small trout flies while fishing for trout in New York's Willowemoc, and the lower Beaverkill has them. It has run up the East Branch of the Delaware River and its tributaries since New York City built its big Pepacton Reservoir at Downsville, N. Y., and the last time I fished Dry Brook, one of the

197

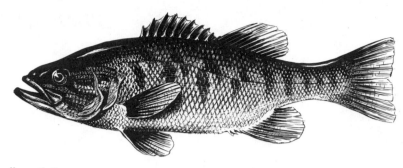

Smallmouth Bass

tributaries of the East Branch, I caught several on wet flies while fishing for trout. One of them weighed just under 3 pounds. Bass fishermen will be surprised that far from being happy over taking these fish I was considerably annoyed, despite the fine fight each of them gave me. In each instance I thought I had hooked a granddaddy of a trout. My wife was fishing with me and some distance below. I heard her shout, left the stream to join her thinking she needed help, and found her with a smallmouth weighing 2½ pounds. She had had a tough time trying to land it with her 3½-ounce rod. She couldn't get it over her landing net, and finally, lucky that her leader hadn't broken, had dragged it out by sheer strength. She was using a No. 10 Royal Coachman wet fly and I a No. 12 Coachman.

Some fishermen are unable to tell the difference between a smallmouth and a largemouth. There are two prominent identifying marks. In the smallmouth the upper jaw extends backward only to the center of the eye. Place a ruler or straight stick vertically across the eye and it will touch the extremity of the upper jaw. In the largemouth the upper jaw goes back beyond the eye. In the smallmouth there may be vertical bars on its sides, never horizontal. The largemouth has a dark band extending along its sides.

The color of the smallmouth varies with its type of habitat. The first smallmouth I ever caught was in Massachusetts when I was a youngster. With the exception of its white belly it was actually black. Generally it is greenish gold with a bronze tone.

The food of this bass consists of small fish, worms, crawfish, frogs, and insects. Spawning, depending upon the water temperatures, usually takes place in May and June, but may be delayed until well into the summer where the water is cold and deep. A favorable water temperature for spawning is above 55 degrees. Like others of the sunfish family to which the smallmouth belongs, it prepares a spawning bed in the gravel, which it clears of silt and minor debris with its fins. The eggs hatch within a period of from several days up to ten, depending upon the water temperature. The male then dutifully guards the nest to keep predators away. The baby bass begin their feeding with water fleas, then graduate to aquatic insects, and when they become adult feed voraciously on almost any of the smaller aquatic organisms, particularly the smaller fishes.

Smallmouth fishermen are successful with quite a variety of lures, both natural and artificial: bass bugs, plugs, spoons, pork-rind lures, minnows, nightcrawlers, spinner combinations, dry and wet flies, bucktails, and streamer flies.

These underwater photographs of a smallmouth (top) and a largemouth bass show the differences between the two species. Note that the smallmouth's upper jaw extends only as far as the eye, whereas the largemouth's upper jaw extends beyond the eye. Also, the notch between the dorsal fins on the smallmouth is shallower than on the largemouth. *Michigan Conservation Dept.*

FLY FISHING

Fly fishing for smallmouths, with its light tackle, gives the utmost in sport. Here, as is true in trout fishing, your water thermometer is invaluable. Wait until the temperature of the water you intend to fish reaches a reading of between 60 and 65 degrees. At such a temperature smallmouths take to shallow water if on a rocky shore, as well as gravel and rocky bars. The water may be as shallow as 1 foot deep, so shallow as to expose the dorsal fin of the fish, or as deep as 8 feet. If fishing from a boat, approach such bass water with caution, avoiding such noises as the thump and rattle of a tackle box on the boat bottom, the careless drop of an anchor, or the splashing of the oars. You will have to make fairly long casts from a position well away from the water you fish, for smallmouth water almost invariably is clear and the bass are wary.

For tackle use a fly rod of glass or split bamboo in the 8- to 10-foot range, weighing from 4 to 5½ ounces according to its length. Use a fly line which fits the rod. (Consult the table in Chapter 2.) Use a 9-foot leader tapered to 1X or 2X. Bass are not as leader-shy as are brown trout, and the finer leaders tapered to such diameters as 3X to 5X aren't needed. Bass bugs do splendidly on smallmouths. Cork-body frogs with bucktail legs are also very good. Streamers such as Gray Ghost, Black Ghost, Edson Tiger, Mickey Finn, and Supervisor often are taken savagely.

One June I spent a fortnight fishing Damariscotta Lake in Maine, a state which has many cold and clear lakes eminently suited to this bass and which give fine fishing for it. During the time I was there the state law provided a special season of fly fishing only on bass, with a limit of three a day. This special regulation is allowed since the bass in Maine waters usually are spawning in June, and is still in effect at the time this is written. As you may catch as many bass as you wish, returning to the water all fish over your bag limit of three, I had a swell time taking these jumping acrobats with streamers and bucktails. Taken on the fly, no smallmouth suffered any injury and could be returned to the water as good as ever. I was using a 10-foot split-bamboo fly rod weighing 5½ ounces. I decided to do a little experimenting, and changed from streamers to a No. 10 Royal Coachman dry fly on a 9-foot leader. I cast along rocky shores, putting the fly into pockets among the rocks, to a sunken log, or any place that seemed a likely spot for a fish, let the fly rest on the water for a few seconds, then with a trembling movement of the rod tip made the fly quiver, and followed with a slow retrieve. Sometimes the rise would

The smallmouth is one of the gamest fishes in North America. Here one jumps and plunges in Manitoba's Winnipeg River. *Manitoba Dept. of Industry and Commerce.*

come when the fly touched the water, but more often when it quivered after the pause following its landing, or when it began its slow retrieve. These bass did not run big, weighing from 1 to 2 pounds, but they really were fighting fools, making jumps and strong runs. On the fly rod they gave better sport than they would have on a bait-casting rod or a spinning rod.

There are flies of bucktail that imitate crawfish, which are very lifelike when retrieved. The bucktail hair vibrates as it is drawn through the water on a slow retrieve and makes the lure seem alive. Many smallmouth lakes are wadable along the shore, and fly fishing for these bass while wading is a fascinating sport. Here, because of the clear water, long casts are usually required, and a leader tapered to 1X and from 9 to 12 feet long will get you more bass. Cast the fly close to any cover under which a bass may be lying. The smallmouth often will refuse to travel any distance for his food. He wants it to come to him.

Fly fishing for river smallmouths in the hot months is more productive if done with wet flies fished near the bottom, weighting the leader with several split shot. Or, if fishing with a spinner and fly, no additional weight is needed. After the June spawning is over, the bass often tend to school. If you can locate such a school by seeing swirls in the water, streamers fished near the surface can give you a lot of fun. They should be given action with slow and twitchy retrieves. Often in such fishing you will see a bass chase the fly and quit without taking it. The natural impulse in such a case is to slow up the retrieve to let the fish take it without any effort. Do the opposite. When the bass gives up his approach, speed up the retrieve to imitate a frightened minnow eager to make a fast getaway. Sometimes the bass will get new energy and rush to take the lure before it can escape. If this doesn't tease him to strike, make your new cast well upstream from him, and let it drift down to him.

The best streamers and bucktails for smallmouths are chunky of body and are dressed with bucktail hair from 3 to 5 inches long. Carry a hook hone with you. Rocks probably will often dull your hook, which may require frequent honing to keep it sharp.

BASS BUGS

There comes a period in early summer, before the water surface warms to a temperature that sends the bass to deep water, when the water is somewhere between 65 and 70 degrees. Smallmouths then will stay in shallow water ranging up to 8 feet deep. They will be found among the rocks along shore, on bars near deep water, but almost always on a gravel bottom. If the day has been pretty warm, you may have to do your fishing in early morning or at evening to find these temperatures. Bass bugs do well under such conditions.

For bass bugging use a split-bamboo or glass fly rod 8 to 10 feet long—rather whippy in action—weighing between 5 and 5½ ounces, an HCH tapered line, and a level 7-foot leader of about 10-pound test. Use poppers on No. 1 hooks. During the day the better surface fishing is to be found near such cover as weed patches, floating logs, boulders, or brush heaps.

Pork-rind lure rigged with two hooks is a deadly early-summer bait for small-mouths. Cast it among rocks or weeds, and retrieve it at varying speeds until you find the method that works best.

PORK-RIND LURES

Pork-rind lures are also excellent under early-summer conditions. Cut with a sharp knife strips of fat pork rind about 8 inches long, and tapering from about ¾ inch at the head to a sharp-pointed tail. Leave some with the natural coloring. Color others with black dye. Use two hooks, one a 5/0, the other 7/0. Cut two holes halfway down each strip you have prepared. Thread a 16- or 18-pound-test line through the eye of the smaller hook, and then join the ends of the line through the two holes you have punched in the strip, tying firmly with a square knot. Punch one hole through the head of the rind, and insert the bend of the larger hook through this. Tie the end of your running line, that on your reel, to the eye of this hook and you're set. Cast this into pockets among the rocks or weeds and retrieve at varying speeds until you find the speed which is most effective on that day.

PLUGS

You can't be didactic in discussing fishing methods and fish characteristics and say "this is true all times and all places," for experiences may vary. But in my experience the smallmouth is far from being the plug taker that its largemouth cousin is, particularly in the daytime. However there are occasions when baits such as crawfish, minnows, or hellgrammites, and artificials such as flies, bass bugs, and silver spoons don't seem to work. Then a switch to plugs may give you some sport. The larger plugs such as you can use with success on the largemouth usually are ineffective on the smallmouth. The small plugs definitely outfish them. Those plugs with shiny, flashy bodies of silver or gold do better than the others, with those

A quartet of shimmering smallmouths provided this fisherman with plenty of thrilling, rod-bending action. *Manitoba Dept. of Industry and Commerce.*

with red head and white bodies coming next. Fish them around bars, emergent boulders, boulders on the bottom, and along underwater ledges. Why small plugs? The smallmouth is not the gross feeder that his cousin the largemouth is, and the small size is the more appealing to him.

Night fishing with surface plugs is not practiced by many bait casters because of difficulty with backlashes. However, skilled casters with educated thumbs, and spin casters, can have a lot of fun night fishing with good surface lures.

After making your cast, be patient and let the lure rest on the water for thirty seconds or more. Then twitch the rod tip gently to make the lure send out little ripples on the water. Wait until you think the ripples have died away, and then repeat.

The strike of a smallmouth at night is an indescribable thrill. The fish, because of the darkness, has lost much of the caution it shows during the daytime. You hear a smash in the dark that raises your goose pimples and your rod tip is likely to be brought violently to the water.

LIVE BAIT

In the heat of summer, smallmouths betake themselves to cooler water at depths of from 15 to 35 feet. Then they like rock or gravel bars and ledges at those depths. Then nightwalkers, live minnows, crawfish, or deep-running plugs are the bait called for. However, the fish will often feed at night in the shallows over bottoms of rock or gravel. Either artificial flies, bugs, poppers, or bait will take them. Hot and humid nights bring out hatches of aquatic flies upon which the bass feed hungrily. Small minnows also range the shoreline, and streamers that imitate minnows or small silver spoons that are minnowlike and retrieved with the pause-and-darting action of little fish take many smallmouths.

In river fishing for smallmouths, the hellgrammite is hard to beat as a bait. It is tough, stands repeated casts without going to pieces, and is a natural bass food. You can get your own supply by turning over rocks in riffles on the river bed, and making a quick grab behind the mean pinchers on their head. The miniature catfish caught from under rocks in such smallmouth rivers as the Delaware make a fine bait. Hold a net below a rock on the river bottom, lift the rock with the other hand, and if there is a little cattie there, let the swift current wash him into the net. Be sure to check your state laws to know whether taking natural bait from streams is legal.

CHAPTER 19

The Largemouth Bass

THE LARGEMOUTH BASS, a game fish of warmer waters, is probably the most popular of all fishes over much of its range. In my home state of New Jersey the crowds that fish the trout streams elbow to elbow are greatly thinned once the bass season opens. Most fishermen reject 10-inch trout in favor of jumping largemouth weighing from 2 to 5 pounds. A spectacular fighter, when the largemouth takes to the air, the sight is impressive; when it falls it sounds as though someone were throwing big rocks into the water.

The largemouth black bass (*Micropterus salmoides*) had an original range from southern Canada down into Florida, Texas, and northeastern Mexico. But its adaptability to sluggish waters unsuited to either smallmouth or trout has encouraged its introduction into areas where once it was unknown. For example, California now has many rivers and lakes where this fish is abundant, and Washington and Oregon have some fine bass waters. The great increase in dam building in recent years has added greatly to the number of prime largemouth waters. This bass is the Number One freshwater game fish of the South, where they reach weights considerably larger than in the North, due to the longer feeding season. The largest largemouth bass of authentic record taken on rod and line weighed 22 pounds, 4 ounces, and was caught in Montgomery Lake, Georgia, in 1932.

The largemouth has many local names, including Oswego bass, green trout, green bass, straw bass, bayou bass, slough bass, lake bass, moss bass, grass bass, and marsh bass.

Comparison of the fighting ability of the largemouth with that of its cousin, the smallmouth, is inevitable. There are some lakes in which both

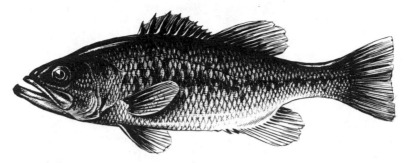

Largemouth Bass

are found, where the water is clear and cool, yet not cold enough to be unsuited to the largemouth. There it is possible to compare the two. Pound for pound the smallmouth will fight longer and more stubbornly than its bigmouth relative.

It is not difficult to distinguish the largemouth from the smallmouth. Take a ruler or any straight-edge and lay it vertically across the rear of the bass's eye. If it doesn't touch the rear extremity of the upper jaw, it is a smallmouth. If the rear extremity passes the straight-edge, it is a large-mouth. Also, the coloring and markings differ. The smallmouth is likely to have shadowy *vertical* dark stripes on the upper half of its body. These are lacking in the largemouth, which has a dark *horizontal* band along its median line. This marking is responsible for the name "linesides" affectionately given it by many fishermen.

The chief food of the adult bass is forage fish, though it also relishes crawfish and frogs. Young bass feed principally on water insects and tiny crustaceans such as daphnia. The spawning time varies between the South and the North. In the North spawning is in May or June; in the South it comes in late winter or early spring. Like its distant relative, the bluegill, the largemouth prepares a nest by removing any silt from gravel, leaving it clean. After the female deposits her eggs and they are fertilized by the male, the latter stands guard over them, and stays to remain a protector of the fry until they are several weeks old.

The largemouth likes water weeds and beds of water lilies such as are found in the shallower water, and so this fish is the bait caster's delight. Thus, when the water temperature is favorable, surface-running plugs and bugs are effective as well as such baits as minnows, crawfish, and frogs. The smallmouth in the northern part of its range in winter goes into a state of semi-hibernation and eats little. The largemouth, on the other hand, is likely to stay on the prowl for food most of the winter.

In northern largemouth waters the best fishing months are June (where there is a legal season in that month), July, August, and September, with September leading. In the South the colder months are likely to provide better fishing.

The largemouth's food is likely to be more abundant in shallow water where minnows, frogs, crawfish, and other small creatures are plentiful. So even when the surface of this water is warmer or colder than they prefer, they will feed there, and afterwards descend to the depths where the temperature is more to their liking. In hot weather this feeding period is likely to be early in the morning or at night. Lures fished on the surface will then take them. In shallow water look for largemouths where good cover is close to natural food, such as openings among the weeds and lily pads, heaps of sunken brush, logs, and rocks large enough to give them shelter.

Early in the season when the water is cold—that is, somewhere in the middle fifties—the bass do little feeding, and rarely can you interest them in any bait or lure. When the water temperature reaches around 60 degrees, they take an interest in satisfying their hunger, especially in early morning or at night. For daytime feeding in shallow water they wait until the temperature there gets into the sixties. The most favorable water temperatures for largemouth feeding lie in the broad band between 60 and 80 degrees. In hot weather, when shallow water has become so warm as to make the bass uncomfortable, they usually can find in the deeper water temperatures in the 70- to 75-degree range.

LURES

Considering the largemouth's appetite for live fish, it is interesting that this bass hits artificials. We know that fish have the sense of smell. That is why catfish go for the rightly named "stink bait." Scientists have found that in returning to the stream of their birth, salmon are guided by the smell peculiar to that river. Bass, if hungry, will sometimes take the dead, or motionless and almost dead, minnow of the still fisherman. They are guided by their sense of smell.

But artificial lures do not have the flesh smell. If they are motionless, the fish are indifferent to them. So it is primarily the action of the lure which causes the fish to strike. They will hit a lure when hungry because it has

Exploding from the depths, a hooked largemouth on Lake Bradford, Florida, shows he won't quit without a fight. *Florida State News Bureau.*

an alluring motion which makes them think it is alive and edible. I believe they also hit a moving lure which comes near them out of pure cussedness, even when they are not hungry. They resent what they think is a living creature invading their territory. Often you can cast into good bass water without response. But continue casting, putting the lure right into the bass's lair, and it gets into a fury and attacks the lure as though it wanted to tear it apart.

Successful lures all over the largemouth's range include spoons, spinners, bass bugs, poppers, plugs, bucktails, pork-rind lures, artificial frogs, plastic worms and eels, jigs, and wet and dry flies.

Surface Lures. Fishing for largemouths with surface lures is the most fun of all. The lure is in sight all the time and when a bigmouth hits it, the splash is electrifying. To me this form of bass fishing rates with dry-fly fishing for trout and for the same reasons.

Top sport in surface fishing is provided by the popping bug. With a stiff-action 9- to 10-foot fly rod you can get out pretty long casts with the little lure, and reach spots where a bass is lurking, without approaching close enough to warn the fish. Make your cast, then let the bug lie motionless on the water for at least half a minute, or until the ripples it made when it hit the water have disappeared. Then make it tremble and quiver a bit by twitching the rod tip gently. Wait until the ripples again have faded away. If nothing happens, then make it pop and gurgle on the retrieve. The popping often will excite a bass to murderous frenzy. When the fish hits, strike hard and quickly before it can spit out the lure. Use a 6-foot, 15-pound-test leader.

There are several other types of bugs that are mighty successful in shallow water. Most of them are made of cork or balsa wood. If you see swirls in the water or fierce smashes, which indicate that bass are chasing and feeding on minnows, try one. Unlike the poppers, which are made with concave heads to make them chug and pop on retrieve, the heads of these bugs are rather blunt and flat-faced. Some are made with spread wings which help to cause more water disturbance on the retrieve. Fish them the same as poppers, picking openings in the lily pads or weeds, along the sides of sunken logs, or by rocks.

Then there is that doughty little fly-rod bass catcher, the artificial frog, which like the poppers and bugs is excellent in shallow water. An effective type of frog is made with cork body and bucktail legs. Work the lure in imitation of a natural frog, in the same pockets among the weeds that you would cast a bug. After the cast, let the froggie lie motionless upon the water for at least a half minute, twitch it several times to set up motion in the hair legs, give a slow forward jerk, followed by a fast one, then repeat. Frogs are a favored food of largemouths, but they are found only in shallow water where there are water weeds to provide shelter.

These surface lures can be used with the same fly rod and leader as the popping bug. Of all methods of fishing for the largemouth they give the best sport. They are suited to water up to 6 feet deep if it is clear. If the water is muddy or stained their effectiveness is limited to water up to 3 feet deep.

Plugs.   The number and style of plugs is legion. The beginner is bewildered by the many styles and colors in a sporting goods store, and is tempted to load up with more than he can use. Some of them have a record of success that is impressive. Others are just hunks of wood, plastic, or metal. The reason for this radical difference in effectiveness is action. The

Popping bugs are fished on the surface. With a stiff-action fly rod,
you can get out long casts and drop them in good bass spots.

successful plugs are those with tantalizing wiggles, twists, turns, darts, or
dives which make them act alive and excite the bass to strike.

Plugs fall into three and different distinctive types—surface, medium-
depth, and deep-running. The beginner should get one of each type as a
starter, asking the sales clerk to select for him the biggest seller in each
type.

In my opinion, among the many types of surface plugs the chugger is
hard to surpass. It makes a real fuss when it is retrieved at a steady pace,
due to its collar, which also gives it an enticing wobble. Another excellent
surface plug sports blades or arms which flog the water when it is retrieved and make more fuss than a catfight. With these plugs it is the
action and noise which attract the fish. The color of their backs makes little
difference. What the fish see is their undersides, which should be light in
color—white or yellow.

Among medium-depth plugs, the crippled minnow often shows good
results. An injured minnow usually finds it impossible to get to the bottom,

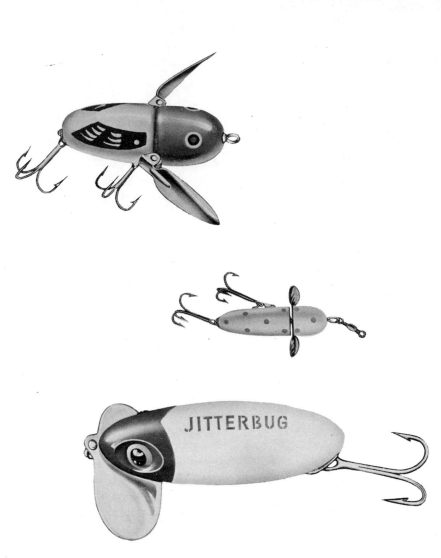

Surface lures for largemouths that kick up a fuss when retrieved (top to bottom): Heddon Crazy Crawler, Pfleuger Globe, Arbogast Jitterbug.

though it is always trying. It will get down a foot or two, and then reluctantly return to the surface. These plugs are made so that when given a jerky retrieve they will dive and dart. A silvery or light-yellow color is desirable in this type of plug.

Underwater plugs float when not given action but dive on the retrieve. A fast retrieve causes a deeper run in some, while others are limited to a course of not deeper than 2 to 5 feet. Because they float, these plugs have the decided advantage of enabling the fisherman to work out a backlash without fear of the plug sinking and getting fouled.

For that period in the hot season when the bass have retired to deep water, the deep-running plug should be used. It sinks when not retrieved, and also swims deep on the retrieve.

In the early days of plug fishing, the plugs were almost invariably large and equipped with three gangs of treble hooks, with usually a propeller at front and rear. They were fearsome-looking things and, armed as they were with so many hooks, after you got a bass into the landing net it was a chore getting it out. The hooks would catch in the cords of the net, and while you were freeing one hook, too often another would foul. In that era New Jersey, for instance, would ban more than three hooks on a lure, and after buying some of the monstrosities I would have to spend time with a wirecutter removing the surplus hooks. Times have changed. The spinning rod with its monofilament line has proven that bass will take, and even seem to prefer, small lures. Some small lures were available in those early days but they were tough to cast with the usual bait-casting equipment. Spinning rods will cast light lures, even those weighing as little as ¼ ounce, a country mile, and they have opened up avenues of great sport. Get these light lures in various colors, in copper, brass or nickel, and in different actions. Some days the fish will take one finish and spurn the others. That applies to the other finishes, too. Be prepared. If one doesn't work, try another.

For plug casting for bass I like a glass rod about 6 feet long, weighing 5½ to 6 ounces, with a fast, whippy tip, and a light quadruple multiplying reel that is level winding. A waterproofed 50-yard line of braided silk or nylon and a 3-foot leader of 10-pound test complete the outfit.

Jigs. How about those times when the bass leave the shallows to get into deeper and cooler water? A good way to get them is with a jig, a dressed hook with a molded-lead head for bumping the bottom. The hook dressing varies: some are made of nylon strands, bucktail, rubber strips, or feathers, or some coarse hair such a polar bear or caribou; others are made of plastic and imitate eels or worms. Unlike plugs, wobblers, and other lures, jigs have no alluring motion of their own to attract the fish. This must be given by the fisherman. Cast into the water and let the jig sink until it hits bottom. When it does, the line will momentarily go slack. Then

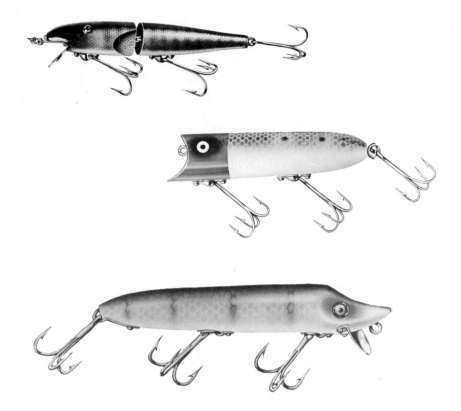

Floating-diving lures (top to bottom): Pfleuger Pal-O-Mine Minnow, Heddon 2500 Lucky 13, Heddon Vamp Spook.

quickly take in the slack and let the jig lie motionless for a short time. Then jerk it upward for about a foot and lower your rod enough to let the jig drop to the bottom again. Repeat this routine until it is time for another cast. Jigs can be fished from a drifting boat, or, if you have a fishing partner to handle the oars, from a boat that is moving slowly.

You can use about any type of rod for jig fishing—a long and stout fly rod, a spinning rod, a bait-casting rod, or a long cane pole. A stiff spinning rod of glass about 7 feet long is hard to equal. You will lose some jigs on the bottom, on rocks or underwater logs, while learning the art, but luckily they cost a lot less than plugs and most other types of artificials. Experienced jiggers cultivate an ability to judge the bottom by the "feel" of the

Deep-running lures for hot weather: Pfleuger Muskill Bait (upper left), Heddon Deep 6 (upper right), Heddon Sonic (lower left), Arbogast Lil' Bass (lower right).

jig. Almost by intuition they get to know when the jig is in the weeds or up against a rock or other obstacle. This intuitive sense, if it may be called such, is similar to that of the nymph fisherman who does not see a trout take and does not feel a hit, but strikes just the same and hooks the fish.

A good place for fishing with a jig is where the water deepens rapidly from shallows to a depth of 20 to 30 feet. Often you will find such water along or off the tip of a point of land. Approach such spots with caution. Give the boat enough headway so that it will drift for some feet to a suitable anchoring position. Don't drop the anchor into the water with a loud splash and a shower of spray. Lower it hand over hand until it reaches bottom without a bump. You should select an anchoring spot near enough to the drop-off so that you can fish it with short casts. Such casts will be effective if your approach has been stealthy and quiet. Fish the jig from shallow water to deep.

You can anchor in the shallow water near the drop-off and fish up the underwater incline instead of fishing down it. These drop-offs are fine bass holes; they have the cooler water the fish prefer in hot weather, yet are near enough to the shallows so they can reach them easily at night when on a feeding foray.

Plastic Worms.   I recently saw the report of the week's catch of bass weighing more than 4 pounds in Lake Norfolk in northern Arkansas. Of the twenty-five busters recorded all except three were caught on plastic worms. These worms are something new in game-fish lures and their success has been terrific. They come in black, pink, white, and brown. You fish them much like you do a jig, though you jerk them higher to give the dangling plastic a lifelike action, not only on the upward jerk but as the lure sinks.

In addition to the steep inclines off points, you will find similar good bass holes off rock or sand bars. If the state where you are fishing publishes a biological survey of your favorite lake, showing water depths, inclines, bars, etc., it will save you a lot of time in hunting these bass holes. Some shorelines, as shown on such maps, have water that deepens rapidly in a series of steps. Fish such water by casting into the shallows near shore, and working the jig or worm downward into deep water step by step. Watch the lure closely. If you see it stutter or pause, strike. It may be a bass. If it is a rock or snag, what of it? These lures are cheap.

Plastic Eels.   Plastic eels, preferably black in color, are also good largemouth lures. They are fished the same way as the plastic worm. A good feature of a plastic worm and eel is that it is soft and fleshlike in texture, and the fish don't detect at once that it is phony, as they do with a plug or spoon. Therefore, they will often hang on to it and try to gorge it. So when the lure is on bottom, and you get a gentle hit, give slack line and wait until the bass moves off with it. Quite likely the bass took the worm by the tail and is working up on it to take the whole lure into its mouth. This is the same procedure you use when fishing with live minnows, frogs, and a gob of nightcrawlers. Many good bass are lost by not giving them enough time to get the whole bait into their mouths. You've got to give the bass time for its getaway movement before you strike.

Pork-Rind Strips.   Bottom bumping also works fine with pork-rind strips. Use a strip about 6 inches long, with a 5/0 weedless hook through the head of the strip, and a No. 3 slender spinner attached. The pork strips are sold commercially dyed black, red, or natural. Try the different colors until you've found which color works best on that particular day. Use a spinning rod with plenty of backbone but a fast tip, and a line of 15 or 20-pound test if the water you fish has a lot of underwater stumps and other debris. Thread the line through a ½-ounce sinker and tie to it a snap swivel to prevent line twist. Fish the pork rind slowly along the bottom with a jerk at frequent intervals to raise the bait into the water about a foot, and let it drop back to bottom. This causes the pork rind to flutter on both rise and fall.

There is some difference between the way bass hit the bottom-crawling baits in shallow water and the same baits in deep water. In shallow water— that is, up to 4 feet—they hit the worm with fury and can be struck at once; while in deeper water they generally tap it gently several times before they move off with it. Perhaps the reason for this difference is because in shallow water the fish feel more exposed to danger and are anxious to gobble the delicacy and make a fast getaway.

Natural Worms.   Speaking of plastic worms brings natural worms to mind. Big nightcrawlers are fine bass takers. Use a No. 1 or No. 2 thin wire hook and thread a couple of the crawlers on the hook so that both ends of the worms are free to twist and wiggle to attract the fish. Heavy wire hooks mangle the worms when you hook them on, and you want to use worms that are lively and not half dead. For a leader attach a piece of nylon about 4 feet long, of 6-pound test. For fishing shallow water less than 6 feet deep—and it is shallow-water fishing that is the most effective for drift fishing—fasten a bobber just above the leader. Then let your boat drift and cast ahead of it, letting the bait lie until the boat is almost on it before making another cast.

In this fishing a very slow drift is advisable. If the breeze is such as to make the boat drift too rapidly, try slowing the boat with some sort of drag. A friend of mine claims good results by dragging a window sash weight behind the boat.

A bait-casting rod or spinning rod about 6 feet long is good for this type of fishing. But such extremes as a long cane pole or a fly rod may be used. The bobber, if properly adjusted, keeps the worms just off bottom, and when it sinks out of sight, sock it to the fish. Chances are that you have got a bigmouth, and they are a prize to any fisherman who loves a battle and a bending rod.

CHAPTER 20

The 100 Best Bass Lakes

IT TOOK THREE years and eight months for Wynn Davis, angling editor of *Outdoor Life,* to compile this valuable list of the best bass lakes in the United States. Two hundred expert anglers in all the states were sent questionnaires, and 107 answered, naming the best bass waters they knew of. It is quite likely that some lake not mentioned in the list will at some time show really superior fishing, but those that are named will, year in and year out, season after season, prove to be champions over the long haul. The list was published in *Outdoor Life* in July, 1958, and is so useful as to warrant republication here.

Alabama
 Bartletts Ferry Lake
 Guntersville Lake
 Jordan Lake
 Pickwick Landing Reservoir
 Wheeler Lake
 Wilson Lake

Arizona
 Apache Lake
 Lake Havasu
 Lake Mead
 Roosevelt Lake

Arkansas
 Bull Shoals Lake
 Lake Greeson
 Norfolk Lake
 Ouachita Lake

California
 Shasta Lake

Florida
 Apalachicola Chain of Lakes
 Lake George
 Lake Hatchineha
 Okefenokee Swamp Lakes
 Panasoffkee Lake

Georgia
 Lake Burton
 Lake Chatuge
 Clark Hill Lake
 Sinclair Lake
 Woodruff Lake

Iowa
 Okoboji Lake

Kentucky
Lake Cumberland
Dale Hollow Reservoir
Dewey Lake
Herrington Lake
Kentucky Lake

Louisiana
Bistineau Lake
Black Lake

Maine
Belgrade Lakes
Big Lake
East Grand Lake
Grand Falls Lake
Grand Lake
Kennebec Lakes
Pocamoonshine Lake
Schoodic Lake
Sebago Lake

Maryland (including Delaware & Virginia—Eastern shore)
Delmarva Lakes

Massachusetts
Cape Cod Lakes

Michigan
Lake Charlevoix
Lake Gogebic
Lake Huron (Thunder Bay)
Manistique Lake
Michigamme Lake
Lake Michigan (Beaver Island area)
Munuscong Lake

Minnesota
Bad Medicine Lake
Basswood Lake
Brule Lake
East Bearskin Lake
Greenwood Lake

Little Vermilion Lake
Loon Lake
Rainy Lake
Saganaga Lake
Turtle Lake

Mississippi
Grenada Lake

Missouri
Lake of the Ozarks
Lake Taneycomo

Nevada
Mohave Lake

New Hampshire
Squam Lake

New Jersey
Swartswood Lake

New York
Black Lake
Lake Chautauqua
Oneida Lake
Lake Ontario (near Thousand Islands)

North Carolina
Fontana Reservoir
Hiwassee Reservoir
Lake Lure
Nantahala Reservoir
Outer Banks Pond (between Kill Devil & Nags Head)
Lake Santeetlah

Ohio
Clendening Lake
Indian Lake
Lake Erie (Port Clinton, Sandusky Bay areas)

Oklahoma
Lake of the Cherokees
Lake Murray

Rhode Island
Flat River Reservoir
South Carolina
Lake Greenwood
Lake Murray
Santee-Cooper area
Tennessee
Center Hill Lake
Reelfoot Lake
Watts Bar Lake
Texas
Lake Texoma
Possum Kingdom Lake
Lake Whitney

Vermont
Lake Memphremagog
Virginia
Lake Drummond
Kerr Reservoir
Washington
Regulating Reservoir
Wisconsin
Balsam Lake
Chippewa Flowage
Lac Court Oreilles
Squirrel Lake

CHAPTER 21

Atlantic and Landlocked Salmon, and Grayling

ATLANTIC SALMON

THE ATLANTIC SALMON (*Salmo salar*) for many years has been called the "King of Game Fishes." Pound for pound it could be argued that a fresh-run steelhead of the Pacific Coast has just as good a claim to that proud title as the salmon. But the Atlantic salmon is a glamor fish which in North America has a rather limited range, and for which there is little or no inexpensive fishing. Relatively few anglers ever have the opportunity of fishing for it, though the dedicated efforts being made by the state of Maine give hope that salmon fishing may become somewhat less exclusive. Newfoundland, Labrador, Quebec, New Brunswick, Nova Scotia, and Maine have practically a monopoly on this grand fish, though an occasional straggler is reported in Massachusetts and Connecticut. Once the salmon was abundant in New England rivers and even farther south in New York and New Jersey. The Delaware River was probably the southern limit of their range.

Times have changed for the salmon and not for the better. Jordan and Evermann's *American Food and Game Fishes,* published in 1902, has this to say: "Nova Scotia, New Brunswick, and Maine have many salmon rivers. New Hampshire, Massachusetts, and Connecticut, a very few good ones." That was true at the time it was written, undoubtedly, but try to find any salmon today in the last three states mentioned! Burgeoning populations and industrialization, with the inevitable dams and heavy pollution, have made the rare salmon that sometimes appears in those once "very good ones" a matter of news. A few years ago Maine's Dennys River offered about the only angling chance for salmon in that state. Now, however, a vigorous campaign on stream improvement is being carried out in that state which is showing encouraging results. Dams that prevented the Atlantic salmon from going upstream to ancestral spawning redds have been removed or equipped with fish ladders. Regular stocking is being done. So now the Dennys, Pleasant, Narraguagus, and Machias are yielding increasing catches to the sport fisherman, and the Sheepscot shows promise. It also has been stocked in the Aroostook, Penobscot, Orland, Piscataquis, Saco, and Tunk Rivers. Thus a highly prized fish that not long ago was threatened with extinction in the United States seems to be fighting its way back.

The Atlantic salmon is not confined in its range to North America. It also occurs in fishable numbers in Greenland, Iceland, Norway, Sweden, England, Ireland, Russia, and Spain. Today the fishing rights on European salmon rivers are highly prized and bring large sums. That is also true of most of the finer salmon rivers in Quebec and New Brunswick. In Quebec several salmon rivers have been reserved by the province for public fishing, with special daily rod fees and the number of permits restricted. Some water in Newfoundland is open to public fishing, and various commercial sporting camps have rights on stretches of salmon rivers open to their guests. Nova Scotia and New Brunswick have resisted the temptation to lease their salmon rivers, and have saved them for sport fishermen who can fish them by purchasing the proper licenses.

The Atlantic salmon is silvery in color with a darker back which may be a steely blue or brownish. The head, body, and fins are spotted with black X-shaped marks. An anadromous fish, it is likely to spend about half of the year in the ocean putting on weight by feeding heavily on shrimp, crabs, herring, other small fishes, and eels.

For many years fishermen have argued about whether the salmon ever eat while on their runs into fresh water. The proponents of the theory that the fish don't, cite as proof the fact that rarely is any food to be found in the salmon's stomach, whether it is caught on the fly or in a commercial fisherman's net. My friend the late Fred Hollender, a skilled salmon fisherman who spent much time fishing for them in New Brunswick, was convinced that they do feed in fresh water. He maintained that their digestive juices are so strong that any food taken in is quickly digested and dissolved. Some scientists state that a salmon with food in its stomach, when taken on a hook or captured in a net will at once disgorge the food in its fright.

Salmon enter a river on their spawning run when the water is warm

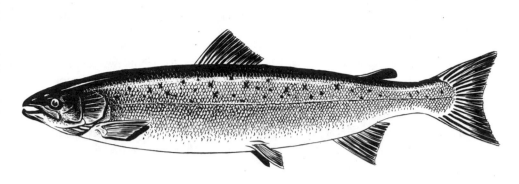

Atlantic Salmon

enough to please them, and their time of entry varies from the South to the North. Thus though the first run may come in Maine in early May, the peak fishing in the Machias is likely to be found in mid-June to mid-July. Several runs may occur during the season. It is said that there have been runs as late as October in New Brunswick's famous Miramichi.

Spawning is in the fall and normally when the water temperature drops to about 50 degrees. The young fish run down to the ocean at about their second or third spring. They return as grilse, when they may weigh a maximum of 6 pounds. Grilse are splendid fighters, often making spectacular leaps. The average weight of adult salmon runs from about 10 pounds up to 20 pounds. The record of one taken on rod and line is held by a magnificent specimen of 79 pounds, caught in Norway in 1928.

One aspect of salmon fishing that I don't like is that so much of it is done from a canoe. You don't have much freedom of action in such fishing, and you feel cramped casting from a sitting position. For that reason I remember with pleasure a salmon river I fished in Nova Scotia which was like a large brook, where I could wade or fish from the bank as I preferred. In wading you have a sense of oneness with the water and are master of your actions and not governed by the whims of a crank canoe.

Fortunately for the good of the sport, fishing for Atlantic salmon is almost universally restricted by law to artificial flies. Despite the belief of many fishermen that the salmon does not feed while in fresh water, and that it rises to the fly from curiosity or annoyance, the fact remains that in British salmon waters bait fishing with prawns, a form of shrimp life, is an effective way to take salmon.

Tackle.   Good tackle for North American salmon includes a fly rod either of split bamboo or glass, from 9 to 10 feet long, and weighing from 7 ounces to 8¾ ounces. This is for waters where the fish average from 10 to 15 pounds. For the bigger salmon rivers, where the fish may run up to 35 to 40 pounds, a two-handed rod is preferred by many. These rods run from 11 feet long up to 14½ feet, and weigh from 10⅞ ounces up to 20¾ ounces. I would prefer to lose a salmon rather than toil all day with a two-handed rod weighing 20 ounces.

For leaders, a 9-foot length is preferred. These are available in tapers running in test from 7 pounds at the point to 17 pounds. They are graded as extra light, light, medium, heavy, and extra heavy. The reel should have a capacity of 40 yards of salmon line plus 100 yards of backing. A good salmon reel may be had in weights varying with the size of the rod, from 5¾-ounce up to 12-ounce. The heavier weight is of course suited to the heavy two-handed rod. A tapered line should be used in a size to fit the rod. These tapers run up to such belly weights as B and A, the tapers being described as GBF and GAF.

Good wet-fly patterns for salmon include the Black Dose, Durham Ranger, Dusty Miller, Jock Scott, Mar Lodge, Night Hawk, Silver Doctor, Silver Gray, Thunder and Lightning, and Wilkinson. The typical American streamer patterns—Black Ghost, Gray Ghost, and Dark Tiger—are also effective. Good sizes are 2, 4, 6, and 8. Good dry-fly patterns are the well-known Wulff varieties of Brown, Black, Gray, White, Grizzly, and Royal. The dry flies are most effective in clear and low water.

Fly Fishing for Salmon.   In fishing for salmon with either wet or dry flies, the same techniques are employed as in trout fishing. Timing is important. Salmon not only wait for favorable water temperatures before they come into a river, but also plenty of water. If a river is lower than normal they are likely to wait for a good rain to raise the water before entering. Also, a river may have only one good run, while others may have several. It is therefore advisable to have the proprietor of the camp where you plan to stay wire you when the salmon are in.

Generally the salmon that will take a fly is fresh-run, which means it is difficult to get those salmon that have been in the river for some days to rise. Sometimes it is possible to see clearly in a pool a number of good fish which stick to their positions and refuse to rise to any fly pattern no matter how skillfully it is cast. It is likely that these fish have been in the river for some days and are waiting for higher water before they go upstream. When the fish are lying deep, it is a good plan to soak the fly in a sinking preparation to get it down to them. Then work the fly up and down in movements of a foot or so.

If a salmon rises in deep water, it is a mistake to cast directly to the spot. Apply the same method used in trout fishing: cast the fly above the spot of the rise and let it drift down to the location of the rise. The trout fisherman, accustomed to the swift rises of most trout, is apt to miss the rise of a salmon. Be deliberate and wait for the salmon to turn, after it rises on its way back to the depths. Also, instead of striking upward as is the tendency, strike sidewise. An upward strike is liable to pull the fly out of the fish's mouth. Some expert salmon fishermen make no strike at all, letting the fish do its own hooking as it makes its turn, merely keeping a taut line.

But a fisherman accustomed to striking at a trout's rise, as I am, finds it hard to school himself to remain passive when he sees the rise of a salmon. I have found it difficult to make the momentary pause, my inclination being to strike at once. The salmon I have lost have almost invariably been due to striking too soon. Also, since in my eagerness to hook firmly one of these magnificent fish, I too often have struck with a heavy hand. I have had to teach myself to strike from the reel. This has been an improvement, and I have broken fewer leaders. But from my own experience, and watching other salmon fishermen, I am convinced that the man who keeps his nerves under control, waits on the rise for the fish to turn, and then strikes with a firm but not too strong hand, is the one who takes the most fish.

When the water is high and rather colored in spring, you can use heavier leaders than would be advisable in lower and clearer water later in the season. Thus, on high and colored water, with the heavier leader and a light and responsive rod, you can strike hard at a rise. Your leader can stand it, and you will sink the barb into the fish's mouth, if you are lucky and the point of the hook is not directed at a bone instead of a cartilage.

If a rising salmon misses the fly on a rise, it can be induced to rise several times again, if the casts are careful and well delivered. But once a salmon detects the nonedible feathers and hackle of the fly, and the angler misses the strike, it is doubtful that the fish will rise again.

Let the hooked salmon run, though under control if humanly possible. The more the fish runs against the play of the rod, the sooner it tires and is ready for the net. Keep as much pressure upon it as your tackle will stand. If the fish seems to want to fight in top water, try and get it to go under by easing up a little on the rod. It is usual to lose more hooked fish at the surface than in deep water. Sometimes a fish will wrench its body from side to side in the top water and tear away the hook. At other times it will leap and free the hook on its return to the water.

To the fisherman who has hooked a salmon, it is a relief when the fish runs upstream, for he knows that then the fish is not only fighting the rod but the current and will tire more quickly. Try and keep below the fish and if possible prevent it from running downstream past you. Your guide, should you have one, on seeing the fish turn and race downstream, will probably rush into the water and by vigorous splashing try to scare it back. Sometimes a stone hurled ahead of the fish will turn it. If the salmon stops running, and sulks on the bottom, a stone thrown at it will often put it into action again. Remember that a sulking fish is resting and recovering its strength, and that should be prevented. It often happens that a salmon will sulk because the fisherman has played it too gently. Twanging a taut line on the sulking salmon is sometimes effective, also, or rapping the rod butt. The raps are literally telephoned to the fish over the taut line and leader and it doesn't like this one bit.

If the pattern of the fly you are fishing stirs no interest, change to another that is markedly different. If you have on a large fly, try another that is smaller. This is sometimes effective as the fish are pretty choosy. If a salmon has risen to your fly, and you felt a momentary resistance before the fly comes free, examine that fly. You may find a wing or some hackle twisted under the bend of the hook. Then shorten the wings or hackle so that the barb of the hook will be free to take hold. Also, the tangling of the feathers in the bend of the hook will give the fly an unnatural drift.

LANDLOCKED SALMON

The landlocked salmon was once thought to be a subspecies, *Salmo salar sebago,* of the sea-run fish, but today the American Fisheries Society lists it with the Atlantic salmon under the scientific name *Salmo salar.* Because it is known to decline access to the sea, this fish is "landlocked" by choice, not by physical barrier. The minor changes in its physical appearance are doubtless due to its changed environment. It is smaller than the Atlantic salmon and has larger scales. Its back may be either black or blue-green, the sides are silvery, and it has black X marks on the upper body. It also has larger eyes and longer fins. Its food primarily is smelts, insects, and occasionally other small fishes. It runs up tributary streams in the fall to spawn, then re-

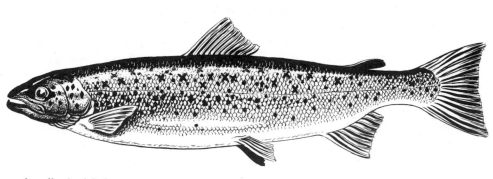

Landlocked Salmon

turns to the lake. The smelt also run up streams to spawn, but in the spring, and landlocks follow this run to gorge upon them.

The range of this grand game fish originally was restricted to four lake regions in Maine—the Sebago Lake area, Green Lake, Scbcc Lake, and the Schoodic Lake-St. Croix River basin. Its outstanding qualities as a game fish have caused it to be stocked in suitable lakes in many parts of Maine as well as in New Hampshire, Vermont, and New York. It has taken hold in a number of these northern New England waters and several in New York state, but many other such attempts have failed. It is particular in its requirements. It must have cold, deep, well-oxygenated water, with cold tributary streams for its spawning. Also, it is noteworthy that those lakes in which it survives have abundant smelt. Those Maine rivers in which it is found throughout the season also have access to lakes which satisfy this salmon's requirements.

In the spring, after the ice is out, smelt and other small fishes in a landlocked-salmon lake school in the shallows. They are followed there by the salmon. They stay in the shallows for about two weeks. When the smelt get the spawning urge and run up tributary streams, the salmon follow them, and when the smelt return to the lake after spawning, the salmon follow them and stay until the following spring.

Lures for Landlocks. In shallow-water lakes these fish will take silver-bodied streamers and other flies which resemble minnows. They will also take such spinning-rod lures as silver wobblers and spoons. In rivers small salmon flies and spinning-rod lures are effective.

I have trolled for landlocked salmon in northern New Hampshire lakes, using salmon flies, with success. These fish are jumpers, often making several spectacular leaps. I have used my 10-foot split-bamboo fly rod, which weighs 5½ ounces, with a 7½-foot leader tapered to 1X. When they go down into deep water, as the surface water warms, you can troll for them as you would lake trout, with a metal line and wobbling spoons of silver finish. As may be expected, when hooked in the depths on such heavy tackle they do not give as spectacular play as in the spring when they are on the surface.

Landlocked salmon taken on rod and line will average from 1½ to 3½ pounds. The largest on record was caught in Maine's Sebago Lake in 1907 and weighed 22 pounds, 8 ounces. It is noteworthy that this lake, which gave the tag *Sebago* to the salmon's scientific name, still produces the heaviest fish.

A similar landlocked salmon is the ouananiche (*Salmo salar ouananiche*), the Canadian landlock, found in the Upper Saguenay River in Quebec and its tributaries, Lake St. John and its tributaries, and some rivers that empty into the St. Lawrence River. In physical appearance it closely resembles the *Sebago,* but averages smaller, rarely going to 8 pounds, and usually weighing 2 or 3 pounds. The leaping qualities of this fish are spectacular, and probably are due to the swift and tumultuous waters which it favors. The tackle and methods used on this lively fish are the same as those for the *Sebago.*

ARCTIC GRAYLING

The Arctic grayling (*Thymallus signifer*) is a game fish with so restricted a range in the United States that relatively few sport fishermen are acquainted with it. Once the fish was abundant in the cold rivers of northern Michigan, but as a consequence of deforestation and siltation, the rivers warmed up, and by 1900 the grayling had become scarce. By 1930 it was extinct in this area.

The early lumbermen were under little or no conservation con'rol. They talked largely of "inexhaustible" forests, skinned the ground bare of trees, dumped tree tops and forest litter into the streams, and left no tree fringe along the banks to shade the water and help hold back with their roots the floods of spring. They often left a biological desert.

The natural range of the grayling in the United States is in the Upper Missouri above the Great Falls. It is found in Alaska and Canada, in a few waters of Montana, and in northern Wyoming. In 1960, when fishing the Madison River for trout, I caught a grayling on a dry fly. I studied it with

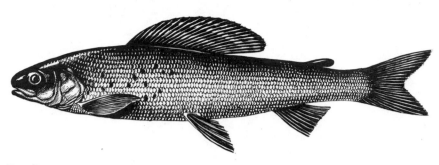

Grayling

as much interest and curiosity as I would have had it been an Atlantic salmon. It was dotted with purple spots ringed with green, and the lower part had rosy lines. The sides were silvery with a purple flush, the head small with a bronzy-blue color. There were also small dark spots on the body. Relative to the size of the fish, the dorsal fin was huge when I pulled it to its full height. The average grayling taken in the United States outside of Alaska is only 10 to 12 inches long, with perhaps 2½ pounds as top weight.

Michigan recently has been trying to bring the grayling back into the state's water by stocking it in a lake where it will not be in competition with other fish. It also has been introduced into several lakes in the Northwest and into Yosemite Park.

The grayling's habitat is cold and clear streams with sandy or gravel beds. Since its natural food is insects, it is a fine game for dry- or wet-fly fishing, though it is partial to such natural baits as grasshoppers, crickets, and angleworms. Grayling have small mouths, so use small flies, a No. 12 or smaller. They like a fly with a plump body of an iridescent cast, such as a Gray Hackle with peacock body, or a Coachman. They also are partial to colorful patterns such as the Grizzly King and Queen of the Waters.

They spawn on gravel beds in April or May, depending upon when the water is at a proper temperature.

The grayling puts up a scrappy fight and will jump. If you are dry-fly fishing, use a leader from 9 to 12 feet long tapered to a tip of 1- or 2-pound test. As these fish run rather small, the fly rod should be light— not more than 4 ounces—permitting you to meet them on equal terms with tackle suited to their size, which will allow them to show their mettle.

CHAPTER 22

The Pikes

ALL THE MEMBERS of the pike family, like Cassius, have a "lean and hungry look." Whether it is the chain pickerel, which is big at 5 pounds, or the muskie, which occasionally weighs over 50 pounds, all members of the tribe are slim in proportion to their length, have long, flattish heads, and a sinister appearance. I have never brought one to the boat without feeling they are malevolent and evil.

The pikes all resemble one another, but there is one infallible way to tell them apart: the pickerel's cheeks and gill covers are scaled all over, the northern pike's cheeks are completely scaled but its gill covers are scaled on the upper half only, and the muskellunge's cheeks and gill covers have no scales on the lower half.

CHAIN PICKEREL

The chain pickerel (*Esox niger*), sometimes called eastern pickerel or pike, is common east and south of the Alleghenies, from Maine to Florida and Alabama, and in Louisiana, Arkansas, and Tennessee. It is green with a golden tinge, but lighter on the lower part of the body. There is a series of dark markings on its sides, which resembles the unjoined links of a chain and from which its name is derived. Like other members of the pike family, it is gluttonous and feeds on smaller fishes and frogs. It frequents clear weedy lakes, ponds, and placid streams. Its average size is from about 15 inches up to 2 feet. The record weight of one caught on rod and line was 9 pounds, 3 ounces, taken from Medford Lakes, New Jersey, in 1957. It is a favorite with ice fishermen, particularly in New England.

As a game fish the pickerel is only fair, and that is a proper rating for

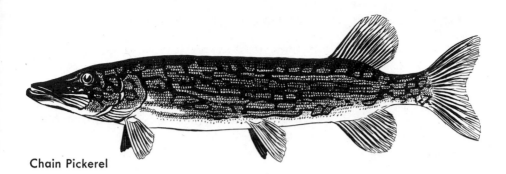

Chain Pickerel

it as food. It makes a thrilling rush to seize the bait, a pretty good run after it has taken it, will sometimes jump, but soon quits.

It is caught by bait and spinner casting, still-fishing with minnows, frogs, or nightwalkers, trolling, and skittering. It primarily is a fish of shallow water and loves weed beds. It will take an artificial fly, particularly those patterns which are a gaudy red, or red and white, such as a Scarlet Ibis, a Parmachene Belle, or a Royal Coachman. Skittering has always been a popular form of pickerel fishing. Today it is not practiced as much as it used to be. The fun of bait casting and spinner fishing has relegated it to the background, yet it is a deadly and fascinating method of catching almost any game fish in shallow water.

The equipment for skittering is cheap and coarse: a long cane pole, a stout cotton or linen line double the length of the pole, and a package of 3/0 hooks. Tie the line at about its middle to the tip of the pole, fasten one end to the butt of your pole, tie the hook to the running end of your line and you are ready to go.

Your bait can be a minnow, a strip of pork rind tapered from about ¾ inch at the head to a point at its tail, a chunk of pork, or a frog. If you like less primitive lures you can use a noisy surface plug like the chugger. With this rig, you skip the lure over the top of the water off weed beds and in pockets among lily pads.

BARRED PICKEREL

The pickerel has a small relative, the barred pickerel (*Esox americanus*), which gave my boyhood friends and me good sport. We called it the brook pickerel. Those we caught averaged 9 to 10 inches, though it is said to reach 12 inches. It is green, has a black bar below the eye and curved dark bars along its sides. It has a range from Maine to Florida and Alabama. Its gill covers and cheeks are entirely scaled. It is found in placid lowland streams, small brooks, and swampy pools.

We would kill a small bullfrog, cut off its hind legs, skin them, and fasten one to a No. 4 snelled hook. Then, stealing quietly to a dark little pool under the alders, we would jig the frog's leg up and down. Being skinned, the leg would be easily visible in the dark water. Before long we would see the dark snout of a little pickerel clamped onto the frog's leg. We would wait to give the hungry fish a little time to gorge the leg and make off with it, then give the alder pole a heave and bring out the twisting and turning captive. We claimed these miniature pikes were good to eat despite their size and boniness. I remember them with nostalgic affection for we could find them in almost any small marshy stream and they rarely refused to take that skinned frog's leg.

NORTHERN PIKE

The northern pike (*Esox lucius*) rates next to the muskellunge as the prized member of the pike family. It has a number of aliases, including great northern pike, common pike, Great Lakes pike, pickerel, snake, and jackfish. Its range includes the Connecticut River in New England, eastern New York, all over Canada, Alaska, the Ohio Valley, Great Lakes, Missouri, and Nebraska. It is olive-green with white or yellow belly. It has short, oval spots, single and not joined, on its body. The lower half of the gill cover is without scales. It is a gross feeder, gorging on fishes and leeches. It is cannibalistic. Some anglers have had the experience of hooking a small member of the family weighing a pound or more, and having it seized viciously by a larger northern. Its habitat is slow-moving streams, and shallow, weedy water in lakes, but it is even found in cold, clear, rocky rivers suited to trout. The average run of these fishes is about 5 pounds and under, but they grow larger in waters having plenty of food. The largest of authentic record to be taken on rod and line weighed 46 pounds, 2 ounces, caught in New York's Sacandaga Reservoir in 1940. Because of its size and its fair game qualities, the northern is a favorite fish with anglers in Wisconsin and Minnesota and that part of Ontario lying north of those states.

There are two schools of thought among fishermen as to the merits of this fish. One school defends it passionately as a worthy game fish and a tasty food. The other school decries its gameness as a fighter and its taste

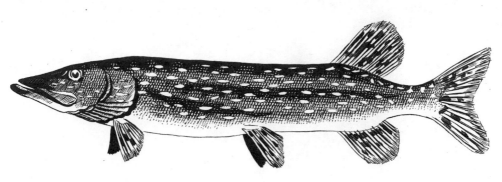

Northern Pike

as a food and calls it a "snake." In my opinion neither school is justified in its claims and the truth lies somewhere in between. I would class the fish as "fair" in both qualities, reckoning its gameness on a pound for pound basis.

Admittedly, the northern has suffered somewhat from the widespread use of heavy tackle by most fishermen. Spinning fishermen, with their lighter tackle, get a lot more fun out of these fish than do bait casters. So if the fisherman equips himself wth a 7-foot glass spinning rod, a salt-water spinning reel, and a 10-pound-test Stren line, he will be well equipped for the average northerns, which run between 3 and 6 pounds. This rig handles well lures of ½ to 1 ounce. As northerns have sharp teeth, you should attach a 10-inch wire leader of 20-pound test between lure and line. Where the pike run big, you will need a 20-pound line with the same wire leader.

Northerns are found in about the same type of water as largemouth bass. Look for them in beds of lily pads, over underwater weed patches, among stumps, and under tangles of driftwood. The smaller fish will be near shore in small weedy bays, the same sort of water in which you will find pickerel in the East. The larger fish will be in deeper water but not at the depths at which you will find largemouth bass in the heat of summer. About the minimum depth for largemouths in the heat of summer will be around 20 feet, which is just about the depth limit of large pike, which generally haunt water from 10 to 20 feet deep. The best time of the year for the true busters is in late season, October and November, but May and June are fine months for run-of-the-mill northerns, just as they are for pickerel.

A northern pike rockets out of the Winnipeg River in a last, desperate attempt to shake the hook from its mouth.

After a seesaw battle, angler brings fish boatside so his partner can get a net under it.

A lunker! October and November are the best months for big babies like this one. *Manitoba Dept. of Industry and Commerce.*

The color, type, and style of the lure doesn't make much difference to this ravenous fish, which takes less skill to catch than any of our popular game fish. About anything with action will get its attention in shallow waters, except in those months of July, August, and the first half of September, when it takes to deeper water. Cast close to stumps, logs, pockets in the lily pads, and weed patches. When a pike hits the lure, sock it to him. That hook is up against a tough, bony mouth, which explains why a pike often seems to strike hard enough to hook himself but gets away.

If the pike have taken to the deeper water—from 10 to 20 feet—fish for them with jigs or plastic worms (discussed in Chapter 19). You will find good water for this fishing off rocky bars and points of land where the water deepens abruptly.

Often a northern will fool you. You think you have it licked, for it stops fighting and follows the resisting rod toward the boat. But the sight of the boat has an effect on the fish like a piece of paper blowing before a skittish horse: it is shocked into violent action and may break off. To prevent this, jerk the rod upward when the pike is faking defeat, and sting him into action away from the boat. Wait until the fish turns on its side before you get out that landing net and prepare to scoop it in. Almost any game fish lies on its side after it has been beaten in a vigorous battle.

MUSKELLUNGE

The muskellunge (*Esox masquinongy*) reaches the largest weight of any of the pikes and is the glamor fish among them. Its range is from the Great Lakes area northward into Canada, and includes Ohio, Pennsylvania, New York, Tennessee, and Kentucky. It has no scales on the lower half of the gill cover. It may be green, green with a brown tinge, or grayish. It has dark markings on body and fins. It is a flesh eater, preying on fish and frogs primarily. Its chosen waters are clear, cool, and weedy lakes and rivers. There are two subspecies, the Chautauqua and northern, which differ chiefly in their coloring but are similar in their habits. It is a doughty, stubborn fighter—a grand game fish. Jordan and Evermann in *American Food and Game Fishes,* state that the muskie reaches a length of 8 feet and a weight of 100 pounds or more, but the record taken on rod and line is 69 pounds, 15 ounces, caught on the New York side of the St. Lawrence River in 1957.

As food the muskie is the best of the pike family and rates among the

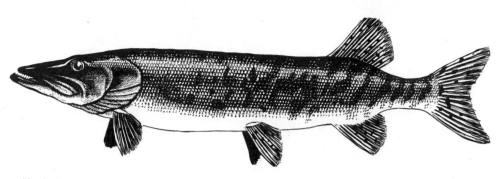

Muskellunge

finest of the game fishes. In the opinion of some its flesh is equal in flavor to that of the salmon, which is high praise indeed.

Spawning is in the spring, generally in April and May. It is a "lone wolf" among fishes, probably because of its voracious habits. It requires such a large amount of food that it must of necessity be solitary.

Favorite methods of fishing for muskies are trolling and casting. A few fishermen try for them with light tackle, which means rod, reel, and line suited for largemouths in waters where the fish may run up to a maximum of 7 to 10 pounds. That is stunt stuff and not to be recommended. Muskies run so large that your tackle should show respect for their size, strength, and vicious disposition. But that doesn't mean that the muskie fisherman should go to the other extreme and equip himself with tackle better suited to giant tuna.

A heavy-duty spinning rod, about 7 feet long and weighing around 8 ounces, and which will handle lures ¼ to ¾ ounce will subdue a big muskie if used properly. A spinning reel with a capacity to hold 100 yards of 10-pound-test monofilament line, and a good drag, should complement the rig. Attach a 10-inch braided-wire leader to the end of the line. You probably have seen the huge plugs offered as muskie lures and question the suitability of this rig to use with such plugs. But big plugs are not needed in muskie fishing. They take fish, it's true, but much smaller lures do just as well and even better over much of the season.

For lures the fisherman should get a supply of spinner-bucktail combinations. The spinners should be sizes ranging from No. 3 to No. 5, and be either all gold or all silver color. A particularly effective lure of this type is a No. 4 gold spinner with a No. 2 treble hook equipped with

Spinner-bucktail combinations are lethal muskie lures from August to October (from top): Heddon Whispurr, Heddon Spinfish, Heddon Bear Hair Hep.

white bucktail. As spinners can twist a line into an unholy mess a small ball-bearing swivel should be used on this rig. This hook-up is most effective from early season until about the first of August. During August, September, and October the bait caster can have fun with big spinner-bucktail combinations, big underwater plugs, and lures which imitate large wounded minnows.

For bait casting with these larger lures use a heavy-duty glass rod about 5½ feet long. Heavy plugs aren't suited to one-arm casting, so the rod butt should be long enough to permit use of both hands. The reel should be level winding, hold 100 yards of 25-pound-test line, and be made to prevent backlash.

As in fishing for northerns and pickerel, fish the weed beds. The tops of the weeds may come to within a few inches of the surface or they may be as much as 8 feet deep. Fish over the tops of these weed beds. Also cast off their borders, letting the lure sink and then retrieving.

Along in October artificial lures take a back seat as muskie catchers. Never dainty feeders and always hungry, they want meat—and suckers are their favorites. Use a sucker large enough to give a bass fisherman hysterics—about 10 or 11 inches long. Doll up that sucker with a belly band. Take a piece of stout line, and tie it around the sucker's body right back of the gills. Take the loose end of the line, bring it forward, wrap it tightly around the sucker's snout, tie that loop to make it stay put, then carry back the running end of the line and tie it securely to the loop back of the gills. Tie a large hook to the body loop, a 1/0, 2/0, or 3/0. Then tie your fishing line to the eye of the hook. Look for the muskies in shallow water close to shore, off weed beds and above them, near sunken logs and rock ledges. Cast under the branches of trees that extend over the water.

If a muskie strikes, give it plenty of time to gorge the sucker. Often it will take a lot of time before deciding to move off with the bait. When

Method of tying hook to sucker as described in text.

Pfleuger 5" Mustang, adjustable to any depth, is typical of the large, deep-running plugs for use on muskies.

it does, strike hard. Its mouth is bony and it takes a sharp hook and plenty of strength to sink that hook into it.

The best method of landing a muskie is with a big aluminum-handled landing net. Don't expect a muskie with every cast. Muskie fishing is a sport for those with patience. Many men fish for them for years before they land one.

WALLEYE

The walleye (*Stizostedian vitreum vitreum*) is included here because it is called a pike, though it is not a true pike. It has as many aliases as a confidence man—pike-perch, jack salmon, blue pike, green pike, yellow pike, yellow pickerel, dore, dory, pickerel, walleye, and yellow pike-perch. It has a wide distribution from waters entering Hudson Bay east to New Brunswick, southward and west of the Appalachians to West Virginia into Alabama, and west to Arkansas and Iowa. It is common in the Great Lakes region and abundant in Lake Erie. Though found in rivers it prefers clear and moderately deep lakes with hard bottoms of rock, gravel, sand, or clay. It is a fish eater of voracious habits and when in inshore waters feeds readily upon crawfish.

This fish is a dark olive-green with faint, brassy, oblique bars; its belly and lower fins are tinged with pink, with the two fins on the back mottled. However, the color markings vary considerably according to the water from which it is taken. It is one of the best flavored of our fishes. The average size of the walleye caught by fishermen is from 2 to 5 pounds. The record caught on rod and line is held by a specimen weighing 25 pounds, caught in Old Hickory Lake, Tennessee. Its large eyes, which look as though the fish were half or wholly blind, give it its name, and its strong, sharp teeth bespeak the character of its food.

Spawning is in early spring. If in a lake fed by large streams, the walleyes will run into them to spawn. If streams are lacking, they like shallows near deep water, such as along bars, where the bottom is hard and clean.

The best fishing for walleyes comes in spring or fall. Effective lures include small plugs or spinners baited with minnows or worms, trolled in deep water; sinking plugs; the good old June Bug spinner baited with worms; and showy spoons in various colors. The best time of the day is between sunset and midnight, when bats are fluttering swiftly around and the bullfrogs are bellowing.

During hot weather, walleyes in rivers like to lie off the mouths of cold entering streams, provided they can find relatively deep water there. In lakes they like to hang around rocky, gravelly, or hard sand-bars. All things considered, trolling is the best way to catch them, for these fish are wanderers. Live minnows or worms behind an attractor spoon, fished near bottom behind a boat, is a good method. If you are using a live minnow without a spoon, move slowly. If you are using an attractor spoon, step up the movement to avoid continual snagging. When you catch a walleye it pays to troll back and forth over the same stretch of water. You may have come upon a concentration of fish. If the state has published a topographical map of the water you fish, it will help you greatly by showing water depths, bars, etc.

In the spring walleyes are likely to be found near shoals and bars looking for minnows. You can fish such water by anchoring quietly at casting

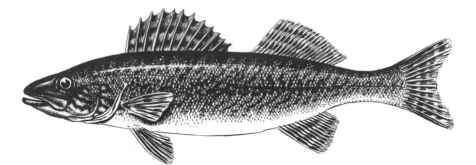

Walleye

distance. Minnows, crippled-minnow plugs, and wobbling spoons that dart and wobble when retrieved are good casting lures here. In hot weather, when the fish lie deep, try several hooks in tandem behind a flashing spoon and a sinker a yard ahead of the hooks. Put a nightwalker on each hook. As you troll slowly with this rig the sinker drags along the bottom, with the worms riding a few inches above it.

I have found that in summer fishing can be good during the day if the sky is heavily overcast or a light rain is falling. If the day is sunny and the sky clear, wait until sunset.

CHAPTER 23

The Panfishes

THE PANFISHES ARE the most widely distributed of our North American fishes. Almost all of our warm-water streams, lakes, and ponds have one or more varieties. Generally it takes neither skill nor fancy tackle to catch them, nor long and expensive trips to find them. Given water that is not badly polluted, and a fair amount of food—aquatic insects, small crustaceans, minnows, grubs, and worms—they flourish like the green bay tree. Prolific spawners, they withstand much harder fishing than most of the game fishes. In fact, most panfish waters tend to be underfished, the result being overpopulation and small size. Many farm ponds suffer from this condition. Hard fishing in such waters would result in catches of larger fish and more sport in the end.

For our purposes in this chapter we will consider only the typical panfishes, all of which are excellent food, and which are to be found in every section of the country. They are the bluegill, yellow perch, crappie, catfish, and white bass.

BLUEGILL

The bluegill is the most representative of the sunfishes, which include the red-breasted bream, scarlet sunfish, long-eared, red-spotted, McKay's, shellcracker, common sunfish, and red-eared. Scientifically the bluegill is known as *Lepomis macrochirus*. Locally it has a number of aliases such as blue bream, blue sunfish, copper-nosed sunfish, and dollardee. Its original range was in the area of the Great Lakes, in the Missippi Valley, from western New York and Pennsylvania west to Iowa and Missouri, and from Minnesota to Florida and the Rio Grande. But its value as a sporty food

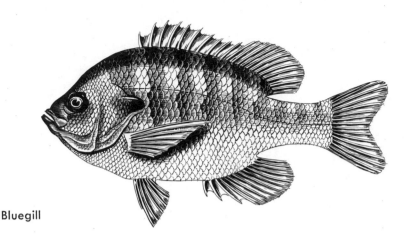

Bluegill

fish has resulted in its being introduced into many waters outside of its original range so that now it is present in many ponds, lakes, and streams on the Pacific Coast and in New England. It does well in quiet streams and even better in ponds and lakes. It is one of the most popular of fishes for stocking farm ponds which, during the past twenty years, have become legion. For instance, Iowa alone has more than 21,000.

The bluegill is olive-green on the back, paler on the sides, with bluish cheeks. The gill cover (opercle) has a dark flap, which, in one color or another, is the trademark of the sunfish family.

One reason why the bluegill is so popular among farm-pond owners as well as fishermen is that it is the largest of the panfishes, reaching a weight of about 1½ pounds and a length of more than a foot. A bluegill of that size puts up a fine fight on a fly rod, matching many game fish of equal weight. Taken on a light rod it presents its chunky body side on to the angler, which considerably increases its resistance. Anyone who has eaten a freshly caught bluegill will agree that it is the best tasting of all the panfishes, a little superior even to the yellow perch. Its flesh is not mushy, but firm and flaky, with a flavor all its own. The biggest on record, taken on rod and line, weighed 4¾ pounds and was caught in Alabama.

Another virtue of this broadsided sunfish that adds to its popularity is that it is not a seasonal fish. It feeds in spring, summer, autumn, and winter, and it is one of the popular fishes for ice fishing. It takes the bait well throughout the entire year, even during the hot months, when so many fishes are choosy and hard to take. It is not at all particular about bait and will accept about anything within its size range. Angleworms are the best all-round bait, but grubs, gallworms, grasshoppers, crickets, cut bait, bits of shellfish, and even little minnows are good for the larger blue-gills. And it will take a small spoon with a small strip of pork rind on the hook.

The bluegill travels in schools, so when you catch one stick around, for there surely are others to be caught. If you are in an anchored boat, avoid noise such as rattling oars or tackle box. Seek a location just off a patch of bottom weeds in 5 to 15 feet of water. Do not neglect the heaps of brush so often found in ponds and lakes, open spots among the lily pads, emergent or sunken stumps, around the piles supporting a bridge or dock. During the heat of the day this sunnie likes deeper water or the shade of bridges or docks.

Along toward evening the bluegill comes into shallower water, and then the fly fisherman can have rare sport. Look among the weeds near shore and in coves. If there is a good bluegill population present, you are likely to see miniature rings on the water. Bluegills are rising, not with the eager and emphatic splash of a trout or bass, but with an audible gurgle. The many little rises show that here is a school ready to take a wet or dry fly. Cast a fly over the ring in the water that tells of a feeding sunnie. If a dry fly, let it rest motionless for a moment, then with a little twitch of the rod tip give the fly a movement to resemble a struggling insect. Then retrieve slowly with the hand-twist. If you have been quiet in your approach, chances are that there will be a little splash and you are fast to a bluegill. Your fish is not likely to be a jumper. Rather, it bores for the bottom like a brook trout.

For dry flies I like the Coachman and Black Gnat, particularly the former at dusk when its white wings are readily seen. I prefer No. 10 or No. 12. Wet flies are also good, and here also I like the Coachman and Black Gnat in the same sizes. Remember that the bluegill's mouth is small, and it prefers food that it can take into its mouth with little effort.

An artificial that works splendidly is a spider, not the dry-fly pattern known by that name but one of those plastic or rubber lures with rubber legs cut from slender rubber bands. These rubber legs are probably the reason why the fish like them so well, for they vibrate as they sink into the water or are slowly retrieved. These spiders work best when on a long leader, say about 9 feet, and tapered to about 1-pound test. Let them sink slowly and those rubber legs will do their work.

Wading a lake or pond inshore where the bottom is firm enough, and

A lady angler on the Suwannee River in Florida lands a panfish—with her husband's help—on light spinning tackle. Panfish are found in most of our warm-water lakes and streams, and are always a tasty meal. *Florida State News Bureau.*

casting dry or wet flies and spiders with a 4-ounce fly rod is productive and really good sport, and the early evening is the best time to do it. Advance slowly and quietly as though you were after a wary trout. Do not splash the water with your casts or slash it on your back cast. The bluegill can hear and, despite its willingness to feed, has some native caution. Look for a school of sunnies rising. Fish that school with care and finesse. You may be able to take a number out of that one school, one after another, and each one can give you real fun if your fly rod is light and fairly whippy.

Bait fishing for bluegills is done from the bank, from a boat, from a dock or bridge, or from a dam embankment. A bobber or float is usually employed. Almost any type of rod will do—a long cane pole, a spinning rod, or a fly rod. A bait-casting rod is too short and stiff. The long cane pole with a slender, whippy top is ideal, for with it you can reach out and cover a lot of water, swinging out your casts so as not to whip off the bait. A No. 5 hook of light wire is small enough to take an angleworm without mangling it. Sunfish are great bait stealers. Select a small and lively worm and impale it on the hook as follows: Start at one end of the worm, leaving a little end of it to squirm. Run the hook through and leave a small loop. Do this three times. This can be done with a long-shank hook. Watch that bobber. When it goes completely under, strike.

YELLOW PERCH

The yellow perch (*Perca flavescens*) comes next to the sunfish family in popularity with panfish fishermen, and like the sunnies has a wide distribution. It is typically a fish of the Central and Eastern states, though it has been planted in the Pacific states and also in British Columbia. It abounds in the Great Lakes and in rivers, ponds, and lakes from Nova Scotia as far south as South Carolina. It is variously called the ringed perch, raccoon perch, red perch, and striped perch. Its back is olive-green, its sides golden yellow, its belly white, with the sides strongly marked with vertical broad stripes which go from the back down to below the median line of the body. From its eyes to the start of the dorsal fin there is a distinct inward curve; its body is deepest from the dorsal fin down to the pectoral fins, giving the fish a humped appearance. It is very prolific, and if not kept under control by hard fishing soon becomes overabundant in the smaller ponds and the fish become stunted. Years ago, when state fish commissions were less informed than today, yellow perch were introduced into some good trout ponds. The two species of fish cannot live together successfully. The less prolific trout yielded to the extremely prolific perch and soon disappeared.

The yellow perch is a flesh eater, feeding upon small fish, water creatures of various kinds, worms, crustaceans, and insects. It likes to be close to weed beds where there is plenty of food; and where such weed beds are scarce or nonexistent, the perch will haunt deeper water where there are bottoms providing such vegetation. Like the sunnies they are a school fish, and when you catch one, stick right there until the school moves on.

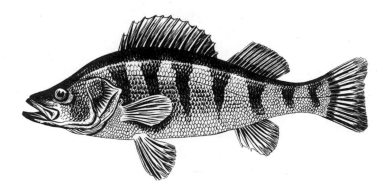

Yellow Perch

Yellow perch may be found in water where the bottom slopes from a depth of 10 feet down to 50 feet. They seem to like the shallow water in the evening, taking to deeper water with the coming of dawn. In every season except summer they hold close to bottom. Spawning in spring along the shorelines, with the coming of hot weather and warmer water, they go back to the depths, preferring water from 35 to 55 feet deep. In winter they are in the deepest water they can find, provided enough oxygen is present. The biggest perch are found in the deepest water.

The average yellow perch caught probably runs from 8 to 10 inches long. The biggest on record, caught on rod and line, weighed 4 pounds 3½ ounces, and was caught at Bordentown, New Jersey, in 1865.

This fish spawns in March or April, depending upon water temperatures. A favorable temperature for spawning is around 50 degrees. And though this ringed critter bites well at all seasons of the year, including winter (it is popular with ice fishermen), it is at its ravenous best as a baited-hook taker in the spring. When the fish are on their spawning runs in sluggish streams feeding perch lakes, the fishing population is likely to turn out in droves. Furthermore, the flesh is at its best when the fish is caught in cold water.

Perch caught in shallow water are almost invariably small. The lunkers, as has been said, lie in the deeper water, and such fish caught on light tackle put up a very pretty fight. These deep-water perch love small minnows or crawfish. If live minnows are not available, try those preserved minnows sold in tackle stores, usually in small jars, and keep them moving by jigging.

A small nickel spinner with a worm on the hook often gets a perch to strike. Or an unbaited spinner moved slowly through the water gets their eager attention. In deeper water, where the lunkers lie near bottom, fishing a spinner as jiggers fish their jigs will probably get you some fish that you can show with pride. For still-fishing, a float adjusted to the depth at which you are fishing is a must. A light spinning rod is good in perch fishing, or you use a long cane pole, like most perch fishermen. A size 6 or 8 hook is right. If bait fishing, let the fish run for a short distance with the bait before trying to hook it. In handling the yellow perch to take it off the hook or to dress it, avoid the sharp spines on its dorsal fin. They hurt.

CRAPPIE

The crappie is one of the numerous sunfish family, with its original range extending from southern Canada, the Great Lakes, and the Mississippi Valley south to northern Florida and into North Carolina, and from Vermont and New York westward to the Dakotas and south to Texas. It has many other names, among them bachelor, campbellite, croppie, newlight, tinmouth or papermouth, sac-a-lait (in Louisiana), bridge perch, goggleye, speckled perch, and even shad. It is plentiful in ponds, lakes, and sluggish waters. Its range has been extended by planting it in waters from New England westward to the Pacific Coast.

Science recognizes two members of the crappie family, the black and

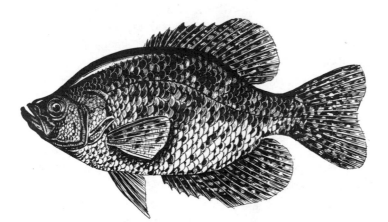

Black Crappie

the white. The black crappie (*Pomoxis nigro-maculatus*) and the white crappie (*Pomoxis annularis*) are quite similar in appearance, the principal difference being that the black has seven or eight dorsal spines, while the white usually has but six. The black also is darker in color, with mottled sides, while the white is silvery, with eight or nine vertical dark bands on its sides. Both have the striking large dorsal and anal fins from about the center of the body extending rearward to near the tail.

The average crappie caught weighs about a pound, though larger specimens are not uncommon. The record for a black crappie taken with hook and line is 5 pounds, caught in Santee-Cooper Lake in South Carolina. The record for a white crappie is held by one of 5 pounds, 3 ounces, caught in Enid Dam, Mississippi. The natural food of each is small fishes, insects, and crustaceans. The black crappie is principally a northern fish, the white southern. The black is found in lakes and large, rather warm streams, and the white in sluggish ponds and bayous. If it is caught in clear water that does not get too warm during the summer months, the crappie is good to eat.

The best crappie fishing comes in April, May, and June, and late in the fall, with the peak of it during April and May when the fish are on their spawning runs. About mid-June the crappies retreat to deep water, from 25 to 30 feet, but may come in to shallower water from dawn into early morning, usually where depths are from 5 to 8 feet, and feed near the surface. As morning advances they go back to deep water. At twilight again they feed on the surface until dark. Like the bluegill and yellow perch they are a school fish.

Crappies may be caught by drifting, trolling, still-fishing, and casting. For bait fishing there is nothing quite as good as a small, lively minnow up to about 2 inches long. Among artificials, small spoons, minnow-shaped and silvery, and wooden wobblers are good. Also, when the fish are surface-feeding and you see the rings they are making on the water, dry flies, wet flies, and small streamers will interest them. They are tender-mouthed, as the local name "papermouth" suggests, and your strike must be delicate or the hook will tear out of their mouths.

If trolling during the daytime with a wooden wobbler, you must sink the lure down to where the fish are lying. Sinkers or split shot will likely give an unnatural motion to the lure. Try a light, short wire leader with a swivel fastened on one end and a snap catch on the other, and fasten this to your short nylon leader. You can buy these ready-made at any tackle shop. These wire leaders are light enough to carry down the lure and yet not prevent its natural action. Let the boat move slowly. If the lake or pond you are fishing has stumps sticking out of the water, move the boat among them. Crappies love such stumps. They also like weed beds, so troll just off such beds also. Along toward twilight when the crappies are surface feeding, as you will see from their dimpling rises, you will need to fish nearer the surface. So take off the wire leader and attach the lure directly to the nylon leader.

Many fishermen use long cane poles, with lines just double the length of the pole. The line is tied at its middle to the pole top, one half being brought down and tied at the butt of the pole and the business end of the line attached to the leader. A bobber is fastened on the line a few inches above the hook, a lively minnow is put on the hook, and then fished near stumps, sunken brush heaps, emergent rocks, and other likely places. This rig is very successful.

When the crappies are feeding in shallow water early and late in the day, small streamers of white or yellow with silver tinsel bodies make good imitations of the small minnows which crappies adore. With a fly rod cast such a streamer among the feeding fish and retrieve it with little jerks. They often go for such a lure and a crappie on a light fly rod gives much better play than one on a stiff pole.

For still-fishing during the day when the crappies are in deep water, get the depth and the proper type of bottom by putting a treble hook on a line with enough sinker weight to take it down. Dredge the bottom with it at a depth of 25 to 30 feet, pull it up, and see if there are bottom weeds clinging to it. If there are, then fish there, using a small minnow on a No. 5 hook, and fishing just off bottom.

Drift fishing is at its best when there is just enough breeze to move along the boat very slowly. In the deeper waters of 25 to 30 feet you let out enough line so that your minnow moves along about a foot off bottom. Should you get no strikes at that depth, raise the minnow by so adjusting the bobber that the bait is a foot or two nearer the surface, and try it at that level for a while. Keep raising the minnow until you find the depth at which the crappies are feeding.

WHITE BASS

The white bass (*Roccus chrysops*) has a range in the Great Lakes area west to Manitoba, southern Ontario to New York, south in the Mississippi Valley to Arkansas, and in eastern Texas. Its color is striking—gold

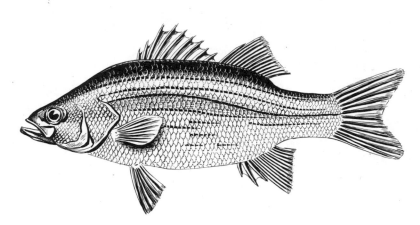

White Bass

and silvery, with narrow, dark, horizontal lines of closely associated spots from the gill covers to the tail on its upper sides. It averages 1 to 3 pounds, 1 foot in length. The top length is around 18 inches. There are no figures available as to the record weight of this species caught on rod and line. Within its range it is locally called striped bass and barfish. The name "striped bass" applies properly, of course, to *Roccus saxatilis,* known in the South as rockfish or rock. The white bass is generally found in the deep lakes within its range.

Like the other panfish discussed in this chapter, it is a school fish which spawns in the spring, either near shore or in feeder streams. It often is found feeding on the surface or near to it. Its food is minnows, crawfish, shrimp, worms, insects, and larvae. As is true of the crappies, minnows make up the chief part of its diet.

Favorite baits of white-bass fishermen are small minnows, worms, and crawfish. Artificial lures that are successful are flies, small spinners with small and slender pork-rind strips on the hook.

The best fishing for these fish is on their annual spawning runs when they ascend the feeder streams of the lake. Then they are ravenous and go for minnows, small spinners, small plugs fashioned so they're minnow-like, and small streamer flies with tinsel bodies resembling minnows. Later in summer, big schools of shad minnows swarm on the surfaces of white-bass lakes, and these bass embark on a campaign of slaughter. The surface of the lake where the minnows are is broken by the little fish trying to escape their pursuers, and by the hungry bass closing in on their prey.

Fishermen seeing and hearing the commotion are drawn to the scene. Small silver or nickel spoons or small streamer flies then can give some fine sport.

Drift fishing, still-fishing, trolling, and fly casting with weighted flies, while productive during the spring runs and summer carnival with shad minnows, are all uncertain at other times. Then deep trolling with minnows, small shiny spinners, and small plugs that imitate minnows, will take these fish if they are in a feeding mood, which often is not the case. If you hit a school of them that is willing at this time, stick to it, for if you take one, its schoolmates may be equally obliging.

CATFISH

The common bullhead (*Ictalurus nebulosus*), otherwise classified as the brown bullhead, goes under the name of speckled bullhead, horned pout, squaretail catfish, black catfish, Sacramento catfish, and yellow catfish. It probably has the widest distribution of our catfishes, being found in southern Canada and North Dakota, the Great Lakes region south to the Ohio Valley, New England to Virginia, from eastern Illinois and eastern Arkansas to Florida and the Carolinas. Not native to California, it has been put into the Sacramento River and various lakes in central and northern California as well as in southern Oregon. Its color is somewhat variable and may be dark brown, almost black, or even yellowish. It generally is abundant in about every weedy pond or small lake within its range, as well as many streams. It has a straight-edged tail and sharp spines, one at the dorsal fin, and one by each pectoral fin. Many a time as a boy, when fishing for these fish, I've seen a comrade dance around when he had handled one of these bullheads incautiously, and heard his howl of anguish as he speared his hand on one of these spines.

The average bullhead caught is about 10 or 11 inches long, though they may reach a weight of 7 pounds. The largest I ever caught was 17 inches long.

To return to those sharp-pointed spines—the youthful angler learns by experience not to close his hand on the forward body of the fish when attempting to unhook the bullhead. He learns to straddle his fingers over these fishy stilettos so as to avoid them.

If a boy's first fish is not a sunnie it is likely to be a bullhead. They're very easily caught. When I was a moppet about six years old, my uncle took me fishing to a weedy pond within walking distance of my home in the country in Essex County, Massachussets. My pole was a jointless cane affair about 12 feet long, the line was coarse and of braided cotton, the bobber was a cork from a bottle, and the hook was about a No. 4. The bait of course was a lively angleworm dug from ground heavily fertilized by cattle droppings just outside of the barn. My uncle guessed at the depth of the water by probing with the tip of his cane pole, and adjusted my bobber to suit the depth so that the baited hook would rest close to the bottom. It wasn't more than three minutes before my bobber jiggled at the top of the water and then disappeared under it. I gave a mighty upthrust with my pole and a small black object sailed over my head and into the weeds back of me. I ran at top speed, seized the fish, and got speared for my rashness. Being only a child I bawled a little, then went back to my fishing, sucking at the wound. We caught some fifteen or twenty bullheads that day, and as we caught them put them in a heap in the sunshine, there being no shade handy. When we gathered them up to take them home, without having dressed them, they appeared shriveled. Before cleaning them, my uncle put them in a dishpan of water, and I was amazed to see most of them recover and wiggle around.

Bullheads spawn in early spring or summer, and in some cases will guard the eggs and later the young. They will eat about anything—insects, tadpoles, worms, and crawfish. They feed most actively at night, and it is a common sight to see the lanterns of fishermen as they put out from landings in their boats to take advantage of this habit. The chief thing to remember in fishing for these popular fish is to get your worm bait down so that it is just off bottom. Lower the worm so it touches bottom, then raise it several inches.

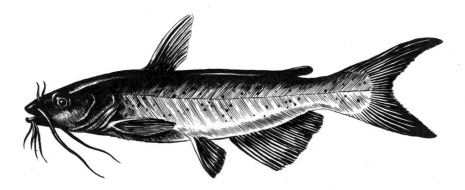

Channel Cat

They are very good eating. Their flesh is firm and usually reddish when dressed. I found early that to skin them it is well to nail head and tail to a board, start to peel the skin with a sharp knife, then finish the job with pliers which give a good grip.

The channel cat (*Ictalurus punctatus*) is the only one of the large catfish family to have a forked tail. It has local names such as speckled catfish, fiddler, white cat, and silver cat. Its range is from the prairie provinces of Canada to the Great Lakes-St. Lawrence basin, Montana to Lake Champlain, and south through the Mississippi Valley to Florida and the Gulf of Mexico. Its color is slaty gray and silvery, and it is usually black spotted. Its average weight is 4 to 5 pounds, with the record on hook and line being a whopping 55 pounds for one caught in South Dakota. You can start an argument about any time in channel-cat country by calling it a panfish. Channel-cat fishermen will object and say that it is just about as good a game fish as any.

Its natural food is small fishes, crawfish, mussels, and insects. It likes clean and rather fast-flowing streams with gravelly bottoms, though they sometimes inhabit slow-moving and muddy-bottom streams. A bass-bugging rod weighing 5 or 6 ounces and from 8 to 10 feet long is a good rig for this fine fish. Pick a line suited to the rod, in either a D or C level, according to the weight of the rod. A leader from 6 to 9 feet long is suited to the type of fishing. Select a flashy silver-color spinner, size No. 1 or No. 2. Bait the hook on the spinner with a nightwalker. Don't try to cast with this rig, for that would likely snap off the worm, but swing the spinner out sidewise, with coils of line in your left hand ready to be released when the baited spoon goes out.

Using the spinner-worm combination, cast upstream and let the current bring the lure down toward you, keeping the rod tip pointed at the lure, and taking in line as needed to keep it reasonably taut awaiting a strike. Let the spinner bump along the bottom. Remember how in wet-fly fishing, as the fly reaches the end of its arc as it comes to the end of its drift, you draw it back toward you for several feet, then let it drop back? Do the same here. A fish may have followed the lure to the end of its drift, and then, when seeing it go upstream, think it is escaping and nail it.

For bait fishing, nightwalkers lead, with ordinary angleworms, live minnows, catalpa worms, crawfish, and shrimp all close behind in yielding good catches.

CHAPTER 24

The Shad

THE AMERICAN SHAD (*Alossa sapidissima*), as a splendid sport fish, was overlooked until about twenty-five years ago when Connecticut anglers fishing the Connecticut River below the Enfield Dam found that this silvery and toothsome fish would take certain types of artificial flies and spinners, and that few game fish could put up a better battle. Yet Jordan and Evermann in *American Food and Game Fishes,* published in 1902, make this comment: "After entering the rivers, the shad take but little, if any, food previous to spawning, but after casting its eggs it will strike at flies or other small shining objects, and it has been known to take the artificial fly." Right there was a tip for sport fishermen, but the tip was practically disregarded until a generation later.

Originally this fine fish was confined to the Atlantic Coast from Florida to Newfoundland, the rivers best known for its runs being the St. Johns in Florida, the Potomac, Susquehanna, Delaware, and Connecticut. Because of pollution in their lower stretches, the Delaware and Potomac have seen their best days as shad rivers. Other rivers along the Atlantic Coast once had good shad runs, but the erection of dams on them has kept the fish from ancestral spawning grounds so that their runs have stopped or become greatly diminished. A parallel case is that of the Atlantic salmon, once common in a number of New England rivers but now gone except in a few.

However, though its range has shrunken along the Atlantic Coast, it has been nationally increased by the introduction of the fish into Pacific Coast rivers. In the decade between 1870 and 1880, shad were stocked in California's Sacramento River and also in the Columbia. The plantings suc-

256

Shad

ceeded admirably. Now shad are common from San Diego in Southern California all the way along the Pacific Coast into Alaska.

The average shad taken on rod and line probably weighs from about 2¼ pounds up to 5 pounds. The Pacific Coast shad top weight seems to be a little heavier than those along the eastern coast, being 14 pounds as against 12 pounds for the latter.

Like the Atlantic salmon, the shad is anadromous. Most of the year it spends in the ocean, but to spawn it must seek fresh-water rivers. The time of its spawning runs seems to be determined by river temperatures. It has been found that water temperatures must be within a range of ten degrees, from 56 to 66 degrees, to induce most shad to enter them, and that when the water goes over 66 degrees the runs markedly shrink.

As would be expected, since this is so, the runs are earlier in the South, and are progressively later in northern rivers. For example, shad enter the St. Johns River as early as November, with the largest runs in February and March. In South Carolina rivers they appear in January. But in the Connecticut River the first arrivals are in late April or May, with the height of the run in the first half of June. In Canada they come the last part of May and in June. In California they come from late April to the middle of July, with the peak run in late May and June.

According to "Atlantic Coast Migrations of American Shad," Bulletin 142, U.S. Fish and Wildlife Service, adult shad from the Chesapeake Bay to the Connecticut River go northward to spend summer and fall in

Not only is the shad a fine fighting fish, but it is also a table treat. The roe, shown here along side a shad, is considered a rare delicacy. *Florida State News Bureau.*

the Gulf of Maine. It appears that they spend the winter months along the Middle Atlantic areas in deep water.

The female shad lays a tremendous number of eggs which are emitted in open water and left without parental care. They hatch within a week from time of spawning, and the youngsters stay in fresh water until the fall when, having reached a length of 4 to 6 inches, they go down to salt water.

On the Atlantic Coast, the St. Johns River in Florida probably yields more shad than any other river along the coastline. The yearly catch there is somewhere in the neighborhood of 65,000. It is likely that the Connecticut River is second with a catch of nearly 40,000 in good years. Best catches have been made, according to a bulletin published by the Farmington River Watershed Association and Windsor Rod and Gun Club, both of Connecticut, when water temperatures reached 67 and 68 degrees.

In Florida most of the shad taken in the St. Johns River are caught by very slow trolling, using a small silver spoon and a jig to keep the spoon near bottom. An alternate method is to cast small yellow or white jigs close to undercut banks or by using the same lures close to bottom in the deeper holes. The largest fish come usually about the middle of November. About three weeks later comes a second run. The last run of the usual four stays in the river until about mid-May. The peak of the season is usually from mid-January to mid-March. From upper Volusia County to the head of the river the fish may be caught only on artificial lures.

Use a spinning or fly rod weighing between 5 and 6 ounces. If using a small jig, let it go to the bottom, take up any slack, then give a little twitch to the rod to lift the jig from the bottom, reel in the lure slowly for a few inches and then repeat. These fish have tender mouths, so if you get rough with them you will lose the fish. The average weight of shad taken in the St. Johns River is a little over 2 pounds for the males and a fraction over 3 pounds for the females.

Fly fishing for shad is a great sport, for the fish can be as aerial-minded as a rainbow trout, and gives fine play on a rod of 5 to 6 ounces and a tapered line of HDH or HCH, depending upon the weight of the rod. A 50-yard backing on the reel of 4-pound test monofilament is desirable. Streamer flies, sizes No. 2 or No. 4, skimpily dressed, red and white with tinsel bodies, are effective, especially if topped with several red beads. Pools with some current and the tails of riffles are good places to cast. Put enough split shot on the leader to get the fly down near bottom, casting across the current and letting it take the lure downstream. On the retrieve bring in the line very slowly.

Spinning with small silver wobblers, Colorado spinners, and other small shiny lures is very effective. Weighted flies with tinsel bodies will also take these fish. With such flies a swivel and keel are employed to prevent line twisting, the keel being attached about 3 inches above the lure.

The shad is overlooked by most sport fishermen who think of it only as a commercial fish to be taken with nets. But as a fighter and food fish it ranks right up among the better of our game fishes and it is so productive that it is underfished.

CHAPTER 25

Ice Fishing

WHEN I WAS a youngster, fishing through the ice was left almost entirely to boys. Rarely did you see an adult hovering over a hole in the ice, or huddled near a fire on shore watching for a tip-up flag to fly over one of the holes so arduously chopped through the ice with a hatchet. Now the sport has become popular for all ages. For example, at Lake Winnipesaukee in New Hampshire, during the winter thousands of little fishing shanties dot the ice, and the hardy devotees of the sport even elect a "mayor" of the ice village. Ice fishing has caught on all along the ice belt to the West, particularly in Michigan, Minnesota, and Wisconsin. Villages of ice shanties spring up almost overnight when the ice gets thick enough to be safe. Then eager fishermen drive their cars right to the doors of their shanties. Oil stoves, gas lanterns, and bottled-gas stoves make shanty interiors comfortable despite plummeting temperatures.

The tools of the sport have improved. We used to use an old hatchet to cut holes in the ice. Now Swedish ice augers can cut a hole through ice 3 feet deep in just about nothing flat. To be exact, a muscular performer of the art can do this in about half a minute. It took us kids about fifteen times as long to get down to water through thinner ice, and we used up a lot of muscular energy in doing it. With the ice auger, take along a metal skimmer to skim off the ice that continually forms in the hole, and to remove the ice chips as you dig the hole.

If you don't use an ice auger, then you will need a sharp spud to chop the holes. This looks like a large, long-handled chisel. You will need to tie a strong cord or leather thong to the spud and then fasten the other end to your wrist, for not infrequently an unfastened spud will slip from your numbed hands and disappear into the depths.

A common error is to cut the hole too big. The chief fish to be caught in ice fishing are crappies, yellow perch, and sunfish, all of which are relatively small. If your quarry is going to be bluegills, a width of about 6 inches is enough. If you are fishing good crappie water where the fish reach respectable weights, 10 inches should do. See that the edges of the hole are cut smooth enough to avoid any fraying of your line in bringing up a fish.

The crappie is the most popular panfish in those ponds and lakes where it is found. It not only attains a better size than other panfish popular with ice anglers, but it travels in schools. Thus, if you catch one, you know there are others in that immediate location, so you stay right there until the school quits biting or moves on. While this fish likes shallow water during the warm months, in the winter it takes to the depths and feeds near the bottom. Look for them in water 20 to 30 feet deep which is relatively free from weeds. If you have had success in catching this fish at a certain location during the summer, try to locate a deep hole or pocket not far away. The chances are that you will be able to pinpoint such a spot by seeing where most of the ice fishermen have gathered.

Successful equipment consists of No. 8 hooks, light split-shot weight to carry the hook down into the water, line of 4-pound-test monofilament, and a short springy glass rod 3 or 4 feet long. Use two hooks, one at the end of the monofilament, and the second on the line about 18 inches farther up. One small split shot is clinched onto the line about 4 feet from the tip. Best distance from the bottom for the lower bait to swim is 3 or 4 feet. Should that distance prove unproductive, try it higher or even lower. Adjust your bobber, which should be very light and only large enough to keep the bait at the desired distance. By far the best bait for crappies is small minnows 1 to 2 inches long. Live-bait dealers, usually located near popular ice-fishing lakes, stock such minnows. Dealers offer insulated minnow pails of 10-quart capacity, for around $3.50, which keep minnows alive in either hot or cold weather.

Hook the minnow between the dorsal fin and tail, being careful not to pierce the backbone, to keep the minnow alive and active. Don't expect the crappie to hit viciously. It seems to take the minnow gently in its mouth, as though to enjoy its savor, and then move off with it. If a bobber too large or a sinker too heavy is used, the fish is quick to detect unnatural resistance and will drop the bait. So watch that bobber closely, and don't strike until it is well under water.

The bluegills and other sunfish outnumber the other panfish in most

Ice fishing setups may range from a lone angler with pail and bait bucket, to the snug trio behind the windbreak cooking a hot lunch, to a more elaborate shelter replete with chairs, stoves, and wooden warm-up hut. *Michigan Conservation Dept.*

ponds and lakes in which they are found. Once it was thought they wouldn't bite in winter, but the tons of them caught through the ice every winter disprove that belief. Unlike crappies they rarely if ever can be caught at night. Like the crappies they have the schooling habit, and in winter are found in deeper water than in summer. Just off submerged weed beds in about 12 to 20 feet is a good place to try. Explore the bottom with a line weighted with a heavy sinker and a treble hook tied to the tip. If the hook brings back weeds, it is likely you're close to good bluegill water. Vary the depths at which you are fishing to learn at what level they are hitting. A springy glass rod about 3 feet long, and a monofilament line of 4-pound test is good. Use a short shank No. 8 or No. 10 hook.

Good sunfish baits are small grubs, gallworms, meal worms, angleworms, and the larvae of aquatic insects found under rocks on stream bottoms. Or you can find larvae in ponds and mud bottoms. Dump a mass of the mud onto a fine screen, then sift it.

An effective jigging rig for these panfish is a small silver or gold spoon with the hook brazed on, and a bit of bait on the hook. Jig gently, raising and lowering the spoon with little twitches that make the spoon flutter up and down in a distance of less than an inch.

Yellow perch can be taken through the ice by jigging. Fish for them in water up to 60 feet deep. Use a jigging stick, available at dealers for about half a dollar. This usually is about 15 inches long, with the lower part notched to hold the line, and a hole at the upper end through which the business end of the line is passed. The line can be adjusted to the depth at which you propose to fish. Your jigging spoon should be worked at no more than 12 inches off the bottom, or that distance above any bottom weeds. Jigging spoons are effective where minnows are hard to get. They are heavy and sink rapidly with a fluttering action.

If using bait when jigging, fasten to your line a 3-ounce sinker, tying on a No. 4 to 8 hook about one foot below it. Lower the sinker into the water and pay out line until the sinker hits bottom. Then take in enough line so that the bait is about one foot off bottom. Now comes the jigging. Raise and lower the wrist, not the arm, in regular movement for a few seconds, then abruptly bring up the jig stick to nearly shoulder height. Keep at this routine and you will find you have hooked a perch.

Live minnows only an inch or two long make excellent bait for perch, particularly the larger ones. The eye of a perch you have caught is excellent bait. Nightcrawlers and ordinary angleworms are good, as are catalpa worms collected the previous summer and kept in your freezer. Salmon

A simple tip-up made of bamboo cane, as described in the text, can be an effective ice-fishing rig.

eggs are good; they are sold in glass containers in many tackle stores.

Or, if you want some sport without the luxuries of an ice shanty, an oil stove, and other oddments, make a number of tip-ups out of lightweight bamboo canes. The crosspiece that goes over the hole should be long enough so that it can't be dragged into the water by an active fish. Lash another stick at right angles to the hole stick and extending about 4 inches beyond the lashing. To the long end of that stick fasten a scarlet cotton flag. Then tie your line firmly to the short end of the flag stick, first finding the depth at which you are to fish by letting the sinker go to the bottom, then raising it about a foot from the bottom. When a fish takes the bait, the pull on the flag stick raises it into the air and gives the glad report that you have a fish on. When the holes have been chopped in the right places, and there are fish around, you may see three or four flags in the air at once. Then you leave the fire on the bank at which you've been thawing out, and race madly to reach the flags before your fish can get away. Believe me, it's fun.

Ice fishing is productive. In one recent winter on the Canadian portion of Lake Erie, over 56,000 ice fishermen caught more than 1,800,000 yellow perch. The average fisherman caught more than 44 fish on each trip. Contrast this with the average catch per trip in summer, which is usually about three fish!

CHAPTER 26

The Importance of
Water Temperature

THE FLY FISHERMAN often is frustrated at finding both wet and dry flies ineffective early in the season, while bait fishermen are having a field day. Likewise, the bass fisherman cannot understand it when shallow, weedy waters that were so fruitful earlier in the season prove so barren in summer. Water temperature is the reason. There is a close relationship between water temperature and the feeding activity of the fish. There also is a decided difference in locations where fish may be found, and that difference is determined by temperature. Fish go to the places where the temperature is the more congenial. Scientists have definitely proved these facts which expert anglers have suspected and used to their advantage.

Fishery biologist Norman S. Baldwin at the University of Toronto studied feeding activity and growth of brook trout at different water temperatures. With water temperature at 55 degrees F. the trout ate weekly a number of minnows that totaled about half of their own weight. When the water temperature rose to about 63 degrees, the trout feeding became less. At 70 degrees the feeding urge declined so markedly that the food intake fell to 6 per cent weekly of the weight of the fish.

Furthermore, while trout feeding increased as water temperatures rose from cold to warm, the ratio of gain in bodily weight to amount of food eaten decreased with the rise in temperature. Baldwin concluded this was due to the increased need for body maintenance. Another scientist at the University of Toronto, J. H. Graham, found that the preferred temperatures of trout are between 57 and 67 degrees, the most favorable being just over 59 degrees.

As for the relationship between the feeding activity of black bass and water temperatures, Dr. H. S. Swingle, a pioneer in the study of fish ponds,

266

studied black bass kept in tanks, in each of which the water was maintained at a constant temperature, which varied according to the tank. These temperatures varied from a low of 40 degrees to a high of 90 degrees.

At 40 degrees the bass refused to feed. Dr. Swingle force-fed one bass in that tank with a minnow and examined it four days later. The minnow showed no sign at all of any digestion. At one week after the forcible feeding the minnow showed slight digestion.

Likewise the bass kept in the tank held at a 90-degree temperature were just as reluctant to feed as in the tank of 40-degree water. The best temperature for feeding activity and digestive ability was discovered to be 79 degrees.

The fisherman who takes advantage of these demonstrated facts, carries a water thermometer, and is guided by what it tells him, is many jumps ahead of the hit-or-miss angler. If he is after brook trout, and finds the water below 50 degrees, he should look for the fish at the bottoms of deep pools and undercut banks. If bait fishing with worms or minnows, he should use enough split shot to get his bait down to the bottom where the trout are lying. At such times dry flies are a waste of time. The fly fisherman should tie on a wet fly or nymph with leader similarly weighted. This advice applies also to water up to 55 degrees. At temperatures from 55 to 60 degrees there still is little feeding at the surface and the wet fly, nymph, and bait still are much better than the dry fly.

When the water temperature climbs above 60 degrees, insect life in and on the water becomes active. The dry-fly fisherman has his innings at last. The trout now move out of the deep water into the riffles, into the potholes in fast and shallow water, to choice feeding stations above and below emergent or underwater rocks where the current brings food to them.

As the water temperature goes above 68 degrees, the trout feel discomfort. They retreat to deep water which usually is cooler, to places off the mouths of feeder streams which are likely to have cooler water, or where cold springs enter. Brown trout and rainbows are more tolerant than are brook trout of higher temperatures and will continue to feed in water several degrees higher than 68.

But brookies, browns, and rainbows in water of temperature above the preferred range will come out of the depths, the cut banks, and spring holes to range shallow water at night in search of food. Then is the time to take the trophy fish, the big ones rarely seen during the day except in the larger streams. The darkness gives them confidence and they are less wary.

In general, fly fishing is at its best in the northeastern and northern midwestern states during May, June, and early autumn, the latter in those states where trout fishing is legal at that time of the year. In the northern Rocky Mountain states September is the best time for big trout, for the trophy fish begin to take in late August and right through October. They seem to want to put on fat to last them through the cold winter.

Coming to black bass, the bass-fishing vacationist who takes his vacation during the hot months of July and August, and is back at his desk or bench right after Labor Day, if in the northeastern or northern midwest states, loses out on the best bass fishing of the season. Water temperatures during the last three weeks of September and the first three in October generally are the most favorable of the season. The bass then are on the prowl, stuffing themselves like black bears do before holing up for the winter. Then the fish are likely to be in shallower water.

In the South, where largemouths reach the maximum weights, the best fishing for them is likely to be in spring and fall. Then the upper levels of water are usually within the preferred temperatures of bass, 70 to 75 degrees. Starting about the middle of September they feed voraciously for seven to eight weeks, and the fishing is quite likely to be the best of the year. At the temperatures named, look for them in shallow water. Use surface lures or baits.

When water temperatures range above the preferred levels, the bass take to deep water. Then use deep-running lures, jigs, plastic worms, or minnows fished close to bottom.

CHAPTER 27

Fishing Weather

ONE CANNOT BE exact in defining the best fishing weather. The feeding activity of fish is governed by a number of variables such as water temperature, air temperature, wind direction, barometric pressure, the turbidity or clarity of the water, and, to some extent, the phases of the moon.

Anyone who has lived in the country falls heir to the wisdom of the farmer, whose livelihood is so largely dependent upon the weather. Rain in the haying season, frost when the fruit trees are in blossom, a long, wet period or a prolonged drought—these affect crops and in turn the farmer's income. So he has learned to interpret the signs and profit by them. Here are some of those signs I learned as a child in the country.

Cobwebs on the grass in the morning indicate a fair day. The little grass spider is a good fair-weather prophet.

Dew on the grass in the morning, before the sun has had time to dry it, is another omen of good weather. It appears only when the skies are clear.

Swallows fly high in clear weather because the insects on which they feed fly high too, and high-pressure air makes high flight easier. Conversely, perching birds are more likely to be found in trees when a storm is on the way because low-pressure air makes it more difficult to fly. The cuckoo, sometimes called the "rain crow" in the country, often will herald the approach of rain with its call of *cow, cow, cow*. The trill of the tree toad also is a harbinger of rain.

When the smoke from a chimney, seen in the country where wood-burning stoves are often used, rises almost straight in the air, that is a fair-weather indication, for it denotes high pressure. Low-pressure air forces the smoke downward.

When you see dark clouds in the west or northwest, it is probable that rain will fall in your location. If lightning and the dark clouds are in other quarters of the compass, it is likely that the storm will pass you by.

The weather in most of the United States comes from the west since wind movement in general is from west to east. Thus the high and low fronts for the most part come from the west. It is said that the progress of these fronts may reach 500 miles a day in summer and even more than that in winter, perhaps 700 miles. The larger city newspapers publish daily weather maps. By following them you can see from the prevailing front in the west what your weather is likely to be within the next 24 hours, if you're east of it.

The clouds also help you to make a reasonably accurate forecast of the weather. High clouds are fair-weather indications and while they prevail a storm is not likely. Low-hanging clouds are the weather-breeders.

The most favorable winds for fishing are from the south, southwest, or west. However, during a hot spell when the winds shift from the south to the northwest, bringing in cooler weather, it often causes the fish to begin feeding. While occasionally a good catch may be made when the wind is in the east or northeast, usually such winds make for poor fishing. The old doggerel

> When the wind is in the north
> The fisherman goes not forth;
> When the wind is in the south
> It blows the bait in the fish's mouth;
> When the wind is in the east
> The fish bite the least.
> When the wind is in the west
> The fish bite the best.

has considerable truth in it.

The barometer is another reliable guide for fishermen. Rarely have I found good fishing when the barometer shows a sustained low—that is, at or below 29.90 for some time. If it starts to rise, its effect on the fishing is not likely to be immediately apparent, but it means prospects are improving and the fishing is almost sure to be better. As it rises the fish tend to leave the bottom and come closer to the surface.

If the barometer records a low-pressure reading that is sustained, or if it starts to drop slowly, almost invariably trout hug the bottom and what feeding they do is in that area. Usually fishing for them at such times is poor, but sometimes bait, or a well-sunken wet fly or a nymph, will get you some action.

Quick changes in the barometric pressure, either up or down, have a decided influence on fish-feeding activity. The rapid changes in the air pressure seem to disturb them and they go on a hunger strike.

I have considerable faith in my barometer, a "Stormoguide." If it shows low pressure or is falling, I either abandon a planned fishing trip or, if committed to it, go with little confidence that it will be successful. But if the barometer has been showing low pressure, and there have been rains followed by cooler weather and westerly winds, the rising barometer indicates favorable fishing conditions.

In hot summer weather it is necessary to get down deep and fish close to bottom with either bait or artificials. In such weather the fish retreat to the depths where the water is colder. The best fishing then is in early morning and evening. A mild day in spring following a chilly period is likely to bring out hatches of insects, and they in turn bring up the trout from deeper water to feed on the surface.

Overcast skies are favorable provided the wind is not in an unfavorable quarter. A mild day with a drizzling rain is excellent weather for about any type of fishing.

We all know that a clear sky at sunset, or one that paints clouds well above the horizon with scarlet and gold means a fine day on the morrow. But when the sun sets behind dark clouds it means the contrary.

> Red sky in the morning
> Sailors take warning;
> Red sky at night,
> Sailor's delight.

When the weather has been hot, dry, and muggy, a heavy rain which raises the water in streams but does not make it muddy, followed by cooler weather, will usually put the fish on the feed. The rain has washed much food into the streams and the cooler weather has stirred the fish out of their lethargy. If the water becomes muddy, the fish stop feeding, but as it clears the fishing picks up and is likely to be good while the water is lowering.

A long-continued period of high temperature and no wind is almost always a time of poor fishing, particularly on lakes and ponds. The water then is glassy calm. The amount of oxygen in the water has decreased since there has been no wind to kick up waves and generate oxygen. Such weather conditions work specially hard on those waters with rocky bottoms and few weed beds, for water plants are generators of oxygen.

During recent years a school of thought among fishermen has emphasized the importance of storm fronts. These anglers point out that fishing is likely to be extra good at the approach of a storm, at a time when the barometric pressure, preceding a cold front, is low. When cooler air is noted, that means that the front has passed on. Then the feeding activity of the fish will come to a halt.

The oncoming of a warm front is also likely to bring good fishing. This is heralded by the sky slowly becoming overcast. As the front advances, there comes a drizzling rain, low-hanging clouds, and then harder rain. As the front passes, the rain lets up or turns into drizzle again.

Fishing is likely to be poorest just before, during, and after the moon is full. Generally it is better during the dark of the moon and when it is in its first and last quarter. My experienced fishing friend the late Billy Abbott explained that when the moon was nearing, had reached, or had passed its full the fish feed heartily at night and thus are indifferent during the daylight hours.

The time of day also affects fishing. Early in the trout season, the early and late in the day fishing is inferior to that from 10 A.M. to 4 P.M., when the water has warmed up a bit. One can't be positive about it; all that can be said is that certain conditions are likely to be favorable and certain others unfavorable.

CHAPTER 28

The Fisherman's Boat

THE BOAT IS a fisherman's necessity. No matter how devoted he is to fishing small streams, there are often times when he wants to fish in ponds or lakes where bank fishing is impractical or useless. Frequently he finds all the boats at the rental dock spoken for, or has to put up with one that leaks or is otherwise unsatisfactory. So nearly every fisherman would like to own his own boat, which he can take to any water he wishes to fish.

CHOOSING A FISHING BOAT

In buying a boat for fishing, the fisherman is faced with a number of considerations: length, capacity, weight, and material. If the boat is to be kept in one body of water, say by a man who owns a cottage on a lake or at a seaside resort, the question of length and weight are minor considerations. But if the angler has to lift his boat in order to transport it to fishing waters, the question of weight is important. Upkeep also is a consideration. Will painting and repairs be necessary at regular intervals? Are molded fiberglass or aluminum boats the answer?

Here we consider only boats bought primarily for the purpose of fishing; not big luxury boats or boats designed for speeding, but boats for the average man who wants to keep upkeep expense at a minimum. We confine our suggestions to the man who intends to use a boat on small inland waters. A big boat here is not needed and is a problem. What *is* needed is a boat that is short enough to be handled easily and at low speeds, and is not dependent upon a motor but can be shoved along with a pole, rowed or paddled as the occasion requires. It should be light enough so that one reasonably strong man can load and unload it. This is important whether you carry it on a trailer or a car top.

Fiberglass and plywood boats run somewhat heavier than those of aluminum. Aluminum boats average 9 to 10 feet long and weigh about 50 pounds. Weights vary according to the length and thickness of material. Such a boat will seat comfortably two men. If both are to fish, they should be careful casters and not "sidewinders." An aluminum boat is tough and can stand pretty rough treatment from snags and knocks. It is ideal for one-man fishing and handling in quiet inland waters. It will cost somewhere between $100 and $200, depending upon the maker, length, and material. A small outboard motor of low horsepower—1 to 1½—is suited to such a boat. It is much more stable to cast from than a canoe.

Glass fishing boats mostly run to larger sizes and more speed than we have in mind here. If they are well made they are heavier for their length and width than aluminum boats. Some boat makers are putting out 10- to 12-footers, but the really good ones weigh from 150 to 200 pounds in the longer lengths, and about 115 pounds for the shorter. The 12-footer will carry three persons safely. It costs around $265.

Royalite is a U. S. Rubber Company product, and the Thompson Royal-Craft of Cortland, New York, offers a 12-foot Royal-Topper of this material with 4-foot beam that only weighs 115 pounds. It will take a 5 or 7 horsepower motor and also can be rowed.

Improvements have been made in canvas-covered boats. Coverings now are tougher and require a lot less maintenance than formerly. The Old Town Canoe Co. of Old Town, Maine, puts out a 12-footer called the Sport Boat that will carry three persons well, will take a motor up to 7½ horsepower, and can be easily rowed. The weight is interesting—just under 100 pounds.

In aluminum boats in the 12-foot class, Grumman Boats, Marathon, New York, have their Cartopper model. It is 12 feet, 3 inches long, has a 4-foot beam, and weighs 89 pounds. It will take a 6 horsepower motor and carry four persons. However, in my opinion, a boat of that length is better adapted to three persons.

If you get a boat of the types that have been described, see to it that oarlocks are installed and equip it with a pair of oars. For comfort get a chair-back that can be clamped onto your seat. Have a floor-rack to cover exposed bottom frames.

Here are some suggestions for the fisherman with a boat:

Don't smoke near gasoline.

Be alert to the weather. Take to shore if you see a storm coming up, or the wind rising and beginning to stir up a fuss on the water.

Keep an eye open for stumps, sunken logs, rocks, fishermen, and other boats.

When you drop the anchor, lower it, don't toss it.

Should your boat overturn, stay with it, for the tipped-over boat will keep you afloat until help comes.

When in a boat don't engage in horseplay or hasty movement. Be considerate of others, and don't speed past fishermen in anchored boats or those who are trolling.

When you travel with a boat trailer, you will profit by these suggestions from Johnson Motors:

1. Use safety chains. This is now the law in many states.

2. After driving a few miles, check your trailer hitch and tie-downs and see if they are secure.

3. When the trailer is parked for overnight, loosen the tie-downs.

4. Check your insurance policy to assure yourself that your car is covered by the policy when towing a trailer.

5. Be sure that your trailer fits your boat. The boat should be supported in at least three places. If a motor is carried on a boat, it must have transom support.

6. When towing a trailer, remember that extra length. It takes more room to pass another car, requires more parking space, and a greater distance to stop. Drive at lower speeds.

7. For safety and better performance, a frame hitch is better than a bumper hitch.

8. Check the vehicle laws of your state to see if a license is required for the trailer.

GOVERNMENT REGULATIONS

By act of Congress, motor-propelled boats are divided into four classes. *Class A* includes those craft less than 16 feet long. *Class One* covers boats 16 feet long or longer but less than 26 feet. *Class Two* includes boats from 26 feet up but less than 40 feet. *Class Three* includes boats of 40 feet and up but not more than 65 feet.

Here are the legal requirements for equipment for boats in the classes designated above:

Class A. *Lifesaving Equipment.* Required are one Coast Guard-approved life preserver, a ring buoy, buoyant vest, or buoyant cushion, in good condition, for each person aboard.

Lights. Combination light in front of boat showing red to port and green to starboard from straight ahead to two points of compass behind the beam; visible one mile. A white light in the back of the boat showing all around the horizon for two miles.

Rules for boat operation. 1. Boats without motors have the right of way over boats with motors. 2. Keep to the right in channels. 3. When meeting another boat head on, swing to the right. 4. When two boats are approaching each other at an angle, the boat on the right has the right of way. 5. A boat being overtaken always has the right of way. 6. Do everything possible to avoid a collision in an emergency.

Fire Extinguisher. No fire extinguisher is required on pleasure outboards of open construction. However, if an outboard has an enclosed compartment, no matter how small, it must have a fire extinguisher. Any one of the following may be used: 1-quart vaporizing liquid, 1½-gallon foam, 4-pound CO_2, 4-pound dry chemical.

Ventilation. Two or more ventilators with cowls or equivalent capable of removing gases from the bilges in engine and fuel-tank compartments on boats constructed or decked over after April 25, 1940, using gasoline or fuel of a flashpoint less than 110 degrees F. Motor boats with the greater part of the bilges under the engine, and fuel tanks open and exposed to the air at all times, do not require ventilators.

Flame Arrester. Carburetors on all engines of motor boats, other than outboards, must be fitted with an approved device for arresting backfire. Installations made before November 19, 1952, need not meet the detailed requirements of the specifications, and may continue to be used as long as they are in good condition.

Class One. Equipment same as Class A, except that a hand-, mouth-, or power-operated whistle or horn is required, which will produce a blast lasting two seconds and can be heard for half a mile.

Class Two. Lifesaving devices same as Class A.

Lights. Individual running lights (not combination lights), red to port and green to starboard that can be seen for at least a mile. Two bright white lights, one in the rear of the boat visible all around the horizon for two miles, and one up front showing right ahead to two points behind the beam on both sides for two miles.

Bell. One which can be heard for some distance; horn or whistle, one hand- or powered-operated whistle or horn capable of producing a blast at least two seconds long which can be heard a mile. Fire extinguisher, any two of types specified for Class A. Ventilation and fire arrester, same as for Class One.

Class Three. Lifesaving devices: one Coast Guard-approved life preserver or ring buoy for each person aboard. Horn or whistle, must be power-operated, capable of producing a blast two seconds long and being heard a mile. Fire extinguisher, any of three types specified under Class A. Lights, bell, and flame arresters same as for Class Two.

In all classes boats fitted with a fixed fire-extinguisher system in the machinery space may dispense with one of the required fire extinguishers.

Suggested additional equipment for smaller boats: line for tying up, small anchor, tool kit, some spare motor parts, a powerful flashlight for running at night in addition to those required by law, also fenders.

Boat Numbering. An outboard or inboard boat of more than 16 feet long must be licensed by the Coast Guard and have a number assigned to it. To get a number, apply to the Coast Guard District Commander having jurisdiction over the area in which the boat is owned. To learn the location of this Commander, write Coast Guard Headquarters, Washington 25, D.C., asking for information and forms and instructions to apply for a number.

CHAPTER 29

The Fisherman's Ethics

STATES AN PROVINCES set up laws regulating fishing seasons, creel limits, size limits, and methods of taking. Their object is to provide better fishing for all. But the individual conduct of the fisherman is largely a matter of conscience and decency and not of regulation by law. All those who hunt and fish are mistakenly called "sportsmen" in the public prints, though many of them do not deserve the title. The true sportsman consciously or instinctively follows the Golden Rule—"Do unto others as you would have them do unto you."

The sportsman obeys the fishing laws to the letter. He knows they were drawn up by trained men, better versed in conditions than he, and are designed not to hurt his sport but to better it.

If it is necessary to cross private lands in order to reach a stream or lake, or to fish on private property, the sportsman asks permission from the owner. When crossing privately owned lands, he does not walk over seeded fields or go through uncut hay lands, but follows a fence line where he will do no damage. Should he come to a closed gate, he closes it after him; if the gate is open, he leaves it open. He does not drive over private lands without permission, and then drives only where told he may.

He does not build a fire without permission, and then only where he can build it on mineral soil, using extreme care to remove any combustible materials to a safe distance from the site. Before leaving he douses the fire, stirring the ashes with a stick so that every ember is wet and safe. If a smoker, he does not throw away a lighted cigarette or cigar without being sure that it is out. He will use the same caution with a pipe.

He leaves no litter anywhere he goes. Any tin can or bottle is buried, the tin cans flattened by stamping on them. Papers, even the wrapper of a candy bar, is either burned safely or stuffed into his pockets to carry home with him. He is orderly in all his acts.

He cuts down a tree only with permission. He does not dig up any plant or shrub without permission. He does not camp without permission, and having had it, leaves the campsite clean. On leaving the property he thanks the owner for the privilege that was given him.

The real sportsman conducts himself toward other fishermen just as properly. If he is fishing a stream and comes upon another angler fishing a pool or stretch of water, he goes around him, walking well back from the bank, knowing that the sight of him would alarm the fish and curtail the fellow angler's sport. He throws no trash, caps, or bottles into the water to pollute it or possibly cut the waders of another angler.

If driving a motor-powered boat on a lake or pond, he keeps well away from the anchored boat of another fisherman and cuts down his speed. A high-powered motor boat can set up waves that are a hazard to small boats and may even swamp them. The great increase in the use of motor boats, and the recklessness of their drivers, have blown up a storm among fishermen, who have demanded that the authorities exercise greater supervision over them.

This sportsman, should he fish with you, is modest. He does not boast of his catch, commends you on your casting, and is happy if you creel a good fish. When you come to a fine, fishy-looking stretch of water, he's likely to tell you, "There should be a good fish there. Go ahead and try it. I'll move along a little way." If he puts on a fly that gets fish, and you haven't that pattern, he insists on your taking one or two from his box.

Following these unwritten laws of good conduct is sure to earn a fisherman respect and admiration. It is not strange that such anglers not only add to the pleasure of others but that they themselves get the utmost out of the sport.

CHAPTER 30

The Fisherman's Books

THERE IS NO closed season for the fisherman who likes to read, for there is much pleasure to be derived from sharing the experiences of fellow anglers who are talented enough to write interestingly about their favorite sport. When winter comes and you put away your fishing rods, store your flies in moth preventives, wipe spoons and spinners with an oily cloth, and clean and oil your reels, the sport of fishing need not end. There is ample opportunity to continue your fishing—vicariously—by reading some of the many fine books on the subject that are available.

I have a large library of fishing books accumulated over many years. Often I have bought an alluring fishing book when I could ill afford it. The suggestions in this chapter are limited by personal experience. Doubtless there are many other books also worth mentioning but which I do not know. Many of those I name are out of print but bob up now and again in the catalogs of second-hand book stores; some of them are on the shelves of public libraries.

We who speak and read English are very fortunate. There are many more books on fishing in English than in any other language. Not only are there many such books by English and Scottish authors, but during the past century a large and increasing number of fishing books have appeared by American and Canadian authors.

The British are devoted to fishing, and because of this devotion have produced considerable literature on the subject dating far back in history. There has come down to us the *Boke of St. Albans,* one of the first books on fly fishing and fly tying, credited to Dame Juliana Berners, abbess of a nunnery, and dated 1486. Izaak Walton's *The Compleat Angler* came nearly two centuries later.

The greatest of the angling authors have stressed the fact that the true measure of a happy and successful fishing trip is not the size of the catch but the emotions aroused by the senses of sight and sound; by the companionship of genial and congenial friends; and by the refreshment of body and soul.

Bliss Perry, author of one of my favorite fishing books, *Pools and Ripples,* realized this truth when he wrote: "By some strange trick of memory the fish you take or lose seem in retrospect only a bit of highlight in the general picture. . . . The cardinal flowers blooming twenty years ago on a mossy log upon the shadowed shore of Big Greenough Pond are lovely yet, though not a trout rose that morning from under the log." My copy of that delightful book was published in 1927 by Little, Brown & Company, Boston.

A splendid book for the fly fisherman is Mary Orvis Marbury's *Favorite Flies and Their Histories,* illustrated with thirty-two fine color plates of flies. It is full of anecdotes from expert anglers of the period and makes fine reading. For years it was out of print and a collector's item but was reprinted recently. I am happy to see that the Charles F. Orvis Company of Manchester, Vermont, is now offering the book at $15. It belongs in the library of every dedicated fly fisherman. I am fortunate to own a copy of the original edition, published in 1892 by Houghton Mifflin Company of New York and Boston.

The classic book on the black bass is still, eighty years after it was published, *The Book of the Black Bass* by Dr. James A. Henshall. It was in this book that he made the oft-quoted statement: "I consider him [the black bass], *inch for inch* and *pound for pound,* the gamest fish that swims." The book exhaustively discusses the black bass in all its aspects—distribution, habits, tackle, and methods of fishing for it. My copy was published in Cincinnati by Robert Clarke & Company in 1881.

Angling in America by Charles Eliot Goodspeed is a splendidly illustrated book which traces the history of angling in North America, with special emphasis on the angling literature of the continent since the earliest days. It contains much information not generally known and was the product of exhaustive research. My copy was published in 1939 by Houghton Mifflin Company, Boston, at $15.

One of the best of the earlier American books on fishing is *I Go A-Fishing* by W. C. Prime, published by Harper & Brothers in 1873. Interlarded with chapters on the author's fishing experiences are others of a romantic nature and seemingly fictional. When you come to one of the latter, skip it, and you will lose nothing. The fishing chapters are marked by vigor, freshness, and beauty. Despite its publication date it does not seem to be rare, for I frequently see it listed in the catalogs of second-hand book stores.

Henry P. Wells' *Fly Rods and Fly Tackle* was first published by Harper & Brothers in 1885, and a second edition came out in 1901, which I own. Wells was the originator of the famous Parmachene Belle fly, still widely used and effective, particularly on brook trout. While the book is largely technical, it also contains some interesting anecdotes. It includes chapters on hooks and how they are made, lines, reels, rods and rod materials, rod making, casting the fly, flies and fly fishing. I have found the book useful.

Dr. Henry Van Dyke was one of the relatively few angling writers who have proved that fishing books can be so well written and interesting as to appeal to the nonangling public. *Fisherman's Luck, Days Off,* and *Little Rivers* were published by Charles Scribner's Sons in the 1890's. They were widely read and important in giving to sport fishing a prestige that had been somewhat lacking. Van Dyke also compiled an anthology, *A Creelful of Fishing Stories,* published by Scribner's in 1932, which contains selections by writers whose works may be otherwise unobtainable. Such noted anglers as Thaddeus Norris, Frank Forester, President Grover Cleveland, H. T. Sheringham, G. E. M. Skues, John Buchan, and Earl Grey of Fallodon are represented. Van Dyke was a distinguished advocate of sport fishing. He was a clergyman before becoming professor of English literature at Princeton University. He also served as minister to the Netherlands from 1913 to 1918.

High on my list of enjoyable fishing books is *The Tent Dwellers* by Albert Bigelow Paine, published by Harper & Brothers about 1910. This joyous book tells of a fishing trip to Nova Scotia. There is good reason to believe that the author's companion, referred to as "Eddie," was Edward Breck, author of the valuable *The Way of the Woods,* a manual for sportsmen in the northeastern United States and Canada, published by G. P. Putnam's Sons in 1908. *The Tent Dwellers* is human, humorous, and genuine.

Game Fishes of the World by Charles Frederic Holder is a splendid work, one that any fisherman would be happy to own. Published by Hodder & Stoughton of London, New York, and Toronto, in 1913, in completeness and literary style it ranks among the best of the fishing books. Its title is somewhat misleading, implying that it is a scientific description and classification of various game fishes. Far from that, it is a vivid account of fishing experiences in different parts of the world. Holder authored another book on fishing which I value, *Recreations of a Sportsman,* published by G. P. Putnam's Sons in 1910. This is devoted entirely to sport fishing on the Pacific Coast. The author tells of his experiences in fishing the little "Mission rivers" of southern California, the famed Feather and Rogue Rivers, and Crater Lake.

Frank Parker Day's *The Autobiography of a Fisherman,* published by Doubleday, Page & Company in 1927, is a wistful, tender, and thoughtful book.

Zane Grey's *Fresh Water Fishing* was published by Harper & Brothers in 1928. It tells of fishing for trout and bass along the Delaware River and for steelhead trout on the Rogue River. There are chapters on fishing in Crater Lake, Upper Klamath Lake, and Tyee salmon fishing off Vancouver Island in British Columbia. This is one of the better fishing books published in the first half of this century.

The classic book on dry-fly fishing in America is George M. La Branche's *The Dry Fly and Fast Water,* published by Charles Scribner's Sons in 1914. La Branche is to the American dry-fly fisherman what Halford was to the British, and when dry-fly men get together you are likely to hear the book discussed. It treats in detail the use of the dry fly on American waters, giving many interesting anecdotes.

Among the practical books are those by Edward R. Hewitt, an expert fisherman who devised the great Bivisible flies, still among the best. His *Handbook of Fly Fishing,* published by The Marchbanks Press, New York, 1933, is the most valuable book of its kind and size. Only 116 pages, it is jammed with sound advice. I have another of his books, *Hewitt's Handbook of Stream Improvement,* published by the same company in 1934. It is a mine of information on its subject.

And now we come to the works of Ray Bergman, for twenty-five years the fishing editor of *Outdoor Life.* They are *Trout, Fresh Water Bass,* and *Just Fishing,* published by Alfred Knopf, Inc., and *With Fly, Plug and Bait,* William Morrow & Co. Bergman, a master fisherman, has devoted his life to the analysis of fishing problems and how best to solve them. He does not talk down to his readers and does not profess infallibility. His anecdotes, which cover a wide field of fishing in the East, Midwest, the Rockies, Far West, and Canada, are always interesting and pertinent. At this writing all of his books are still in print.

A fine reference work for the fisherman is *American Food and Game Fishes* by David Starr Jordan and Dr. Barton Warren Evermann, pub-

lished in New York by Doubleday, Page & Co. in 1902. Jordan was the
first president of Stanford University, and Evermann ichthyologist of the
United States Fish Commission. A splendid work, beautifully illustrated
in color and black and white, scholarly and exhaustive, it is a mine of
information on our fresh- and salt-water fishes.

Among the British angling writers, there is a wide field of interest.
Salar the Salmon by Henry Williamson was published in this country in
1935 by Little, Brown & Company, Boston, and republished in 1950. The
story of the life history of an Atlantic salmon told in fictional form, the
book is deservedly well known and interesting.

Francis Francis, a noted English authority on sport fishing, wrote, as
stated in the subhead of his *A Book on Angling,* a "complete treatise on
the art of angling in every branch." It is encyclopedic in detail, enlivened
by anecdote, and his advice will often aid the American angler. It was published by J. B. Lippincott Company in Philadelphia, and Herbert Jenkins
Ltd. in London in 1920.

Sir Edward Grey's *Fly Fishing,* published by J. M. Dent & Company
of London in 1899, is scholarly and interesting.

Harry Plunket Greene, well known as a concert singer in his day, wrote
Where the Bright Waters Meet, the American edition being published in
1925 by Houghton Mifflin Company. Mainly, the volume tells of the
author's angling in the little river Bourne in Hampshire, England. Though
small, this river yielded to him and his friends trout up to 5 pounds, while
two-pounders were plentiful. He describes the joy of fishing vividly and
with touches of humor.

Another delightful book on angling by an English author is *Golden
Days* by Romilly Fedden, which tells of his fishing experiences in Brittany.
The writer is sensitive to the beauties of Nature and his pages are flooded
with sunshine and happiness. It was published in Boston by the Houghton
Mifflin Company in 1920.

Any discussion of the works of British anglers would be incomplete
without mention of Frederic M. Halford, who may well be called the
dean of dry-fly fishing. He wrote *Floating Flies and How to Dress Them,
Dry-Fly Fishing in Theory and Practice, Dry-Fly Entomology, Modern
Development of the Dry Fly* and *The Dry-Fly Man's Handbook.* I own
the last mentioned and value it highly. Published by George Routledge &
Sons Ltd., London, 1913, it is an exhaustive discussion of the sport of
dry-fly fishing with a section on the fisherman's entomology. While much
of it is technical, it also has interesting anecdotes.

A fine book of reminiscences, *Trout Fishing Memories and Morals* by H. T. Sheringham, published in this country about 1920 by Houghton Mifflin Company, contains many interesting anecdotes, which although about English fishing, will appeal to the Yankee reader.

A Canadian author of decided merit is Roderick L. Haigh-Brown. His *River Never Sleeps* and *Return to the River,* a story of the Chinook salmon run, have been widely read not only by fishermen but the general reading public. *Return to the River,* published by William Morrow & Company in 1941, is fictional; *A River Never Sleeps* is factual, telling of the author's British Columbia fishing experiences during each month in the year. Beautifully written, it belongs in every fisherman's library.

Izaak Walton's *The Compleat Angler* has been published in more editions than any other fishing book. Walton was born in Stafford, England, in 1593. His book was first published in 1653, and that first edition brings fabulous prices among collectors when a copy comes up for sale. While the author's nature lore is often derived from folklore, and the narrative suffers from its dialogue form and labored style, Walton, because of his honesty, simplicity, and love of Nature, has exerted a profound influence on fishermen through the years.

CHAPTER 31

Sources of Information

Herewith is given a list of the state and Canadian provincial agencies to whom to apply for any information about fishing laws in their respective areas. Fishing may be banned in some waters, special restrictions may apply to others. Some streams may have special minimum size regulations different from those named in the general law, and restrictive measures on the method of capture: for example, waters that are restricted-to fly fishing only. The use of minnows for bait is sometimes restricted and legal methods for their capture are defined. Play safe. Don't fish until you are informed of the law. Variations and exceptions in the law are designed for one purpose only—to provide better fishing for all.

ALABAMA—Department of Conservation, Administrative Building, Montgomery, Ala.

ALASKA—Department of Fish and Game, 229 Alaska Office Building, Juneau, Alaska

ARIZONA—State Game and Fish Commission, Arizona State Building, Phoenix, Ariz.

ARKANSAS—State Game and Fish Commission, Game and Fish Building, State Capitol Grounds, Little Rock, Ark.

CALIFORNIA—Department of Fish and Game, 722 Capitol Ave., Sacramento, Calif.

COLORADO—State Game and Fish Department, 1530 Sherman St., Denver 2, Colo.

CONNECTICUT—State Board of Fisheries and Game, State Office Building, Hartford 14, Conn.

DELAWARE—Board of Game and Fish Commissioners, Dover, Del.

DISTRICT OF COLUMBIA—Metropolitan Police, Washington, has jurisdiction.

FLORIDA—Game and Fresh Water Fish Commission, 646 W. Tennessee, Tallahassee, Fla.

GEORGIA—State Game and Fish Commission, 401 State Capitol, Atlanta 3, Ga.

HAWAII—Board of Commissioners of Agriculture and Forestry, Division of Fish and Game, Box 5425, Pawaa Substation, Honolulu 1, Hawaii.

IDAHO—Department of Fish and Game, 518 Front St., Boise, Ida.

ILLINOIS—Department of Conservation, State Office Bldg., Springfield, Ill.

INDIANA—Department of Conservation, Division of Fish and Game, 311 W. Washington St., Indianapolis 9, Ind.

IOWA—State Conservation Commission, E. 7th & Court Ave., Des Moines 9, Ia.

KANSAS—Forestry, Fish and Game Commission, Box 591, Pratt, Kans.

KENTUCKY—Department of Fish and Wildlife Resources, State Office Bldg. Annex, Frankfort, Ky.

LOUISIANA—Wild Life and Fisheries Commission, 126 Civil Courts Bldg., New Orleans 16, La.

MAINE—Department of Inland Fisheries and Game, State House, Augusta, Me.

MARYLAND—Maryland Game and Inland Fish Commission, State Office Bldg., Annapolis, Md.

MASSACHUSETTS—Department of Natural Resources, Division of Fisheries and Game, 73 Tremont St., Boston 8, Mass.

MICHIGAN—Department of Conservation, Lansing 26, Mich.

MINNESOTA—Department of Conservation, State Office Bldg., St. Paul 1, Minn.

MISSISSIPPI—State Game and Fish Commission, Woolfolk State Office Bldg., Jackson, Miss.

MISSOURI—State Conservation Commission, Farm Bureau Bldg., Jefferson City, Mo.

MONTANA—State Fish and Game Commission, Helena, Mont.

NEBRASKA—Game, Forestation and Parks Commission, State Capitol Bldg., Lincoln 9, Neb.

NEVADA—State Fish and Game Commission, Box 678, Reno, Nev.

NEW HAMPSHIRE—State Fish and Game Department, 34 Bridge St., Concord, N. H.

NEW JERSEY—Department of Conservation and Economic Development, Division of Fish and Game, 230 West State St., Trenton, N. J.

NEW MEXICO—State Department of Game and Fish, Santa Fe, N. M.

NEW YORK—State Conservation Department, Albany, N. Y.

NORTH CAROLINA—Wildlife Resources Commission, Box 2919, Raleigh, N. C.

NORTH DAKOTA—State Game and Fish Department, Bismarck, N. D.

OHIO—Department of Natural Resources, Wildlife Division, Ohio Departments Bldg., Columbus 15, Ohio.

OKLAHOMA—Department of Wildlife Conservation, Room 118, State Capitol Bldg., Oklahoma City 5, Okla.

OREGON—State Fish Commission, 307 State Office Bldg., Portland 1, Ore.

PENNSYLVANIA—State Fish Commission, Harrisburg, Pa.

PUERTO RICO—Department of Agriculture and Commerce, San Juan, P. R.

RHODE ISLAND—Department of Agriculture and Conservation, Veterans Memorial Bldg., 83 Park St., Providence 2, R. I.

SOUTH CAROLINA—State Wildlife Resources Department, 1015 Main St., Box 360, Columbia, S. C.

SOUTH DAKOTA—State Department of Game, Fish and Parks, State Office Bldg., Pierre, S. D.

TENNESSEE—State Game and Fish Commission, Cordell Hull Bldg., Nashville, Tenn.

TEXAS—State Game and Fish Commission, Austin, Tex.

UTAH—State Department of Fish and Game, 1596 W. N. Temple, Salt Lake City, Utah.

VERMONT—State Fish and Game Commission, Montpelier, Vt.

VIRGINIA—Commission of Game and Inland Fisheries, 7 N. 2nd St., Box 1642, Richmond 13, Va.

WASHINGTON—Department of Game, 600 N. Capitol Way, Olympia, Wash.

WEST VIRGINIA—State Conservation Commission, State Office Bldg. No. 3, Charleston, W. Va.

WISCONSIN—State Conservation Department, State Office Bldg., Madison 1, Wis.

WYOMING—State Game and Fish Commission, Box 378, Cheyenne, Wyo.

CANADA

ALBERTA—Department of Lands and Forests, Edmonton, Alta.

BRITISH COLUMBIA—Fish and Game Branch, Department of Recreation and Conservation, 567 Burrard St., Vancouver 1, B. C.

MANITOBA—Department of Mines and Natural Resources, Winnipeg, Man.

NEWFOUNDLAND—Department of Mines and Resources, St. John's, Newfoundland.

NORTHWEST TERRITORIES—Northern Administration Branch, Department of Northern Affairs and National Resources, Ottawa, Ontario, Canada.

NOVA SCOTIA—Department of Lands and Forests, Halifax, N. S.

ONTARIO—Department of Lands and Forests, Parliament Bldgs., Toronto, Ontario

PRINCE EDWARD ISLAND—Department of Industry and Natural Resources, Charlottetown, P. E. I.

QUEBEC—Department of Game and Fisheries, Quebec, Que.

SASKATCHEWAN—Department of Natural Resources, Government Administration Bldg., Regina, Sask.

YUKON TERRITORY—Game Department, Yukon Territorial Government, Box 2029, Whitehorse, Y. T., Canada.

CHAPTER 32

Maps for the Fisherman

MAPS ARE OF great help to the fisherman. Road maps, published by most of the big oil companies and available free at gas stations, while useful in tracing a general route, are not sufficiently detailed to show minor bodies of water. But the federal government and state and provincial departments publish and sell at moderate prices detailed maps drawn to fine scale which are invaluable to the fisherman. Also, many states now publish survey maps of various lakes within their borders which show depths, underwater contours, bars, patches of weeds, etc.

FEDERAL GOVERNMENT MAPS

The U. S. Geological Survey, Department of the Interior, Washington 25, D. C., publishes the best maps available in the United States. The various states are divided into quadrangles, each about 16½ x 20 inches, with a standard scale of 1 inch to 2½ miles. Contour lines show elevations. They are in such fine detail that streams, ponds, lakes, swamps, roads, and trails all are shown.

An index map of each state is available free which shows all the quadrangles that have been mapped. From it you can select the quadrangle in which you propose to fish, and order from the Survey at the current low price of 30 cents per map. For maps of areas east of the Mississippi River, address the Geological Survey, Washington 25, D. C. For maps west of the Mississippi, address the Geological Survey, Federal Center, Denver, Colorado.

All the states have not yet been completely mapped. Should you find that the particular area in which you are interested is not yet mapped by the

290

Survey, then you usually will be able to get a detailed map from the state agency named herein. Should you find the particular state of your interest not listed here, write the State Highway Department at the state capital.

THE NATIONAL FORESTS

Much of the best fishing available to the general public is to be found in the national forests. These forests hold the finest wilderness now left in the United States—roadless, remote, and unspoiled. Among them are lofty mountains, superb scenery, deep gorges and canyons, and many clear blue lakes and rushing streams which offer a challenge to the fisherman. They are located in all sections of the country. There is one or more within a day's drive of every fisherman, wherever he lives. Hiking and riding trails within them total about 120,000 miles. They are of great importance to the fisherman of today and tomorrow. With the rapidly increasing population and abuses of a very small and willful minority, posting by landowners has barred to the public access to many fishing waters once open to all. The national forests, covering some 181,000,000 acres, and offering much of the best fishing in the country, are publicly owned and open to all for recreational purposes. Here are no "No Trespass" signs. The fisherman who behaves decently, has a state fishing license, and observes the fishing laws, can enjoy the finest fishing available.

General rules apply to every visitor to a national forest. They are simple and dictated by common sense.

1. Be sure to check on local fire rules. Read the signs and posters. Some areas are closed to smoking or to all travel because of fire hazard. Ask the ranger.

2. Discharging fireworks is forbidden in all national forests.

3. Build campfires only in safe places and put them out with water before leaving.

4. At regular camp and picnic areas build fires only at designated places.

5. In areas where smoking is permitted, don't smoke when walking or riding in the forest, and be sure your match, cigarette, cigar, or pipe heel is out before you discard it.

6. Never throw lighted smokes out of a car—use the ashtray.

7. Tables, latrines, and shelters are costly and for your convenience. Don't cut initials, mutilate, or destroy them. Leave them in sanitary condition.

8. Trees, shrubs, and flowers make a forest attractive. Don't cut or deface trees. Leave flowers for others to see and enjoy.

9. Don't pollute ground or water. Fish and clothing should not be cleaned in lakes and streams.

10. Observe state and federal game and fish laws.

The writer has fished in a number of the national forests. He has found the forest rangers friendly and helpful, a good source of fishing information. He has enjoyed these fishing trips immensely and rarely has been disappointed in his catch. He considers them invaluable to the fisherman and the hope of the future. Following is a list of national forests. Fishermen who want a map of any forest should write The Supervisor of the individual park as listed below.

Alabama

WILLIAM B. BANKHEAD NATIONAL FOREST, 178,895 acres, Montgomery, Ala. Bass and bream.

CONECUH NATIONAL FOREST, 83,790 acres, Montgomery, Ala. Bass and bream.

TALLADEGA NATIONAL FOREST, 357,847 acres, Montgomery, Ala. Bass and bream.

TUSKEGEE NATIONAL FOREST, 10,777 acres, Montgomery, Ala. Bream.

Alaska

CHUGACH NATIONAL FOREST, 4,726,145 acres, Anchorage, Alaska. Trout and salt-water fishing.

TONGASS NATIONAL FOREST, North Division, 16,016,140 acres, Juneau, Alaska. Trout and salt-water fishing.

TONGASS NATIONAL FOREST, South Division, 16,016,140 acres, Ketchikan, Alaska. Trout and salt-water fishing.

Arizona

APACHE NATIONAL FOREST, partly in New Mexico, 1,732,891 acres, Springerville, Ariz. Lake and stream trout fishing.

COCONINO NATIONAL FOREST, 1,801,091 acres, Flagstaff, Ariz. Lake and stream fishing.

CORONADO NATIONAL FOREST, partly in New Mexico, 1,196,534 acres, Tucson, Ariz. Some trout and bass fishing.

KAIBAB NATIONAL FOREST, 1,715,190 acres, Williams, Ariz. Various fishing waters.

PRESCOTT NATIONAL FOREST, 1,248,210 acres, Prescott, Ariz. Limited trout fishing.

SITGREAVES NATIONAL FOREST, 744,820 acres, Holbrook, Ariz. Fishing negligible.

TONTO NATIONAL FOREST, 2,902,072 acres, Phoenix, Ariz. Artificial lakes covering 30,000 acres. Bass fishing, limited trout fishing in high country.

Arkansas

OUACHITA NATIONAL FOREST, partly in Oklahoma, 1,542,412 acres, Hot Springs, Ark. Numerous lakes with bass fishing.

OZARK NATIONAL FOREST, 1,046,309 acres, Russellville, Ark. Stream and lake fishing.

California

ANGELES NATIONAL FOREST, 648,754 acres, Pasadena, Calif. Easily reached fishing for a heavily populated area.

CLEVELAND NATIONAL FOREST, 391,682 acres, San Diego, Calif. Warm-water fishing.

ELDORADO NATIONAL FOREST, 640,619 acres, Placerville, Calif. Lake and stream fishing.

INYO NATIONAL FOREST, 1,774,176 acres, partly in Nevada, Bishop, Calif. Lake and stream fishing.

KLAMATH NATIONAL FOREST, partly in Oregon, 1,697,600 acres, Yreka, Calif. Has Klamath River and tributaries with fine salmon and steelhead fishing. Also trout.

LASSEN NATIONAL FOREST, 1,047,372 acres, Susanville, Calif. Lake and stream fishing for rainbows, Loch Leven, and steelhead trout.

LOS PADRES NATIONAL FOREST, 1,740,245 acres, Santa Barbara, Calif. Trout fishing.

MENDOCINO NATIONAL FOREST, 867,425 acres, Willows, Calif. Lake and stream fishing.

MODOC NATIONAL FOREST, 1,688,789 acres, Alturas, Calif. Stream and lake fishing.

PLUMAS NATIONAL FOREST, 1,147,611 acres, Quincy, Calif. Holds the famous Feather River country. Trout fishing, lakes and streams.

SAN BERNARDINO NATIONAL FOREST, 613,912 acres, San Bernardino, Calif. Lake and stream fishing.

SEQUOIA NATIONAL FOREST, 1,118,551 acres. Porterville, Calif. High mountain lakes and streams, golden and other trout.

SHASTA-TRINITY NATIONAL FOREST, 2,036,836 acres, Redding, Calif. Lake and stream fishing. Dolly Varden and other trout.

SIERRA NATIONAL FOREST, 1,295,832 acres, Fresno, Calif. Lake and stream fishing.

SIX RIVERS NATIONAL FOREST, 935,268 acres, Eureka, Calif. Trout fishing in spring and summer; steelhead and salmon fishing in fall and winter in six rivers.

STANISLAUS NATIONAL FOREST, 896,165 acres, Sonora, Calif. Fishing in lakes and 715 miles of streams.

TAHOE NATIONAL FOREST, 694,112 acres, Nevada City, Calif. Lake and stream fishing.

Colorado

ARAPAHO NATIONAL FOREST, 990,371 acres, Golden, Colo. Lake and stream fishing.

GRAND MESA-UNCOMPAHGRE NATIONAL FORESTS, 1,317,865 acres, Delta, Colo. Lake and stream fishing.

GUNNISON NATIONAL FOREST, 1,660,147 acres, Gunnison, Colo. Trout fishing in streams, many high lakes.

PIKE NATIONAL FOREST, 1,084,947 acres, Colorado Springs, Colo. Lake and stream fishing.

RIO GRANDE NATIONAL FOREST, 1,800,322 acres, Monte Vista, Colo. Trout fishing in streams, mountain lakes.

ROOSEVELT NATIONAL FOREST, 784,051 acres, Fort Collins, Colo. Trout fishing in many high lakes, streams.

ROUTT NATIONAL FOREST, 1,145,111 acres, Steamboat Springs, Colo. Trout streams, alpine lakes.

SAN ISABEL NATIONAL FOREST, 1,104,042 acres, Pueblo, Colo. Lake and stream trout fishing. Twelve high mountains of more than 14,000 ft., many timberline lakes.

SAN JUAN NATIONAL FOREST, 1,850,053 acres, Durango, Colo. Alpine lakes. Trout fishing.

WHITE RIVER NATIONAL FOREST, 1,961,798 acres, Glenwood Springs, Colo. Trout fishing in lakes and streams.

Florida

APALACHICOLA NATIONAL FOREST, 556,480 acres, Tallahassee, Fla. Fishing for bass, bream, and perch in many lakes, ponds, and many miles of three rivers and their tributaries.

OCALA NATIONAL FOREST, 361,029 acres, Tallahassee, Fla. Numerous lakes and large clear streams with fishing for bass and bream.

OSCEOLA NATIONAL FOREST, 157,233 acres, Tallahassee, Fla. Bass, perch, and bream fishing in numerous ponds.

Georgia

CHATTAHOOCHEE NATIONAL FOREST, 680,333 acres, Gainesville. Ga. Trout and bass fishing in lakes and streams.

OCONEE NATIONAL FOREST, 96,066 acres, Gainesville, Ga. Bass and bream fishing.

Idaho

BOISE NATIONAL FOREST, 2,629,465 acres, Boise, Idaho. Lake and stream fishing for trout and salmon.

CARIBOU NATIONAL FOREST, partly in Utah and Wyoming, 976,041 acres, Pocatello, Idaho. Stream trout fishing.

CHALLIS NATIONAL FOREST, 2,447,696 acres, Challis, Idaho. Trout fishing in streams and lakes, salmon fishing.

CLEARWATER NATIONAL FOREST, 1,248,455 acres, Orofino, Idaho. Trout and salmon fishing in back country.

COEUR D'ALENE NATIONAL FOREST, 723,217 acres, Coeur d'Alene, Idaho. Lake and stream fishing.

KANIKSU NATIONAL FOREST, 1,625,383 acres, partly in Montana and Washington, Sandpoint, Idaho. Lake and stream fishing.

NEZPERCE NATIONAL FOREST, 2,195,908 acres, Grangeville, Idaho. Holds famous Selway-Bitterroot Wilderness Area. Lake and stream fishing.

PAYETTE NATIONAL FOREST, 2,307,205 acres, McCall, Idaho. Has 154 fishing lakes, 1,530 miles of fishing streams. Trout and salmon.

SALMON NATIONAL FOREST, 1,768,718 acres, Salmon, Idaho. Trout and salmon fishing.

ST. JOE NATIONAL FOREST, 866,269 acres, St. Maries, Idaho. Lake and stream fishing.

SAWTOOTH NATIONAL FOREST, partly in Utah, 1,802,680 acres, Twin Falls, Idaho. Has famous Sun Valley. Trout fishing in lakes and streams.

TARGHEE NATIONAL FOREST, partly in Wyoming, 1,666,370 acres, St. Anthony, Idaho. Trout fishing in lakes and streams.

Illinois

SHAWNEE NATIONAL FOREST, 211,013 acres, Harrisburg, Ill. Stream, river, lake fishing.

Indiana

HOOSIER NATIONAL FOREST, 117,906 acres, Bedford, Ind. Bass, bluegill, and catfish fishing in four rivers and a creek.

Kentucky

CUMBERLAND NATIONAL FOREST, 458,352 acres, Winchester, Ky. Has about 500 miles of fishing streams with bass and pike in the larger streams, and fine bass, crappie, and bluegill fishing in big Lake Cumberland.

Louisiana

KISATCHIE NATIONAL FOREST, 591,726 acres, Alexandria, La. Fishing for warm-water fish in lakes and bayous.

Michigan

HURON NATIONAL FOREST, 414,819 acres, Cadillac, Mich. Trout fishing in Au Sable River and smaller streams. Easily reached from heavily populated regions in southern Michigan, northern Ohio, and Illinois.

MANISTEE NATIONAL FOREST, 445,775 acres, Cadillac, Mich. Like the Huron National Forest, readily accessible from heavily populated areas. Lake and stream fishing.

OTTAWA NATIONAL FOREST, 858,352 acres, Ironwood, Mich. Numerous easily reached fishing lakes and streams.

HIAWATHA-MARQUETTE NATIONAL FORESTS, 830,179 acres, Escanaba, Mich. Lake and stream fishing for trout, bass, northern pike, walleyes, and perch.

Minnesota

CHIPPEWA NATIONAL FOREST, 639,452 acres, Cass Lake, Minn. Lake fishing for walleyes, northern pike, and panfish.

SUPERIOR NATIONAL FOREST, 1,957,981 acres, Duluth, Minn. Best canoe country in the United States, with 5,000 lakes. Lake and stream fishing, walleyes, northern pike, bass, trout.

Mississippi

BIENVILLE NATIONAL FOREST, 175,657 acres, Jackson, Miss. Warm-water fishing.

DE SOTO NATIONAL FOREST, 500,335 acres, Jackson, Miss. Warm-water fishing.

HOLLY SPRINGS NATIONAL FOREST, 143,352 acres, Jackson, Miss. Fishing negligible.

HOMOCHITTO NATIONAL FOREST, 189,069 acres, Jackson, Miss. Fishing for warm-water fishes.

TOMBIGBEE NATIONAL FOREST, 65,232 acres, Jackson, Miss. Fishing for warm-water fishes.

Missouri

CLARK NATIONAL FOREST, 902,662 acres, Rolla, Mo. Fine float trips. Fishing for smallmouth bass and other species. Several large lakes. Current and Eleven Point Rivers.

MARK TWAIN NATIONAL FOREST, 451,085 acres, Rolla, Mo. Clear streams with fishing for bass, walleyes, and panfish.

Montana

BEAVERHEAD NATIONAL FOREST, 2,131,136 acres, Dillon, Mont. Fine trout fishing in outstanding streams such as the Madison, Big Hole, Ruby, and Beaverhead Rivers. Also high mountain lakes.

BITTERROOT NATIONAL FOREST, partly in Idaho, 1,574,563 acres, Hamilton, Mont. Trout fishing in many lakes and streams.

CUSTER NATIONAL FOREST, partly in South Dakota, 1,171,476 acres, Billings, Mont. Trout fishing.

DEERLODGE NATIONAL FOREST, 1,134,639 acres, Butte, Mont. Lake and stream fishing, mostly trout.

FLATHEAD NATIONAL FOREST, 2,336,378 acres, Kalispell, Mont. Lakes and streams with trout fishing.

GALLATIN NATIONAL FOREST, 1,700,139 acres, Bozeman, Mont. More than 200 lakes and thousands of miles of good trout streams.

HELENA NATIONAL FOREST, 966,613 acres, Helena, Mont. Lake and stream fishing, mostly for trout.

KOOTENAI NATIONAL FOREST, partly in Idaho, 1,817,975 acres, Libby, Mont. Lake and stream fishing, mostly for trout.

LEWIS AND CLARK NATIONAL FOREST, 1,862,011 acres, Great Falls, Mont. Good trout fishing, streams and lakes.

LOLO NATIONAL FOREST, 2,502,698 acres, partly in Idaho, Missoula, Mont. Many fishing lakes and streams.

Nebraska

NEBRASKA NATIONAL FOREST, 206,082 acres, Lincoln, Nebraska. Entire forest in game refuge. Some fishing.

Nevada

HUMBOLDT NATIONAL FOREST, 2,507,869 acres, Elko, Nev. Fishing in streams and Wildhorse Reservoir.

TOIYABE NATIONAL FOREST, partly in California, 3,118,966 acres, Reno, Nev. Excellent trout fishing in many fine lakes and streams.

New Hampshire

WHITE MOUNTAIN NATIONAL FOREST, partly in Maine, 723,394 acres, Laconia, N. H. Brook-trout fishing in 650 miles of streams and 39 lakes and ponds.

New Mexico

CARSON NATIONAL FOREST, 1,225,408 acres, Taos, N. M. Trout streams and alpine lakes. Has Wheeler Peak, 13,151 ft., highest in state.

CIBOLA NATIONAL FOREST, 1,696,703 acres, Albuquerque, N. M. Limited fishing at Bluewater and McGaffey Lakes.

GILA NATIONAL FOREST, 2,715,520 acres, Silver City, N. M. Lake fishing in Wall Lake and Bear Canyon Reservoir. Trout fishing in streams, most of it requiring pack trips to little fished waters.

LINCOLN NATIONAL FOREST, 1,087,855 acres, Alamogordo, N. M. A fair amount of fishing.

SANTA FE NATIONAL FOREST, 1,233,550 acres, Santa Fe, N. M. Trout fishing in mountain streams and lakes.

North Carolina

CROATAN NATIONAL FOREST, 152,351 acres, Asheville, N. C. Fishing in five large lakes, some streams.

NANTAHALA NATIONAL FOREST, 448,278 acres, Asheville, N. C. Stream fishing for trout, bass fishing in a number of fine lakes.

PISGAH NATIONAL FOREST, 479,697 acres, Asheville, N. C. Trout, bass and perch fishing.

Ohio

WAYNE NATIONAL FOREST, 106,129 acres, Forest Supervisor, Bedford, Ind. Fishing in numerous streams and lakes.

Oregon

DESCHUTES NATIONAL FOREST, 1,659,368 acres, Bend, Ore. Good fishing for rainbow trout.

FREMONT NATIONAL FOREST, 1,254,595 acres, Lakeview, Ore. Rainbow and brook trout.

MALHEUR NATIONAL FOREST, 1,410,548 acres, John Day, Ore. Fishing for rainbows and steelheads.

MOUNT HOOD NATIONAL FOREST, 1,115,344 acres, Portland, Ore. Stream and lake fishing.

OCHOCO NATIONAL FOREST, 845,876 acres, Prineville, Ore. Trout fishing.

ROGUE RIVER NATIONAL FOREST, partly in California, 839,290 acres, Medford, Ore. Famous steelhead river, the Rogue. Rainbow fishing in streams.

SISKIYOU NATIONAL FOREST, partly in California, 1,046,607 acres, Grants Pass, Ore. Fine salmon fishing in lower Rogue River, streams with cutthroats and steelheads.

SIUSLAW NATIONAL FOREST, 621,044 acres, Corvallis, Ore. Ocean, lake, and stream fishing.

UMPQUA NATIONAL FOREST, 978,704 acres, Roseburg, Ore. Steelhead and rainbow fishing.

UMATILLA NATIONAL FOREST, partly in Washington, 1,075,938 acres, Pendleton, Ore. Stream fishing for steelheads and rainbows.

WALLOWA-WHITMAN NATIONAL FORESTS, 2,285,207 acres, Baker, Ore. Minam River, famous trout stream, other streams and lakes for trout.

WILLAMETTE NATIONAL FOREST, 1,666,036 acres, Eugene, Ore. Stream and lake fishing.

Pennsylvania

ALLEGHENY NATIONAL FOREST, 470,197 acres, Warren, Pa. Has 260 miles of trout streams, 85 miles of bass fishing in Allegheny and Clarion Rivers.

South Carolina

FRANCIS MARION NATIONAL FOREST, 245,650 acres, Columbia, S. C. Fishing for bass and other species.

SUMTER NATIONAL FOREST, 341,624 acres, Columbia, S. C. Trout and bass fishing.

South Dakota

BLACK HILLS NATIONAL FOREST, partly in Wyoming, 1,045,441 acres, Custer, S. D. Lake and stream fishing, including trout.

Tennessee

CHEROKEE NATIONAL FOREST, 595,097 acres, Cleveland, Tenn. Lake and stream fishing, rainbow and brook trout.

Texas

ANGELINA NATIONAL FOREST, 154,392 acres, Lufkin, Tex. Bass and catfishing in rivers and lakes.

DAVY CROCKETT NATIONAL FOREST, 161,556 acres, Lufkin, Tex. Bass and catfishing in rivers and lakes.

SABINE NATIONAL FOREST, 183,842 acres, Lufkin, Tex. Bass and catfishing in rivers and lakes.

SAM HOUSTON NATIONAL FOREST, 158,204 acres, Lufkin, Tex. Numerous lakes and streams with bass and catfish.

Utah

ASHLEY NATIONAL FOREST, 1,282,829 acres, Vernal, Utah. Lake and stream fishing.

CACHE NATIONAL FOREST, partly in Idaho, 651,909 acres, Logan, Utah. Trout fishing.

DIXIE NATIONAL FOREST, 1,839,547 acres, Cedar City, Utah. Lake and stream fishing.

FISHLAKE NATIONAL FOREST, 1,415,673 acres, Richfield, Utah. Lake and stream fishing.

MANTI-LA SAL NATIONAL FOREST, partly in Colorado, 1,237,128 acres, Price, Utah. Trout fishing.

UINTA NATIONAL FOREST, 774,721 acres, Provo, Utah. Trout fishing.

WASATCH NATIONAL FOREST, partly in Wyoming, 827,441 acres, Salt Lake City, Utah. Holds 576 miles of streams, 115 lakes. Trout.

Vermont

GREEN MOUNTAIN NATIONAL FOREST, 230,954 acres, Rutland, Vt. Fishing in about 400 miles of streams and 30 lakes and ponds.

Virginia

GEORGE WASHINGTON NATIONAL FOREST, partly in West Virginia, 1,002,167 acres, Harrisonburg, Va. Trout and bass fishing, 208 miles of cold-water fishing streams.

JEFFERSON NATIONAL FOREST, 542,725 acres, Roanoke, Va. Three fishing lakes, more than 200 miles of fishing streams.

Washington

COLVILLE NATIONAL FOREST, 928,332 acres, Colville, Wash. Lake and stream fishing.

GIFFORD PINCHOT NATIONAL FOREST, 1,263,380 acres, Vancouver, Wash. Lake and stream trout fishing.

MOUNT BAKER NATIONAL FOREST, 1,818,283 acres, Bellingham, Wash. Fishing for steelheads and rainbows.

OKANOGAN NATIONAL FOREST, 1,520,340 acres, Okanogan, Wash. Lake and stream fishing, trout.

OLYMPIC NATIONAL FOREST, 621,744 acres, Olympia, Wash. Many lakes and streams with fishing for salmon, steelheads, rainbows.

SNOQUALMIE NATIONAL FOREST, 1,207,815 acres, Seattle, Wash. Stream and lake fishing. Salmon, steelheads, trout.

WENATCHEE NATIONAL FOREST, 1,728,086 acres, Wenatchee, Wash. Lakes Chelan and Wenatchee. Trout streams.

West Virginia

MONONGAHELA NATIONAL FOREST, 805,668 acres, Elkins, W. Va. About 1,900 miles of trout and bass streams.

Wisconsin

CHEQUAMEGON NATIONAL FOREST, 827,027 acres, Park Falls, Wis. Lake and stream fishing with emphasis on muskellunge.

NICOLET NATIONAL FOREST, 640,075 acres, Rhinelander, Wis. Lake and stream fishing for muskies, pike, bass, and trout.

Wyoming

BIGHORN NATIONAL FOREST, 1,113,597 acres, Sheridan, Wyo. Over 300 lakes. Streams. Trout fishing.

BRIDGER NATIONAL FOREST, 1,699,059 acres, Kemmerer, Wyo. Much wild country with streams and lakes. Trout fishing.

MEDICINE BOW NATIONAL FOREST, 1,063,537 acres, Laramie, Wyo. Numerous lakes and fishing streams. Trout.

SHOSHONE NATIONAL FOREST, 2,429,510 acres, Cody, Wyo. Hundreds of lakes, streams. Trout.

TETON NATIONAL FOREST, 1,700,766 acres, Jackson, Wyo. Wild country back in. Trout fishing in many lakes and streams.

NATIONAL PARKS

A number of the national parks have fine fishing. For information and what maps are available, write The Superintendent of the individual park as listed below.

Glacier National Park, West Glacier, Montana.

Grand Teton National Park, Moose, Wyo.

Great Smoky Mountains National Park, Gatlinburg, Tenn.

Isle Royale National Park, Houghton, Mich.

Olympic National Park, Port Angeles, Wash.

Yellowstone National Park, Mammoth Hot Springs, Wyo.

Yosemite National Park, Yosemite National Park P. O., Calif.

THE STATES. Write for prices to addresses given.

Arkansas

State Highway Commission, Division of Statistics and Analyses, 401 Highway Bldg., Little Rock, Ark. County highway and transportation maps, large, fine scale. Same, scale ½ inch to 1 mile.

California

County and sectional maps of southern and central California, also Inyo-Sequoia, Inyo-Sierra, Mono-Stanislaus regional maps—Automobile Club of Southern California, Figueroa St. at Adams, Los Angeles, Calif.

Department of Fish and Game maps, 722 Capitol Ave., Sacramento, Calif. Anglers Guide for each of following: Colorado River Area, Trinity Divide Area, Marble Mountain Area, Fish Creek Area, Granite Creek Area, Mineral King Area, Bear Creek Area, Salmon and Scott Mountains Area. Salmon and Steelhead fishing map. Fishing, Hunting, and Recreation map of the Sacramento Area.

California Fishing Maps: C. E. Erickson & Associates, 1521 Shattuck Ave., Berkeley, Calif., publishers maps of various good fishing areas within the state, which show streams, lakes, reservoirs, roads, trails, camps, resorts, and lists commercial packers. Also *Inland Fishing Waters of California,* a directory of more than 2,000 rivers, streams, and lakes. Also the *Steelhead-Salmon Fishing Atlas.* Many sporting goods stores in the state sell these, or apply to the publishers direct for list and prices.

Rand McNally & Co., 619 Mission St., San Francisco, has fine scale maps of the state available.

Metsker Map Co., 111 South Tenth St., Tacoma 2, Wash., publishes maps of all California counties.

Sunset Magazine, Menlo Park, Calif., publishes atlases of maps of San Francisco Bay and Delta, Colorado River, the Lake Mead Area, and Southern California and northern Mexico coast. These show boat launchings, boat-repair and rental stations, access roads, where to fish, and where food is available. Also the *Sportsman's Atlas of the High Sierras*—a guide to the high country from Lake Almanor on the north to the Kern River on the south, including Yosemite, Kings Canyon, and Sequoia National Parks.

Humboldt County Fishing Map, the Humboldt Chamber of Commerce, Seventh and F Streets, Eureka, Calif. Shows county roads, trails, streets, where and how to fish, where to rent boats and equipment, gives license fees and limits.

Amador County Chamber of Commerce, Box 596, Jackson, Calif., publishes large detailed map of the entire county, showing trails, rivers, streams, lakes, campgrounds, ranger stations and lookout stations.

Connecticut

Large state map, State Development Commission, State Office Bldg., Hartford, Conn. Contour maps of 154 bodies of water, also fishing data, 395 pages, book, $1.50, Connecticut State Library, Capitol Building, Hartford, Conn.

Florida

County maps, State Road Department, Division of Research and Records, Tallahassee, Fla.

Georgia

County maps, State Highway Board, Atlanta, Ga.

Louisiana

Maps of individual parishes (the equivalent of counties in other states), scale 1 in. to 1 mile, State Division of Public Works, Baton Rouge, La. Also maps of streams and coast lines.

Maine

A total of over 1,000 lakes and ponds have been mapped and they're sold at nominal prices. Listing them is *Sportsman's Inventory and Index,* a free leaflet. Division of Information and Education, Inland Fisheries and Game Dept., Augusta, Me.

Michigan

Book containing individual maps of all 83 counties, showing state game and recreation area land, public fishing sites, trails, airplane landing fields, Michigan Department of Conservation, Lansing, Mich. Also county maps, scale 1 in. to 1 mile. Maps of about 2,500 lakes available.

Minnesota

County maps 36 x 58 in., scale 1 in. to 1 mile, Department of Highways, 1246 University Ave., St. Paul 4, Minn. Canoe Country maps. Portfolio of 15 color maps covering wilderness country along Minnesota-Canadian boundary, each map 17 x 22 in. These maps drawn from aerial surveys of U. S. and Canadian governments, show canoe routes and portages in detail. Write W. Fisher Co., Virginia, Minn.

Montana

County maps, ¼ in. to 1 mile, State Highway Commission, Helena, Mont. Also state map.

New Hampshire

County maps, scale about 1 in. to 1 mile, also state map, scale 1 in. to 4 miles, State Highway Dept., Concord, N. H.

New Jersey

County maps, scale 2 in. to 1 mile, inquire of State Highway Dept., Trenton, N. J. Varying number of sheets to the county. Biological surveys have been made of many lakes in state which show contours, type of bottom, weed beds, etc., also brief general information about fishes present, rental docks, etc. Several volumes paper bound. Write Department of Conservation and Economic Development, Division of Fish & Game, 230 West State St., Trenton, N. J.

New Mexico

State map, scale 1 in. to 8 miles; 127 quadrangle maps covering state, scale 1 in. to 1 mile, county maps, scale ½ in. to 1 mile, State Highway Dept., Santa Fe, N. M.

New York

Detailed large maps of Catskill and Adirondack State Forests, State Conservation Department, Albany 7, N. Y.

North Carolina

County maps, scale 1½ in. to 4 miles, State Highway and Public Works Commission, Raleigh, N. C.

North Dakota

County maps, scale 1 in. to 1 mile, varying number of sheets to a county, State Highway Dept., Bismarck, N. D.

Pennsylvania

County maps, scale 1 in. to 6,000 ft., Division of Documents, Bureau of Publications, Harrisburg, Pa. County maps for fishermen and hunters, 27 single county maps, 19 two-county maps, State Fish Commission, Harrisburg, Pa.

South Carolina

County maps, Transport and Statistics Engineer, State Highway Dept., Columbia, S. C.

South Dakota

County maps, Statewide Planning Survey, Pierre, S. D.

Virginia

County maps, scale ½ in. to 1 mile, State Department of Highways, Richmond, Va.

West Virginia

County maps, West Virginia Geological Survey, Morgantown, W. Va.

Wisconsin

County maps, Chief Clerk, State Highway Commission, State Office Bldg., Madison 2, Wis.

Lake Maps. A number of states have made biological surveys of various lakes and prepared maps of individual lakes which show depths, character of bottom, location of weed beds, and the like. This mapping is still being done. The official agency responsible is variously named the Fish Department or Commission, Fish and Game Department, Game Department, or Conservation Department, depending upon the state. A complete list of these agencies is given in the previous chapter. To find out what lake maps are available in the state of your choice, write the proper agency for information.

Some states have not been included in the list in this chapter. Information as to what maps are available in those states may be had by writing to State Highway Dept. at the capital.

Rand McNally & Co., with offices in Chicago, New York and San Francisco, publishes pocket maps of each state in considerable detail.

These show bays, gulfs, harbors, capes, and points, Indian reservations and subagencies, islands, lakes and reservoirs, mountains and peaks, national monuments and parks, rivers and creeks, and counties.

DOMINION OF CANADA

Price lists available from each agency named. Hydrographic and Map Service, Dept. of Mines and Resources, Ottawa, Ontario, Canada. The National Topographic Series, prepared from aerial surveys, showing rapids, falls, portages, etc. For lists of topographical maps, various parts of Canada, write Bureau of Geology and Topography, Ottawa, Ontario.

Maps of Ontario Province, Maps and Surveys Branch, Dept. of Lands and Forests, Parliament Bldgs., Toronto, Canada. Also provincial, township, lake, and topographical maps. County, district, and township maps, Department of Highways, Parliament Bldgs., Toronto, Canada.

Quebec—Full line of provincial, regional, and canoeing maps. Department of Lands and Forests, Quebec, P. Q.

Saskatchewan—Township, provincial forests, and regional maps. Department of Natural Resources, Regina, Sask.

British Columbia—Sectional and provincial maps, varying scales. British Columbia Lands Department, Survey Branch, Victoria, B. C.

Manitoba—Provincial, canoe route maps. Surveys Branch, Department of Mines and Resources, Winnipeg, Manitoba.

Knots

BLOOD KNOT

This knot is used to tie two strands of leader together, or to join a leader point with a leader. First, bring the ends of the two lengths of leader together so they lie parallel with one another. Wrap one end over the other several times, bring it down between the splice, and hold. Then repeat with the other end. This leaves a small eye at the junction between the two wraps. Pass the other end through this eye. Holding both ends together, pull tight. Clip off the surplus gut.

BARREL KNOT

Although inferior to the blood knot for joining leaders, this knot makes a small, tight join for two lengths of line. Lay the two ends side by side in the same position as when starting the blood knot. Tie a simple overhand knot with one end around the standing part of the other line; then do the same with the other end. Tighten the knots and pull them together so they jam. Cut the ends close to the knots.

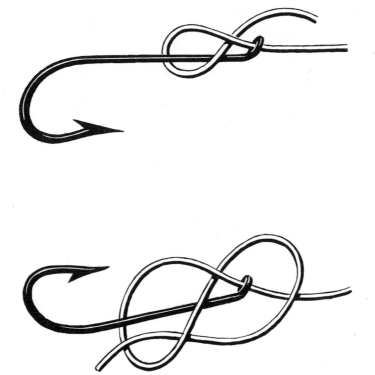

FIGURE EIGHT KNOT

This is a satisfactory knot for tying a hook or a fly to a gut leader, but it is not secure with nylon. Thread the end of the leader through the eye of the hook, then pass it around the hook and under its own loop, coming around the standing part of the line to form a figure eight and finishing off as shown.

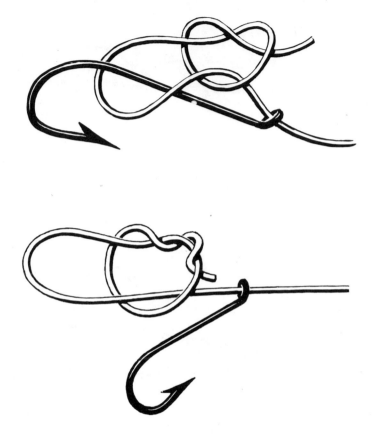

TURLE KNOT

Also fine for tying a hook or a fly to a gut, but not a nylon, leader, the turle knot is many a fisherman's standby. Thread the leader through the eye of the hook and tie a simple slip knot on the end of the leader. Slip the loop over the shank of the hook and tighten it firmly against the eye. The second drawing shows the double turle knot, to be used with nylon or other synthetics.

CLINCH KNOT

This is the knot to use when tying a hook to a nylon leader. It will not slip. Thread the end of the leader through the eye of the hook and wrap it around the standing part four or five times. Then pass the end through the eye formed at the top of the wrap. Pull tight and clip off surplus leader.

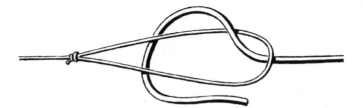

TUCKED SHEET BEND

When it is necessary to join two strands of unequal thickness, such as a line and a leader, the tucked sheet bend is a reliable knot. Pass the end of the line through the leader loop, bring it around and pass it over the loop and under the line. Then tuck the end through the loop formed by the line that encircles the leader loop, and pull tight.

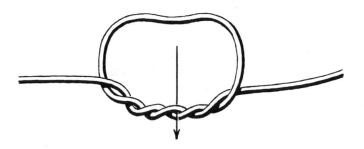

DROPPER LOOP

This knot is used for forming a loop in the center of a leader for tying on a tippet. First, form a loop about 3 inches in diameter at the point you wish to form the dropper. Twist the leader around itself several times. Separate the twisted strands and pull the opposite side of the loop through this opening. The result should look like the illustration, which shows the knot before it is tight.

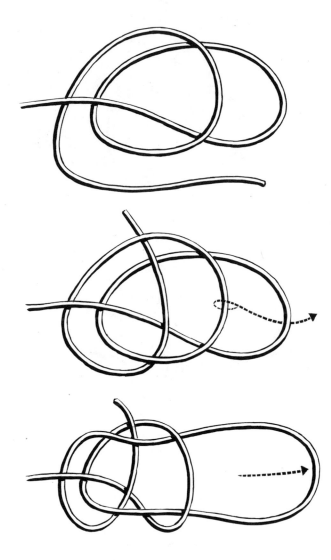

PERFECTION LOOP KNOT

Used for tying a loop in the end of a leader, this knot works well with either gut or nylon. It can also be used to tie a loop at the end of a bait-casting line for attaching a leader. The illustrations clearly show three steps in tying this knot.

Index

Index

M